Canal Ports:

The Urban Achievement of the Canal Age

Canal Ports:

The Urban Achievement of the Canal Age

J. DOUGLAS PORTEOUS

Department of Geography,
University of Victoria, Victoria,
British Columbia, Canada

1977

ACADEMIC PRESS
London · New York · San Francisco
A Subsidiary of Harcourt Brace Jovanovich, Publishers

ACADEMIC PRESS LTD.
24/28 Oval Road
London NW1

U.S. Edition published by
ACADEMIC PRESS INC.
111 Fifth Avenue
New York, New York 10003
Copyright © 1977 By ACADEMIC PRESS INC.

Library of Congress Catalog Card Number: 76-016983
ISBN: 0-12-56 1950-2

Printed in Great Britain by
Willmer Brothers Limited, Birkenhead

in memory of
Phyllis and Mick Porteous
of
York and Howdendyke

Preface

I will not call the canal a liberal
education; it was more of an
invitation to inquiry.

John Masefield

The expansion of the British port system during that period of accelerated urbanization known as the Industrial Revolution has received much scholarly attention. One of the major factors contributing to port growth in the eighteenth and nineteenth centuries was the development of new inland transport systems, notably the canal and the railway. The latter, in fact, was responsible not only for the growth of existing settlements but has also been credited with the creation of a series of completely new ports, notably Barrow and Middlesbrough.

In complete contrast, the urban achievement of the Canal Age has been unaccountably neglected. Studies of the economic, social, technical, and operational aspects of the canal system abound, but the role of the canal as a stimulator of town building has been almost entirely overlooked. And yet it is no accident that, in Britain, the Canal Age and the Industrial Revolution were historically coincident. During the period 1760–1830 the construction of canals was responsible not only for the rapid growth of existing settlements but also for the creation of a large number of small inland ports.

Moreover, canal companies and individual entrepreneurs were directly involved in the founding of a series of important canal ports at the tideway terminals of a number of British canals. The canal-created river port differs markedly from earlier upriver ports based on land carriage connexions, from the later ship canal ports, and also from the railway ports, which almost wholly avoided river sites in favour of seaboard locations. Drawing largely on manuscript sources, notably canal company records held by British Transport Historical Records, and concentrating primarily on four cases, this study develops the concept of the tideway canal port as a distinct type of urban settlement. As a purpose-built town, however, the canal port's adaptive capacity was stretched to the utmost by the development of the more efficient goods handling technologies of rail and road. In the 1970s, two hundred years after the inauguration of the first canal ports, their original function of transhipping from canal to estuarial vessels has become almost completely redundant.

In the broader context, the canal port occupies a unique transitional position in the gradual transformation of Britain's port system from a dependence on upstream locations backed by inadequate wagons and packhorses to the modern emphasis on large coastal installations serviced by an efficient hinterland road and rail system. The relevance of this investigation to port studies is clear, but the author hopes that the study will not only extend the research frontier of the geographer and economic historian, but will also prove useful to the student of urban genesis, planning, and development. The inclusion of a tentative model, or ideal canal port, is indicative of the author's belief that no piece of research is an end in itself, but rather the basis for further investigation.

Howdendyke, East Yorkshire, 1976.   *J.D.P.*

Acknowledgements

For access to and permission to use manuscript rail and canal company records the author is indebted to British Transport Historical Records at York and London. Other information was kindly furnished by: British Waterways; the Manchester Ship Canal Company; the county record offices of Cheshire, Lancashire, Northamptonshire, Worcestershire, and the West Riding of Yorkshire; the public libraries of Birmingham, Chester, Hull, Kidderminster, Leeds, Liverpool, Manchester and York; and a large number of local authority departments, libraries, industrial firms, and individuals in Ellesmere Port, Goole, Grangemouth, Runcorn and Stourport.

A number of individuals provided welcome encouragement and assistance, notably Mr C. Hadfield and Professor H. R. Wilkinson. Above all, the kind help and painstaking criticism of Dr Alan Harris greatly improved the text. Finally, the author extends his gratitude to all those whose technical expertise expedited the production of this book: to Mr Ian Norie and Mr John Bryant for cartographic work; to Miss Renee Stovold for typing the text; to Nigel Banks and Russ Harvey, who worked on the index; and to Carol Porteous, who acted as research assistant, companion, and critic.

The book has been published with the help of a grant from the Humanities Research Council of Canada, using funds provided by the Canada Council. The latter body also kindly provided a grant for library research during the summer of 1973.

J.D.P.

Contents

Perspective

1
The Canal Age, 1760–1830   3

2
The Impact of Canals on Existing Settlements   20

3
The Creation of Settlements by Canals   38

The Genesis and Development
of Canal Ports

Canal Ports and Technological Change

CONTENTS

Figures

Tables

Perspective

Bridges and canals claim attention as fountains from which flows wealth to the public weal; they give subsistence to the industrious indigent, they facilitate and encourage commerce, cause the culture of the ground, the establishment of towns, manufactures, villages, etc., increase population, by multiplying the conveniences of human life, and diffuse universal blessings on every side.

R. Dodd, 1800

1

The Canal Age, 1760–1830

There be three things that make a nation great and prosperous: a fertile soil;
busy workshops; and easy conveyance for men and commodities from one
place to another

Francis Bacon

One of the most remarkable features of the period 1760–1830, that
significant span of British history generally known as the Industrial
Revolution, is its position as a watershed in Britain's population growth.
Whereas the population of England and Wales rose slowly from about 5·6
millions in 1700 to a little over 7 millions in 1750, the succeeding years
saw a rapid expansion to a total of 9·2 millions in 1801 and 14 millions by
1831. This doubling of the population in the short period 1750–1831 was
entirely unprecedented.

Equally unprecedented was the enormous shift in population
distribution which began in the latter half of the eighteenth century. In
1700 the belt of densest population was clearly agriculturally based,
stretching eastward from the basin of the Severn to that of the Thames,
with an extension to cover the prosperous agricultural and textile region
of East Anglia. By 1801, in dramatic contrast, a radical transformation
had pivoted this belt of densest population upon its Severn axis. It now
covered an area stretching northward from the Cotswolds to the central
Pennines. Except for the London region, the most densely-populated
areas of England at the beginning of the nineteenth century were to be
found in Lancashire, Staffordshire, Warwickshire and the West Riding of
Yorkshire. This radical change may best be seen in the changing status of
English towns. Whereas in 1700 the second and third largest towns were
Bristol and Norwich, with about 20,000 inhabitants each, by 1800 only

Bristol remained among the top six, other towns with over 50,000 inhabitants being Leeds, Liverpool, Birmingham and Manchester with Salford. The new orientation was undisputed by the 1830s, when the only towns above 100,000 were Birmingham, Leeds, Liverpool, Manchester and Sheffield.

Clearly, the West Midlands and the regions flanking the Pennines were possessed of some dynamic factor which was responsible for transforming the face of Britain in the span of two generations. These areas, besides having many material advantages in terms of industrial raw materials and power supplies, were relatively free from the guild restrictions and entrenched industrial traditions of the South, whereby that area's progress was hindered. They were thus best able to take advantage of the revolutionary economic climate of eighteenth century Britain. The death of Anne, the rise of the Whigs, the failure of the '15, and Walpole's encouragement of exports increased the insecurity of squire, parson and craftsman—all symbols of the older order of land-based wealth. These same factors helped unleash the combined forces of commercial agriculture, mining and industrialization.[1] Technological innovation, the rise of the factory system, the growth of the division of labour, all heralded nineteenth century industrialization.[2]

The background to this activity was the final attainment of respectability by persons occupied in trade and commerce. Land was no longer the prime source of status, power, and wealth. While Campbell regarded commerce as 'The Life, Spring, and Motion of the Trading World',[3] of which England was naturally the hub, Daniel Defoe, the compleat tradesman, pithily summed up the new attitude in his aphorism: 'An Estate's a Pond, but a Trade's a Spring'.[4] Symbols of this attitudinal revolution, Lords Lumley and Paget began to destroy their carefully-emparked estates in search of coal.

Acting in concert, these interrelated forces aided Britain's metamorphosis from an agriculturally-dependent nation with little occupational specialization and a low degree of integration, into both the workshop and the workhouse of the world. In the period 1760–1830 the doubling of population was matched by a trebling of coal production and a twenty-fold increase in the granting of patents.[5] In response to industrial innovation the productive labour force became increasingly concentrated in towns and industrial villages. Indeed, by 1791 this concentration was such that Wendeborn, in his *View of England*, was already advocating the decentralization of activity from crowded London.[6] Significantly, Wendeborn recognized that this operation was inconceivable without the development of an integrated national canal network.

During the eighteenth century, the shift of population from the rural, agricultural south and east to the industrial, urbanizing north and west was paralleled by a change in emphasis from coastal to interior locations. One of the chief factors behind this movement was innovation in the use of water. The age of steam and steel which completed the transformation of Britain's economy, landscape and way of life, was not to appear fully fledged until the nineteenth century. The initial stages of industrialization were founded upon water. As a source of energy, water power directed the placement of the new textile and engineering mills upon the rapidly flowing perennial streams of the Pennines and Midland Plateau. As a means of carriage of both raw materials and finished products, water transport both permitted and encouraged the growth of new industrial regions. It is no coincidence that the period 1760–1830, previously characterized as the Industrial Revolution, is known to the historians of transport as the Canal Age.

Transport Before the Canal

The canal, instigator of a veritable transport revolution, was a major factor in the process whereby the Industrial Revolution knitted Britain together into a functioning unit by destroying long-established regional autarchies and emphasizing regional specialization in both agriculture and industry. Before the canal Britain's major towns and industrial areas were almost all situated on, or very near, the coasts, and the primitive regional specializations of the time depended as much on the local availability of raw materials as on the movement of the finished product. Consequently, coastal shipping had an importance which is difficult to visualize today.[7]

The writings of contemporary travellers, such as Celia Fiennes and Daniel Defoe, support this picture of a relatively stagnant interior surrounded by the feverish activity of coastal areas.[8] Nottingham, noted Defoe in the early years of the eighteenth century, 'is not esteemed a town of very great trade, other than is usual to inland towns'.[9] Coastal traffic was greatest along the sea coal run between Newcastle-on-Tyne and London, although such products as Cheshire cheese often took the 'long sea' route in preference to the tedious journey overland. Defoe noted sea coal fleets of 500 and 700 sail, and by the early eighteenth century

London's river was already becoming congested. Despite the failure of the agitations of Newcastle, Yarmouth and other east coast ports against the inland navigation projects of the eighteenth century, the coasting trade increased throughout the period, for the expansion of industry and commerce was such that all transport media were constantly oversubscribed.

Interior goods traffic at this time was confined to rivers or the long packhorse trains and lumbering waggons of the inadequate roads. Already in the early eighteenth century there was a growing traffic of agricultural produce from the southern half of England towards London, 'the great vent'. Some of this traffic, however, such as animal produce, was self-propelled. Industry was less well established in the interior, except where the navigability of large rivers and small streams had permitted the development of characteristic specializations at an early date. The edge tool and grindstone exports of Hallamshire, for instance, depended upon Bawtry Wharf, a small port on the river Idle, a tributary of the Trent which itself contributed to the Humber. Derbyshire lead and ironware, Roche Abbey building stone, Nottinghamshire iron and oak timber all found their way to Bawtry, where they were transhipped into small craft for the journey to the seaport of Hull, whence returned groceries, timber, iron ore, copper, tin, hemp, flax, and sundry wares. Through this trade the small inland port, with a population numbered only in the hundreds, had dealings with London, Holland, Norway, and places further afield.

Defoe, excited by the trade of Bawtry, was equally astonished by the flourishing West Riding woollen industry, 'so far out of the way of foreign trade, Courts, or seaports'.[10] He supplied the answer to this apparent anomaly in a discourse on the navigability of the rivers Aire and Calder, also leading into the Humber. A great reciprocal river trade between Leeds and Hull had encouraged the growth of this regional specialization before the Canal Age. The significance of rivers in pre-industrial England was such that no major town lacked access to water, most of it navigable to some degree. Moreover, the demand for water for industrial purposes emphasized the need for industry to crowd onto streams, with such notable examples as the numerous iron forges and mills located on the streams running from the Birmingham Plateau.

A correct inference would be the poor condition of eighteenth century roads. Indeed, the roads suffered a great deal of criticism and adverse comparison with both those of the Romans and the contemporary state-built arteries of France. Although travellers on horseback were not greatly inconvenienced, heavy goods movement by land was seriously impeded. The Midlands, bounded by the Severn, Trent and Thames waterways, and not well served by these because of droughts, floods, shoals and other obstructions, had to depend upon road transport to a greater degree than any other major region. Consequently, much agriculture remained in subsistence form. The sale of produce was limited to markets within a day's waggon journey, no great distance in the Midlands clay country. Despite external connexions via the Trent, transport limitations enabled local semi-subsistence economies to survive in the East Midlands until the last quarter of the eighteenth century.[11] Much of the Midlands' export trade went by packhorse, a form of transport as irregular as that on the unimproved rivers.

Road improvements began in the mid-seventeenth century with government intervention and the establishment of the first turnpikes and regular coach services. But the lack of a surveyor-general was felt throughout the century, and by the end of Anne's reign the Midlands still possessed no turnpikes to speak of. The region remained cut off from metropolitan markets by the wide belt of clays running between Severn and Wash, wherein travellers floundered in such sloughs of despond as at aptly-named Hockley-in-the-Hole, where one slough was capable of engulfing man and beast together. An almost insuperable barrier in winter, these claylands hindered the development of Leicestershire cattle and sheep raising, for beasts had to be sold cheap in October, whereupon Home Counties farmers fattened them until January and thereby amassed large middleman's profits.

As turnpiking gained momentum during the eighteenth century, many of the earlier trusts were set up across the claylands which so impeded traffic between Midlands and metropolis. Yet these turnpikes showed few technical improvements over earlier roads. Jack Metcalfe's pioneer road-building techniques were confined to the north, and Telford and MacAdam did not apply themselves to road construction until the nineteenth century. Manufactured goods remained particularly difficult to move, and their retention of the packhorse as the major medium was regarded by Celia Fiennes as self-evident 'from the narrowness of the lanes where there is good lands . . . and where it's hilly and stony no other carriages can pass'.[12] Certainly enclosure, with its confining of roads into set bounds, made conditions worse. Despite the network of packhorse routes between the heads of navigation of Severn, Thames and Trent it was clear that the heavier Midlands manufactures, together with the fragile output of the growing Potteries, could not long continue to expand if their products were to be carried by such primitive means. Manufacturers and political economists alike realized distribution to be the handmaid of production. The answer to this problem was to make all possible use of water transport.

River Improvement

Until the mid-eighteenth century navigable waterways provided Britain with its cheapest and most convenient form of commercial transport. Although larger seagoing ships were obliged to tranship to river vessels, such as the famous Severn trows and Yorkshire keels, in major estuarial ports, coasters were often able to penetrate for a considerable distance into interior Britain along such rivers as the Yorkshire Ouse, Trent, Severn, Thames and a larger number of East Anglian waterways. Many interior towns which now harbour little more than pleasure boats possessed thriving port facilities; Peterborough, Stamford, Cambridge, Oxford and Shrewsbury all supported a river trade. Such towns were nodal points for waggon and packhorse routes, minor entrepots enabling the produce of the district to be exchanged for a variety of necessary imports, notably coal.

York, for example, was a port before the Roman colonization.[13] In medieval times both trade and politics in the city were dominated by groups of 'merchant adventurers', who were keenly concerned to keep open the navigation of the Ouse and Humber. The city played a major role as a regional distribution centre for imports of grain, coal, iron, spices, wines and salt fish. Exports included Pennine lead, which was floated downstream from Boroughbridge on lighters for transhipment at York. The town also supported a thriving woollen industry, cloth exports being balanced by the importation of alum, woad, and madder. As with many inland ports, a shipbuilding industry arose and port-related entrepreneurial skills were exported, so that as late as the seventeenth century Hull citizens were complaining of the control of their port by York interests.

Before the middle of the seventeenth century, although some attempts had been made to improve the means of passage along naturally navigable rivers, little effort had been expended on the creation of navigable stretches where none had been before. Contemporaries agreed that 'this Island is incomparably furnished with pleasant Rivers, like Veins in the Natural Body, which conveys the Blood into all the Parts, whereby the whole is nourished and made useful'.[14] They were concerned, however, about the sluggishness of flow along some of the aforesaid veins, and the unfortunate frequency of clotting and other obstruction.

Unimproved rivers had many shortcomings as navigations. Many obstacles, such as weirs, fishgarths and mills, were man-made. Other obstructions to trade were inherent in the nature of the river; the Severn may serve as an example. In the days of sail and haulage by men and horses this river carried an immense traffic in coal, iron, pottery, glass, grain, cheese, timber, salt and imported goods; the huge hinterland it served enabled Bristol to hold a quasi-metropolitan status until well into the eighteenth century.[15] A major problem for navigation was caused by the great annual and seasonal variation in the rainfall received by the Severn basin. Consequently, water depth varied tremendously from year to year and from season to season. Freshes, which caused considerable flooding, were frequently interspersed with droughts which caused boats to be laid up and brought trade to a standstill. For example, readings taken by Telford at Coalport indicate an immense variation between good years, as in 1792 when only 24 per cent of the year had less than 2ft 6in depth, and bad years, such as 1796 when the river was deemed impassable for vessels of 2ft 6in draught for 64 per cent of the time.[16]

Further, the uneven nature of the Severn's bed affected current strengths and the distribution of shoals. Although haulage energy requirements along the lower river were about one man per ton, a sharp break of slope at Worcester doubled the requirement above that town. Before improvement, which did not come until the nineteenth century, a 4ft channel was the best that could be expected above Gloucester. Moreover, the combined opposition of local landowners and rivermen prevented the erection of locks and weirs or of training walls designed to increase scour. Even below Gloucester the situation was little improved, for extensive shoaling existed as far downstream as Bristol.

Such problems, common to most British rivers and previously tolerated, loomed larger as trade expanded in the later seventeenth and early eighteenth centuries. The expanding coal trade was most pressing in its demands for ready access by water to all parts of the country. For such a bulky commodity the packhorse was most unsuitable. A packhorse could carry at most 2·5 cwt; the same horse could pull, on an improved river, up to 250 times as much. The proper corrective was clearly river improvement through the provision of training walls, locks, dredging, the removal of man-made obstacles, and the digging of short artificial cuts to avoid the worst stretches. Such river improvement, the first stage in the transport revolution which was subsequently to encompass canal, rail, road and air innovations, reached its height in the period 1660–1730.[17]

During the first forty years of this period a flurry of legislation permitted the improvement of the Yorkshire Ouse, Trent, Dee, Aire, a number of Severn tributaries and several East Anglian rivers, increasing the total navigable length of English waterways from 685 miles in 1660 to 960 miles by the turn of the century. A final burst of legislation came in the period 1719–27 when improvements were authorized for the Weaver, Mersey, Irwell, Douglas, Derbyshire Derwent, Idle and Don. By 1730 about 1160 miles of waterway were navigable. Although a few important schemes came after this period, river improvement had been largely played out by the end of the eighteenth century's third decade.

Existing river ports did not always profit from river improvement. The city of York opposed the Aire, Calder and Don improvements on the grounds that tides would be drawn away from the Upper Ouse. It also, and quite correctly, feared that the West Riding textile trade would gain lasting ascendancy over that of York. More frequently, however, pre-improvement ports sited at important transhipment points, lowest bridge points, or acknowledged heads of navigation, welcomed downstream improvement. Their violent opposition was generally reserved for improvements further upstream. One of the best-known examples of such opposition is that of Nottingham. Previously regarded as the head of navigation of the Trent, seventeenth century Nottingham found itself fighting a protracted battle on two fronts. As early as 1638 Derby had proposed to make navigable the river Derwent so as to facilitate the export of Derbyshire lead and render unnecessary the transhipment of imports at Nottingham. In 1675 the latter town was also engaged in thwarting attempts to improve the upper Trent to Burton. The efforts of these forces of reaction delayed the completion of the Derwent improvement until the 1720s, and of the upper Trent, below Wilden Ferry at least, until the latter part of the eighteenth century. In much the same way Liverpool vainly opposed plans for making the Mersey and Irwell navigable as far as the burgeoning commercial centre of Manchester, and Reading was unhappy about the improvement of the Kennet to Newbury.

The Canal Solution

For the best part of a century the application of canal-building technology to the growing transport problem of industrializing Britain

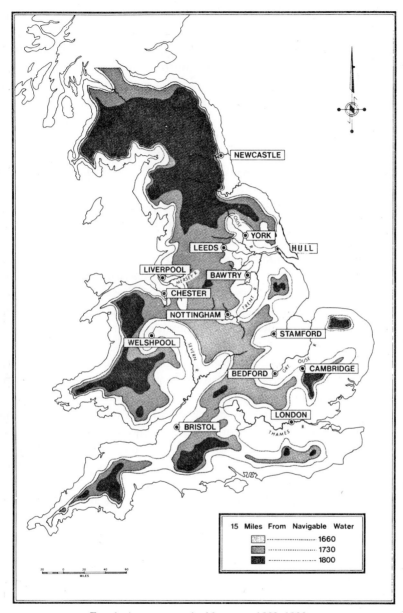

Fig. 1. Access to navigable water 1660–1800.

eased the difficulties associated with river navigations and the painful movement of goods by road. For, despite improvement, rivers still suffered to a great extent from the problems associated with tides, floods, drought, freezing, shifting channels, and the like. Neither an industrial system nor an efficient agriculture could be built up on the basis of the delays and uncertainties inherent in the exclusive use of river and road for goods conveyance. Moreover, not only were many rivers permanently unimprovable and therefore clearly in need of being bypassed, but the piecemeal improvement of rivers still left many areas of interior Britain unprovided with adequate water carriage (Fig. 1). Chief among these areas were the growing textile and engineering regions of the West Riding of Yorkshire, East Lancashire, the West Midlands, and a vast region drained by the Severn. The very regions most likely to benefit from extensive river improvement were to a great extent denied it; even where water transport was available it was restricted in its scope by the arbitrary dictates of physiography. Thus in the mid-eighteenth century, at varying distances from navigable rivers, lay numerous active and potential mines, works, towns, and farms, a constellation of fixed points which required knitting together by a medium more flexible and regular than shoaled rivers and dilatory packhorse trains.

In view of the pressing need for improved goods transportation it is not surprising that pamphleteering dreamers were joined by astute businessmen in the promotion of both local waterways and an interconnecting national system of canals. Having exhausted the possibilities of river improvement, shippers of goods could see that canals were the only possible means of further ameliorating the transport situation. Two interrelated ideas lay behind the profusion of canal schemes in the period 1760–1830: the interconnexion of the seas; and the completion of the internal network of water communication begun in the era of river improvement.

The first of these concepts visualized an internal connexion between the four great English estuaries, to supplement the service provided by the coasting trade. John Phillips, perhaps the first of the great canal enthusiasts, stated the problem succinctly:

'England, in which all the arts and sciences, commerce, and agriculture especially flourish, is an island containing numerous rivers, rendered navigable by art, where not so by nature. The rivers Thames, Trent, Severn, and Mersey, extend far into the country; and almost divide the island into four parts; yet, though four of the principal ports of the Kingdom, London, Bristol, Liverpool, and Hull, are commodiously situated on these great rivers, and incessantly crowded with innumerable vessels laden with the richest productions of the different countries of the world, none of these great commercial ports had, for a long time, any communication with each other except by a tedious and circuitous [coastal] navigation, or a tiresome and expensive land carriage.'[18]

The same writer also eulogized canals as a means of fulfilling the second desire, for an extensive internal communications system of nation-wide extent. He urged England to follow the successful example of foreign nations such as Holland and France, already extensively canalized:

'In countries which have the advantage of canals old manufactories are rendered more flourishing, and new ones established from day to day, in situations where, before, the land was but of little value, and but thinly inhabited . . . As consumers, we are enabled by means of canals to import more cheaply; as producers we export with greater facility. Do the materials of manufacture lie dispersed? Canals unite them, and at the same time supply the persons employed in it with every necessary at the cheapest rate; and the landowner, whether we consider the surface of the soil, or the mines in its bowels, necessarily finds his advantage from new markets, and from having a cheaper carriage both for his productions and his manure.'[19]

Clearly, such an interior communications system would not only support the existing economy, but would everywhere promote new ventures agricultural, industrial and commercial.

Beyond these obvious advantages, other benefits anticipated by canal promoters were far-reaching in their social implications.[20] The seasonal regularization of the supply of coal and food to cities, together with a substantial cheapening of provisions, would improve the lot of the poor and prevent riots. The opening up of Britain's internal frontier would increase rents and promote agricultural improvement. The reduced need for horses and therefore for hay land would release land for food production. The redundancy of boat halers and packhorse drivers would shift their labour into the productive sectors of agriculture and industry. The inadequacies of river navigation would be rectified and land and water carriage monopolies broken. Heavy goods carriage, removed from the roads, would save highway wear and tear and permit improved turnpiking, thus speeding the journeys of market waggons and of the

B

expanding coaching system. In foul weather, goods normally moving coastwise could be transferred from coast to coast on inland waterways free from storms. Similarly, the rapid movement of troops from point to point within the interior would be accomplished without the fatigue of the forced march. And finally, and this to enlist the support of the powerful naval fraternity, canal navigation might prove to be a major nursery for British seamen.

In the face of such arguments the opposition of landed gentry, millowners, farmers, road trustees, rivermen, and land carriers, all with vested trade interests or water rights, proved in most cases to be ephemeral. The first English canals of the new era were being actively promoted in Lancashire as early as the 1750s. The successes of the Duke of Bridgewater, later known as the Canal Duke, made canal promotion fashionable as well as profitable. By 1790 the length of navigable inland waterway had, at over 2,200 miles, almost doubled that of 1730, largely through the construction of nearly one thousand miles of canal. By 1830 the figure had risen to 3,875, and twenty years later had topped the 4,000 mile mark.[21]

By 1790 also, England's four major estuaries had been linked, and the embryo industrial regions of the north and west had at last found canal links with estuarial seaports and thus with external markets and sources of supply. The connexion of the four estuaries was accomplished by the construction of the Staffordshire and Worcestershire Canal, linking Severn and Trent and completed in 1772; the Trent and Mersey Canal, completed five years later; and the Oxford Canal, completed in 1790, which linked the Thames into the national network (Fig. 2). During the same period, no more than one generation, this great St Andrew's Cross of canals centred upon Birmingham, was supplemented by major latitudinal routes designed to facilitate direct access between ports occupying analogous positions on east and west coasts. The Thames and Severn Canal, joining Bristol and London and providing the latter with an alternative route to the West Midlands, was pushed through by 1789. The following year saw the completion of the Forth and Clyde Canal, a venture projected in order to shorten the lengthy and hazardous coastal route between Leith (Edinburgh) and Glasgow. Designed with a similar purpose, the Caledonian Canal, utilizing the natural routeway of the Great Glen, was begun in 1803. A final east-west link, traversing the rugged backbone of the Pennines to connect Hull with Manchester and Liverpool, was provided after the completion of the Rochdale Canal in 1804, soon to be supplemented by the Huddersfield Canal (1811) and the

FIG. 2. The Canal Cross at the close of the Canal Age.

prodigious effort of the Leeds and Liverpool, which finally broke through in 1816. During the 1790s a veritable Canal Mania assured these trunk canals of connexion with numerous smaller lines built to exploit single landlocked resources; all soon bristled with branches.

By linking estuaries and navigable rivers the canal system, by the early nineteenth century, had succeeded in creating Britain's first truly nation-wide integrated system of communications since the road building operations of the Romans. The legal, technical, financial, economic and operational aspects of the British canal system have been extensively discussed.[22] It remains briefly to consider the significance of the network in relation to the anticipated advantages extolled by promoters. Although many of the expected social, political and economic advantages were not realized (the demand for horses actually increased, for example), the canal system effectively upgraded the efficiency of Britain's whole economy. Able to pull about 30 tons on an improved river, a single horse could draw 50 to 80 tons on a canal. Compounded innumerable times in a rapidly industrializing economy, this factor alone is sufficient to justify the canal as a major achievement. It was, in microcosm, the essence of the Industrial Revolution, the replacement of labour by capital in the form of labour-saving apparatus.

Further, canal construction created massive employment opportunities for a rising population, which was later easily diverted to man the mines and manufactories brought forth by the cheap transport it had helped provide. The significance of canals as basic industrial catalysts, unlocking previously unobtainable sources of fuel and raw materials, may be gauged from Phillips' assertion that of the 165 canal Acts obtained between 1758 and 1803, 90 were specifically obtained to serve collieries and a further 47 for the service of iron, copper and lead mines and works.[23] In their activating role during the Industrial Revolution, with ramifications throughout the economy, 'canals can be regarded, not merely as a brief adventure in hydraulics with a hang-over of obsolescence and nostalgia, but as the vital prerequisite of the railways and the great Victorian boom which attended them'.[24]

Obsolescence was, however, built-in. In Britain, though not in continental Europe, the canal's superior position as a medium of transportation was short-lived. Whereas in 1796 Richard Fulton, the American navigation authority, remarked that canals had become 'the subject of general conversation', in 1825 the *Quarterly Review* announced that 'Nothing now is heard of but railroads'.[25] The canal system was disjointed; there was no uniformity of gauge, so that through traffic was confined to the smallest craft, the 30 ton narrow boats of the Midlands. Lack of uniformity in the canal system was mirrored in a conspicuous lack of unity among management; the canals never developed an effective political lobby like that of the 'railway interest'. Moreover, the railways bought up canals which were strategic parts of through canal routes. By 1865 railways controlled about one third, and by 1883 almost one half of the total canal mileage.

Before the middle of the nineteenth century the Canal Cross had been paralleled by a series of railways linking Liverpool, Bristol, London and Hull with major inland manufacturing centres. The effect on the canal trade was not immediate; canals were annually carrying about 30 million tons of goods in England and Wales in the early 1830s, and the figure continued to grow for some time. In 1841 it is estimated that 1 in every 47 active males was directly employed in the inland waterway business.[26] Railways were, in fact, originally conceived as feeders to canals. The superiority of the new mode in terms of flexibility, speed, dependability, efficiency, and cost, however, led to the gradual superseding of canals by railways. By the 1860s the basic railway skeleton had been fleshed with a complex of interconnecting lines with which the canals could not hope to compete.

Although the Duke of Bridgewater's system and several other lines, such as the industrial canals of South Wales, were able to hold their own into the 1870s, the Royal Commission on Canals and Inland Navigations demonstrated that by 1888 only eleven English waterways were able to make a profit of over £10,000.[27] The commission noted that canal traffic had fallen away as railway construction continued, and that even the well-endowed wide canals were receiving more and more of their income from the carriage of bulky cargoes of low cost relative to weight, notably coal. 'Considered as a whole', declared the commission in 1909, 'the waterways have had no share in the enormous increase in the transport business which has taken place between the middle of the nineteenth century and the present time'.[28] After World War I, when canals were challenged not only by railways but also by the rise of trucking on a refurbished road system, traffic was reduced yet more rapidly and many lines fell into disuse. Except for a very few canals which still carry a heavy traffic, notably those lines comprising the Humber system, the canals of the 1970s are either derelict or given over to pleasure boating and angling.

Despite the effective demise of the British canal in the face of technological innovation, the Canal Age has a significance which reaches beyond its purely economic importance as a catalyst of industrial growth and its role in converting Britain from a fragmented coast-oriented state to the cohesive coal-oriented community of the nineteenth century. The canal was also an important agent in the transformation of the island's landscape. It made possible the development of regional specialization in industry, giving rise to characteristic industrial landscapes. Within these regions, and to a lesser extent elsewhere, the canal also promoted the growth of existing settlements, contributed to the stagnation of old river ports, and became a magnet for the location of new industrial establishments. And, a yet greater feat, the canal called into existence new ports and towns in areas where none had previously existed. It is to the consideration of the canal as a shaper of industrial regions, as a selective influence on urban growth, and as a generator of new ports that the next two chapters are devoted.

1. Notes

1. J. H. Plumb, *England in the Eighteenth Century,* Penguin, Harmondsworth (1950).
2. J. H. Plumb, op. cit. p. 22.
3. R. Campbell, 'On the Importance of Commerce (1747)', in D. B. Horn and M. A. Ransome, *English Historical Documents 1714-1783,* Eyre and Spottiswoode, London (1957), pp. 494-8.
4. D. Defoe, *The Compleat English Tradesman,* Kelly, New York (1969).
5. T. S. Ashton, *The Industrial Revolution 1760-1830,* Oxford University Press, London (1948), pp. 2, 39, 90.
6. J. Wendeborn, *A View of England at the End of the Eighteenth Century,* London (1791).
7. T. S. Willan, *The English Coasting Trade 1600-1750,* Manchester University Press, Manchester (1938).
8. C. Fiennes, *The Journeys of Celia Fiennes,* Cresset Press, London (1947).
9. D. Defoe, *A Tour through the Whole Island of Great Britain,* Dent, London (1962), p. 145.
10. Ibid., p. 197.
11. J. D. Chambers, *The Vale of Trent 1670-1800,* Cambridge University Press, London (1957).
12. C. Fiennes, op. cit. p. 250.
13. B. Duckham, *The Yorkshire Ouse,* David and Charles, Newton Abbot (1967), *passim.*
14. *House of Lords Journal* 11 (2 March 1665), 675.
15. W. E. Minchinton, 'Bristol—Metropolis of the West in the Eighteenth Century', *Transactions, Royal Historical Society* Fifth Series 4 (1954), 69-89.

16. W. G. East, 'The Severn Waterway in the Eighteenth and Nineteenth Centuries', in L. D. Stamp and S. W. Wooldridge, *London Essays in Geography*, University of London Press, London (1951).

17. T. S. Willan, *River Navigation in England 1600–1750*, Cass, London (1936).

18. J. Phillips, *A General History of Inland Navigation, Foreign and Domestic*, (1792) reprinted David and Charles, Newton Abbot (1970), p. 84.

19. J. Phillips, op. cit., p. vi.

20. W. T. Jackman, *The Development of Transportation in Modern England*, Cambridge University Press, Cambridge (1962).

21. C. Hadfield, *The Canal Age*, David and Charles, Newton Abbot (1968), p. 208

22. see, e.g., C. Hadfield, *Canal Age*;
C. Hadfield, *British Canals: an illustrated history*, David and Charles, Newton Abbot (1969).
L. T. C. Rolt, *The Inland Waterways of England*, Longmans, London (1950);
Idem., Navigable Waterways, Longmans, London (1969).

23. J. Phillips, op. cit., quoted in H. J. Dyos and D. H. Aldcroft, *British Transport: an economic survey from the seventeenth century to the twentieth*, Leicester University Press, Leicester (1969), p. 103.

24. H. J. Dyos and D. H. Aldcroft, op. cit., p. 103.

25. Ibid., p. 94;
E. A. Pratt, *A History of Inland Transport and Communication in England*, (1912) reprinted David and Charles, Newton Abbot (1970), p. 19.

26. C. Hadfield, *The Canal Age*, op. cit., p. 151.

27. F. C. Mather, 'The Duke of Bridgewater's Trustees and the Coming of the Railways', *Transactions, Royal Historical Society* Fifth Series 14 (1964), 154.

28. *Royal Commission on the Canals and Inland Navigations of the United Kingdom* (1907–9).

2

The Impact of Canals on Existing Settlements

As by means of water-carriage a more extensive market is opened to every sort of industry than what land-carriage alone can afford it, so it is upon the sea-coast, and along the banks of navigable rivers, that industry of every kind naturally begins to subdivide and improve itself, and it is frequently not till a long time after that those improvements extend themselves to the inland parts of the country.

Adam Smith

Eighteenth century canal enthusiasts were of the opinion that a Britain intersected by canals would profit as much as had the Netherlands where, by dint of a painstakingly-created canal network 'our neighbours . . . out of a small tract of marshland, have raised a populous and powerful state, reverenced and courted by all the world'.[1] Indeed, the impact of the Canal Age, felt by all classes of people and in all sectors of the economy, caused ports and inland towns alike to enter reciprocal phases of growth and prosperity.

'Throughout the country, stone for building, paving and road-making; bricks, tiles and timber; limestone for the builder, farmer or blast-furnace owner; beasts and cattle; corn, hay and straw; manure from the . . . mountainous London dustheaps; the heavy castings which were coming into use for bridge-building and other structural purposes—all these . . . moved along the new waterways over what, half a century earlier, had been impossible routes or impossible distances.'[2]

So great was the effect of the canals that Phillips was moved to declare that they 'have entirely changed the appearance of the counties through which they flow'.[3]

Canal-induced landscape metamorphosis may be seen in microcosm in the area served by the Duke of Bridgewater's canal. Built in the 1760s to provide the growing town of Manchester with coal from the Canal Duke's previously landlocked Worsley mines, the canal was almost immediately extended to the Mersey estuary at Runcorn. Thus what had originally been a simple coal canal rapidly became a major thoroughfare for goods passing between Liverpool and Manchester. These major functions apart, the duke's canal was also responsible for a complex series of effects. By opening up an easier passage to Manchester for coal and all manner of merchandise, employment was encouraged, not least in the duke's Worsley mines where housing and social facilities were provided for the workmen.

The growth of Worsley as a coal shipping port was accompanied by the development of boat building, for the canal ran directly into the mines via an adit, thus providing conveyance and drainage in a single channel. Boatbuilders' stocks were flanked by timber yards and stone masons' yards, both being required for canal and mine maintenance. Extensions of the canal provided further support for the whole system by opening up quarries for sand, lime and stone. At Worsley canalside mills, driven by water power, served to grind corn, mix mortar and sift sand. Indeed, so active did this inland canal centre appear that Arthur Young reported that 'the little village of Worsley looks like a river environ of London'.[4] The agricultural commentator was yet further enraptured by his discovery that mud from canal dredging was mixed with dung and spread over the duke's fields. Even more remarkable, the canal was slowly being extended beyond Worsley into a bogland area, manure and stone chippings from mine spoil being used to convert the boggy soil into productive pasture land.

With his control of coal production, goods transport, docks, repair yards, quarrying, shipbuilding, housing, and agriculture, the Duke of Bridgewater had clearly extended the traditional principles of estate management to produce a vast, modern, vertically-integrated, reciprocating commercial system. Young was delighted to witness such enlightened entrepreneurship: 'every part of the whole design acts in concert and yields mutual assistance, which is the grand art of economical management'.[5] If such a transformation could be accomplished by one canal in one small area of Lancashire, the overall impact of the canal system on regional growth, industrialization, port development, and urban growth must have been immense.

Regional Specialization

As has been indicated previously, regional specialization in industry and agriculture was hardly possible on any great scale before the development of a nationally-interconnecting system of communications. Although regional specializations were in evidence before the eighteenth century, the need to devote much energy to the local production of essentials, such as food and fuel, prevented the development of the intensive local concentration upon a few staple products, notably cotton, wool, copper, or iron, which was to become the keynote of industrial Britain. The importance of the canal in influencing this trend may be illustrated by investigating the comparative rise or decline during the eighteenth century of regions with similar manufacturing specializations.

Perhaps the greatest contrast is between the respective fortunes of Lancashire and the West Country. If relative changes in population may be regarded as adequate indicators of regional development, the dynamism of the late eighteenth century was very unevenly spread. Whereas during the century the population of Lancashire rose more than sixfold, in the West Country only Gloucestershire and Cornwall registered increases of over 50 per cent.[6] In terms of total population, Lancashire stood below four of the six West Country counties in 1700, but was double that of Devon, the most populous, in 1801. With regard to the percentage of England's population contained within each region, Lancashire's share rose from 3 to 8 per cent within the century, whereas that of the West Country fell from 19 to 16·5 per cent. In this context of population shift and concentration, it must be remembered that Lancashire is only about one-fifth the size of the southern region.

Lancashire's upsurge was not based upon agricultural improvement. Eighteenth century commentators were largely in agreement that many agrarian innovations had yet to reach the region from the centres of improvement in East Anglia. Almost half the area was waste at the end of the century, rotations were poor, and sheep were grazed even in lowland areas. In marked contrast, West Country agriculture was relatively rich, notably in Gloucestershire and Somerset where enclosures were well established and reclamation was taking place both on moor and in marsh. Somerset, indeed, was beginning to develop a dairying specialization, necessitating the import of grain. The region's richness, however, depended as much upon its textiles and its seaports as upon its agriculture.

Textiles and seaports were closely related for, despite local production, the expanding cloth industry was demanding increased supplies of Kentish, Irish and Spanish wool. In the early eighteenth century, when wool dominated the domestic industry of both regions, sparsely-populated Lancashire could hardly compete with the larger production and steady markets of the West Country going concern. In the latter part of the century, however, Lancashire's former manufacture of woollens, linens and fustians began to give way to cotton. Lack of traditional corporate and guild restrictions in the north encouraged manufacturers and inventors alike, and the newly-invented machinery was found to be better adapted to cotton than wool. The application of steam power to the northern mills gave further impetus to Lancashire, for the small North Somerset coalfield was ill-adapted to modern needs. While the West Country textile industry remained largely dependent upon the traditional hand wheel, the north wholeheartedly adopted the spinning jenny, powered by local coal.

And coal was increasingly carried by canals. Initially better provided with inland waterways, Lancashire was able to capitalize upon a landscape more amenable to canal cutting. By means of canals not only was the textile industry fostered, but improved accessibility to both Cheshire salt and Lancashire coal promoted the growth of the associated chemical and dye industry. Placed in direct communication with the remainder of Britain by means of the Canal Cross, burgeoning Lancashire contrasted strongly with the West Country, where industrial potential was low, where transpeninsular canal projects repeatedly failed to materialize, and where the Thames and Severn, and Kennet and Avon canals were at best peripheral. At the turn of the century, the contrast between the canalized and industrialized north and the relatively stagnant southern portion of western England is nowhere better epitomized than in the comparative fortunes of Bristol and Liverpool. Although Defoe in the early part of the century had thought the trade of the two ports to be divided 'upon very remarkable equalities', he found the rapid growth of Liverpool 'one of the wonders of Britain'.[7] The loss of Bristol's port functions to Liverpool was so great that by 1825 Baron Dupin was able to remark: 'Of the towns in Britain that I visited, Bristol was the one where the general stagnation was most visible and most alarming'.[8] Between 1700 and 1800 a complete change in relative accessibility had been induced by canal construction. Lancashire had become a major centre of activity, whereas the West Country had achieved a relative remoteness in a nation whose nucleus of industrial wealth and power had moved decidedly north.

There is no need to belabour the canal's influence upon regionalization by a comparable contrast between the fortunes of the wool textile regions of East Anglia and West Yorkshire. The former, clinging to the domestic system whereby the towns organized, rather than prosecuted, the industry, could not compete with the factory system developing further north. In the eighteenth century the West Riding textile region was one of the few English districts which could not support itself agriculturally. On the navigable rivers and canals leading to the Humber and Hull, vessels carrying cloth and coal met others carrying foodstuffs upstream. Such regional interrelationships were evident to Defoe, who commented: 'Thus this one trading, manufacturing, part of the country supports all the countries round it . . . the numbers of people settle here as bees round a hive . . . the country looked as if all the people were transplanted to Leeds and Halifax'.[9] Such a strong wave of rural-urban migration had never before been possible because of the lack of an adequate transport base for large concentrations of people.

Industrial and Urban Growth

Without the development of the canal system the processes of industrialization and urbanization in Britain would have been significantly delayed. Urban-industrial centres depend entirely upon a continuous inflow and outflow of goods, cash, and information. In the unsanitary conditions of the Industrial Revolution, sustained urban growth also demanded a constant influx of immigrants. The canal was the means to these ends. Of the seventy principal towns in Britain in 1841, only Luton had no direct connexion with sea, navigable river, or canal.[10] A re-analysis of Hadfield's data[11] on the relationship between inland navigation and urban growth suggests that the connexion of a town with an inland waterway immediately resulted in a high rate of population growth. Taking the rate of growth between 1801 and 1841 as an index, it is possible to compare the performance of towns given inland navigation before 1760 (mainly river improvements) and in the periods 1760–90 and 1790–1830 (before and after the Canal Mania). The former, including such diverse towns as Leeds, Manchester, Exeter, York and Norwich, increased an average 2·1 times in the forty year period; the second group, including Birmingham, Wigan and Coventry, increased about 2·7 times. The third group, however, including the industrial centres of Blackburn, Derby, Macclesfield and Sheffield, increased by an average of 2·9 times. Clearly, the post-canal growth wave for the pre-1760 connexions had subsided, whereas the upsurge was still in full swing for those towns given canal links after 1790.

The detailed causal interrelationships between population growth, urban expansion, industrial development, and transport innovation are too complex to untangle here, and differ from town to town. One aspect of urban growth was common to all settlements, however. The urgent need for a continuous inflow of food and fuel supplies dominated the thinking of urban dwellers, and was naturally of great moment to farmers and mine owners. Men of politics were also concerned; famines of food and fuel had too often led to rioting by the growing urban proletariat. Fuel crises were common in the early eighteenth century; an overland journey of as little as 15 miles could double or treble the pit-head price of such bulky materials as coal. Such was the demand, by 1695 coastal colliers accounted for over one third of the total tonnage of English shipping, but these vessels were unable to service many inland settlements. 'The fuel famine of the eighteenth century would have stopped the growth not only of industry but of population . . . had not means been devised for overcoming it.'[12]

Though river improvement was the first of these means, the cutting of canals into coalfields previously poorly served by natural waterways proved to be the much-needed catalyst for the eighteenth century coal rush. In many cases a new canal's inaugural vessels were no more than a string of lowly coal boats, which were often treated with much ceremony:

'Friday last a tier of boats, laden with coals, passed for the first time, on the Worcester and Birmingham Canal to Selly Oak, attended by two bands of music, and accompanied by the Committee and others of the proprietors . . . On their arrival at Selly Oak, the Father of the Canal landed the first coal, and the workmen were regaled with a roasted ox and ale. We congratulate the public on the benefit which will necessarily be derived along this line of country and its vicinity by the reduction in the price of coal; and it cannot be doubted but that the proprietors will receive very considerable profits for the tonnage which even this short line of their navigation will produce.'[13]

Price reductions were indeed great. The Canal Duke undertook to charge no more than about half the previous price of coal when his first canal terminated in Salford. The cost of carrying coal from Chesterfield to the Trent by canal was a mere fifth of the charge by road transport. 'Inland coal' soon began to compete with the traditional sea coal on the western and southern coasts. Northumberland and Durham interests, restrictive legislation, and the weight of tradition, however, prevented inland coal from encroaching upon metropolitan markets. As late as the 1830s no more than 10,000 tons of London's annual importation of over 2 million tons of coal reached the capital by inland waterway. The influence of cheap inland coal was most marked in the industrializing canal-intersected regions of the West Midlands and the North.

In these regions the opening up of interior coalfields by canals not only cheapened coal and introduced it to areas previously unused to mineral fuel, but also somewhat reduced the differential advantages previously enjoyed by industrial concerns established near sources of supply.[14] Industrial areas were thus encouraged in their growth even if remote from coalfields. Clearly, however, settlements unserved by canal or river were as badly off as ever, and where canal-induced industry sprang up, it was almost invariably located on the banks of the canal itself. Until well into the Railway Age the canal bank proved a magnet for the location of industrial enterprises (Fig. 3). Eighteenth and nineteenth century town plans illustrate the flocking of industry to canal sides in industrial towns such as Birmingham, Stoke-on-Trent and Wigan. Newspaper advertisements for industrial property frequently indicated the distance of that property from the nearest waterway. Many industrial enterprises built private wharves, and some constructed short canal branches to works situated some distance from the main cut. Boatbuilding yards sprang up to serve the growing demand for vessels, which were often launched directly into the canal.

The Bradford Canal may serve as an example of the canal as industrial site. Less than four miles in length, with ten locks, the canal connected Bradford with the Leeds and Liverpool Canal at Shipley. Opened in the mid-1770s, the canal's influence soon extended into areas traversed by the Leeds and Liverpool. Stone quarrying grew apace, and Skipton began to send large quantities of limestone to kilns established along the Bradford line. Coal mining and iron working were encouraged, the ironworks building tramways to assist the transportation of cast iron to canalside wharves and warehouses. The short line also supported a chemical works. More importantly, the three miles of canal traversing the Lower Swansea Valley supported, in 1823, several collieries, nine copper

Fig. 3. Housing, industry and warehousing facing the Staffordshire and Worcestershire
Canal at Stourport.

works, three iron works, two potteries, a brass works, a tin works and a
brewery. At the other end of the spectrum, the Manchester Ship Canal is
today a major linear industrial site, with large industrial estates, such as
Trafford Park, established alongside it.

Even in the twentieth century the more modern waterways retain their
attraction for industry, and this is especially so on the waterways of
Flanders. Analysis of information presented by de Salis[15] indicates that as
late as the 1920s certain British waterways were still the sites of a
significant amount of industrial activity (Table I).

On the Aire and Calder, for example, the town of Knottingley is still
distinguished by its canalside works producing tar products, bottles,
flour, small vessels and electrical power. But factory location on canal
banks had major disadvantages for the canal companies and the public at
large. Besides abstracting water, industrial plants frequently returned it
to the canal in a polluted condition. Sir George Head, an enthusiastic

Table I
Canalside Activity (de Salis, 1928)

Canal	Length of main line (miles)	No. of waterside works	No. of waterside collieries	No. of waterside coal staiths	No. of wharves
Bridgewater	29·25	11	1	7	27
Staffordshire and Worcestershire	46·13	12	1	0	31
Shropshire Union	66·50	5	0	0	30
Aire and Calder	42·00	37	1	9	44

inland waterway traveller of the 1830s, extolled the bliss of the canal passenger as he 'sits basking in the sunshine, and glides tranquilly onwards through a continuous panorama of cows, cottages and green fields'.[16] Unfortunately the same traveller was too soon brought down to earth 'for within a dozen miles of Manchester, the water of the canal is as black as the Styx, and absolutely pestiferous, from the gas and refuse of the manufactories with which it is impregnated'. Wigan proved even worse, an industrial 'place of purgatory. Nothing can surpass the untidiness and filth of this warm nook, . . . a compound of villanous smells'.[17]

Port Development

Inland towns with canal access, however, such as Wigan, did not simply become manufacturing centres with industries clustering alongside the canal. They also became ports. The role of the canal in port development is complex, but we may distinguish between the canal's influence on existing seaports, on the rise and fall of former river ports, and on inland towns, previously landlocked, which achieved inland port status with the arrival of the waterway.

Major Seaports

Canal connexions had several interrelated effects on major seaports. The most direct and immediate influence was the canal's role in opening up a wider hinterland. The sudden growth of Liverpool is illustrative. Liverpool became potentially important as British overseas trade was gradually reoriented towards Ireland and North America after the seventeenth century. This potential, however, could only be actualized by the development of major domestic staples as exports, and this in turn depended upon better inland communications. Liverpool's agitation was an important factor in the improvement of the Mersey and its tributaries, and in the promotion of the Sankey, Bridgewater, Trent and Mersey, and other essential canals. These connexions gave Liverpool an important trading advantage in Lancashire coal, Cheshire salt, Manchester textiles, Staffordshire iron and pottery, the iron production of the Welsh Marches and many smaller trades. With both foreland and hinterland communications expanding rapidly, the annual increase in tonnage of shipping handled in the Mersey port rose from 0·7 per cent per annum between 1716 and 1744, to a growth rate of 4·9 per cent in the period 1744–1851. That the figure fell to 2·6 per cent after 1851 indicates the importance to Liverpool's economic life of the development of an efficient internal communications system.

As the grand entrepot of the western seaboard, Liverpool soon experienced problems of accommodation for both vessels and goods which now impinged upon it from both sea lanes and inland waterways. In the second decade of the eighteenth century, both Bristol and Liverpool were among the first ports to create a modern wet dock. As Bristol declined, its first wet dock abandoned after the 1750s, Liverpool expanded its dock system. Five new docks were created in the period 1753–1821. 'By this time the acreage of the whole dock area was 47, puny enough when compared with the sevenfold increase which was to ensue in the next sixty years, but as the result of a continuous accretion of one dock after another it was a phenomenon which was in every way exceptional in the eighteenth century'.[18] The town grew in conjunction with the docks and shipping, and this growth was again permitted largely by the intricate system of supporting canals. In 1753 the Prescot Hall mine, with an initial monopoly in the supply of coal to Liverpool by land, raised prices. By 1755 Liverpool promoters had introduced the Sankey Brook Navigation Bill into Parliament, and by 1771 45,000 tons of coal were being carried annually down the Sankey Canal for Liverpool's consumption alone. In the same decade the Bridgewater, and Leeds and Liverpool canals were opened, so far averting the fuel crisis as to convert Liverpool into a prominent coal exporter, with 79,000 tons leaving the port in 1791.[19] The attraction of canals for industry led to the growth of canalside industrial zones within the town. The cramped Liverpool Dock Estate had no room for factories, many of which were established athwart the Leeds and Liverpool Canal, and supplied by lighter from the docks and by coal vessels directly from the interior. In particular, the important sugar-refining, oil-seed and cattle-cake industries are still found in this canalside industrial zone.

Hinterland expansion and port improvement were not, of course, confined to Liverpool. In the 1790s 'a sudden explosion of interest in port improvement' in London, reinforced by the contemporary Canal Mania, resulted in Britain's first dock boom.[20] The first wet dock had been built at Blackwall in 1661; a second, opened in 1700, remained at 10 acres the largest dock in London for a century, but between 1799 and 1830 four major dock companies constructed over 160 acres of docks, including the short canal which in 1829 became South-West India Dock.

In South Wales also, port expansion coincided with the opening up of the interior by canals. The three ports of Cardiff, Swansea and Newport each grew up at points where a river estuary served as a harbour on a coast otherwise ill-provided with havens. Urban and industrial development was stimulated by the exploitation of the copper, iron, and extensive coal deposits of the South Wales valleys. Rivers and packhorses proving incapable of supporting the trade, canals were opened to each port within the short period 1794–8. Before the development of true railways, these canals had extensive tramroad feeder systems. The great volume of coal fed into the canals by these, together with poor sea approaches, stimulated a series of port improvements. In Cardiff in particular, the Glamorganshire Canal, extended seawards in 1798, bypassed the old Town Quay on the river Taff and became the focus of what is now the town's port district.

Estuarial problems eventually led to the abandonment of the South Wales canal termini as port zones. In other areas, however, similar problems of access for seagoing vessels were solved by constructing ship canals. The case of the Manchester Ship Canal, completed in 1894, is too well known to repeat here. Further north in Lancashire, however, the approach to Ulverston was becoming increasingly difficult in the eighteenth century. To eradicate this impediment to the export of the rich haematite of Furness, a short ship canal was completed in 1796. This enabled Ulverston to retain its vitality as a port until the delivery of the death blow by the rise of the railway port of Barrow in the late 1840s. During its canal-based heyday Ulverston built several new streets, established shipbuilding yards alongside the canal, into which vessels were launched broadside, and enjoyed a population increase from 2,932 in 1801 to 5,352 in 1841.[21]

Former River Ports

Compared with its generally beneficial influence on seaports, the effect of the canal upon pre-existing river ports was more selective. Manchester, for example, served originally by the navigation of the improved Mersey and Irwell rivers, was transformed into a thriving canal port by the arrival, from four different directions, of the Bridgewater (1765), the Rochdale (1804), the Ashton (1800), the Manchester, Bolton and Bury (1808) and the Manchester and Salford Junction (1839) canals. As short canal arms were cut, and stone, lime, timber, coal, and general merchandise wharves laid out, three port areas emerged. The first, at the junction of the Bridgewater and Rochdale canals, was developed by the Duke of Bridgewater along the river Medlock. The first wharf in this zone, known as Castlefield, was opened in 1765. Although the Canal Duke remained the only resident carrier until the completion of the Trent and Mersey Canal in 1777, by 1804 there were 12 and by 1821 22 carrying firms operating out of Castlefield.[22] On the other side of the Irwell a second port zone, consisting mainly of coal wharves, emerged at Oldfield Road, near the Irwell terminus of the Bolton and Bury line. And further up the Rochdale cut the Piccadilly Wharves zone grew up at its junction with the Ashton Canal. Late eighteenth century town plans emphasize the basis of Manchester's dynamism, for the planning and laying out of streets was taking place chiefly around the dyeworks, mills, and foundries aligned along navigable waterways. By 1801 the former East Lancashire village had become the second largest city in Britain, a success based in part upon the development of its linear port areas.

In only a few cases was the transhipping function of a river port so triumphantly vindicated as in the case of Manchester. On the other side of the Pennines Selby had been an important junction between the packhorses of the West Riding and the seaport of Hull until the improvement of the river Aire to Leeds eclipsed the Ouse port as a mercantile centre. For more than two generations during the eighteenth century, Selby languished, to be revived only by the completion of the Selby Canal in 1778. Once more the West Riding's major port, Selby experienced a resurgence of activity as a canal-river transhipping point.[23] After the 1770s shipbuilding and repair yards, dry docks, warehouses, and other accoutrements of a small port began to emerge. In connexion with port activities, rope making, sail making, grain milling, and iron founding were encouraged. Textile exports rose, and as an exporter of inland coal Selby was finally able to oust the sea coal trade from the upper Ouse. The associated population increase from 2,861 in 1801 to 4,097 in 1821 was the greatest increase experienced in any twenty year period during the nineteenth century. One third of the working population was employed directly in the waterborne trades, a dependence which was Selby's undoing. For, like Ulverston, Selby was finally eclipsed by the railway, and also by the canal-created port of Goole, the development of which is traced in Chapter Seven.

Not all river ports were as well served during the Canal Age. After enjoying a long period of monopoly, many small ports which specialized in transhipment between road and river media suffered a rude awakening as they found themselves rendered redundant by the more efficient canals. The case of Bewdley, a flourishing pre-canal river port on the Severn, is discussed in Chapter Five in conjunction with the growth of the canal-created port of Stourport. In a similar way, the flourishing river port of Bawtry, long in competition with the river Don for the South Yorkshire–Hull trade, suffered a severe blow to its Derbyshire–Hull trade at the opening of the Chesterfield Canal in 1777. This cut, bypassing Bawtry on the Idle, made direct connexion with the Trent at Stockwith. By 1813 the Idle river trade had become 'inconsiderable to what it formerly was'.[24] Reflecting the decline of river trading, the town's population rose only slowly after 1780, and after 1831 began an absolute decline which lasted until the twentieth century.

Landlocked Towns

One of the most radical changes wrought upon existing settlements during the Canal Age was the sudden elevation, upon the arrival of a canal, of a formerly landlocked town to the status of an inland port. Whereas fortunate river ports might simply be confirmed in their existence as transhipment points by the advent of the canal, a town previously lacking navigable water connexion was subject to entirely novel influences as wharves, warehouses, basins and other indications of canal-based commerce began to develop within its purview. The canal's arrival invariably provided such towns with a much-needed economic boost; soon after the commencement of canal carrying, industries, population, general trade and housing all experienced an unprecedented period of mutually responsive growth.

When the Lancaster Canal reached Kendal in 1819, for example, the effect was more than instantaneous, for the town corporation had begun waterside improvements in the previous year. A basin, together with wharves and warehouses, was constructed, as well as a new bridge across the river Kent for easier access to the canal. For this gesture of public improvement the corporation paid £7,004, but the income from the warehouses and wharves was to reach about £550 per annum.[25] Private interests were not slow to follow the lead, for:

'. . . the spirit of improvement fully manifested itself in 1818 and 1819. The date of the new town may, we conceive, truly be placed here, at the time of the opening of the Lancaster and Kendal canal. This event gave an impulse to the public spirit of the inhabitants, and formed the commencement of a new era in the history of Kendal . . . Kent Lane (which before was very steep, and so narrow that two carts could scarcely pass) was thrown open, and the ascent considerably diminished; Long Pool was widened; Candy Street erected; Kent Terrace and Castle Crescent were built shortly after . . . on every side, numerous habitations were superadded to the town [and] in a very short time, the town assumed a new and modern appearance—so very different that a person having been absent for a few years, could scarcely have identified it.'[26]

Towns of far greater importance than Kendal had remained without water connexion during the era of river improvement and the early years of the Canal Age. Leicester's staple hosiery trade and the growth of the town in general were both held back by poor communications, and in particular by difficulties experienced in the importation of coal. The comment: 'Had it a navigable river, whereby it might have trading and commerce, it might compare with many [towns] of no mean rank', was voiced as early as 1622.[27] However, river and canal improvements in the Midlands benefitted the west rather than the east, and during the first part of the Canal Age Leicester had no navigable water connexion whatsoever. It was all the more galling to Leicester that nearby Loughborough, in combination with Derbyshire coal owners, was benefitting by the Erewash Canal and the river Soar Navigation, both in operation by 1779. Moreover, having become the new head of navigation on the Trent–Soar system, Loughborough used its position as a major distributing centre to manipulate and delay Leicester traffic, thus contributing to the stagnation of the latter town.[28]

After weathering a good deal of opposition from the Soar Navigation and the West Leicestershire coal owners, who had a quasi-monopoly in the town, Leicester interests saw the Act passed in 1791 for the Leicester Navigation, completed three years later. As built, the navigation consisted of the 'river line' and the 'Charnwood Forest Line'. The former was essentially an improvement of the river Soar involving extensive artificial cuts. The latter, a canal, was never really viable, though some coal did pass down to Leicester in the early days.

As in Kendal, the effects on the town were anticipatory. Wharves and factories were built and a land boom occurred along the lines of the intended navigations. Though Leicester's population increased from about 6,000 in 1700 to 16,833 in 1801, its subsequent connexion with the trunk lines of the Canal Cross was in part responsible for a further doubling by 1821. The population continued to rise by about 10,000 every decade until 1851, after which the arrival of the railways caused even further acceleration of the trend begun by the canal. Urban development responded to canal connexion not only in general expansion but also in direction of growth, the major thrust of new building being towards the public wharf. New streets, such as Wharf Street, arose, and formerly elite open areas like the Vauxhall Gardens and Black Friars gave way to more profitable commercial buildings. 'Industrial Leicester did not owe its origins to canals. But without them, and without the coal-supplies they made possible, comparatively little advance could have been made until the Railway Age'.[29]

Further examples would serve only to confirm the extreme effect of canals upon towns previously without navigable connexion. But the case of Birmingham, the most important of these, cannot be omitted. In the West Midlands the Birmingham Canal was constructed expressly to connect 'the numerous hearths and furnaces of industrial Birmingham with the prolific coalworks of the contiguous district of South Staffordshire'.[30] Within two decades of its completion in 1772, Birmingham had become the undisputed focus of the whole Canal Cross, a position referred to by Jackman as the 'Kremlin' from which radiated major canals joining the country's four great seaports.[31] Within the region itself, a tangle of coal-feeding canals, on three distinct levels, straggled northwestwards into the chief coalmining areas. The impetus to canal construction given by the expansion of canal-based Birmingham led to a duplication of routes during the Canal Mania, the town being provided with three alternative routes to the Severn. The town itself expanded towards the terminal wharves of the Birmingham Canal in the shape of the New Hall estate, and this movement was furthered by the termination of the Worcèster and Birmingham Canal in the same district.

As the first canal boats arrived, as early as 1769, the cost of coal in Birmingham was cut by half, a great stimulus to industrial production and population expansion. By the end of the eighteenth century, by which time the main pattern of canals in the district had been defined, factories were clustering along canal banks to take advantage of the ease of movement, special low tolls on coal destined for canalside works, and free water for steam engines. By 1811 no less than 124 works and wharves were crowded on the two miles of canal between Aston and Bordesley.[32] Faujas de Saint-Fond, a traveller in the area during the 1780s, was surprised to discover that 300 new houses per year had been built even during the course of the American War of Independence. He unhesitatingly accorded coal the honour of having led to this unprecedented rate of expansion: 'It is the abundance of coal which has performed this miracle and has created, in the midst of a barren desert, a town of forty thousand inhabitants'.[33]

It is clear, however, that canals were the chief instrument in permitting the conversion of the Birmingham region from a mass of small, often unrelated enterprises, into the urban-industrial complex known as the Black Country, capitalizing by means of improved transport on its strategic position within England. The rapid growth of inland Birmingham in a watershed position previously without water transport must have come as a surprise to those whose ideas were moulded in the coast-oriented early eighteenth century. From the viewpoint of 1791, however, the *British Directory* was unequivocal in its assertion of the role of the canal in making possible this phenomenon:

'Let it be remembered ... that in 1690 Birmingham, the first manufacturing town of the British Empire, contained only four thousand inhabitants. She has been raised, IN AN INLAND SITUATION, to her present wealth and population, by means of the numerous canals which connect this opulent place with every part of Europe.'[34]

2. Notes

1. T. Lowndes, (publisher) *The History of Inland Navigation, Particularly that of the Duke of Bridgewater*, London (1779), p. 3.

2. J. R. Clapham, *An Economic History of Modern Britain*, Cambridge University Press, Cambridge (1926), Vol. 1, p. 79.
3. J. Phillips, *A General History of Inland Navigation, Foreign and Domestic*, (1792) reprinted David and Charles, Newton Abbot, (1970), p. vii.
4. A. Young, *A Six Months Tour through the North of England*, London (1770), Letter XIX.
5. Ibid.
6. Calculated from Rickman's 'Observations . . .', *Census of England & Wales*, (1811).
7. D. Defoe, *A Tour through the Whole Island of Great Britain*, Dent, London (1962), p. 255.
8. Dupin, quoted in J. R. Clapham op. cit., p. 6.
9. D. Defoe, op. cit., pp. 199–200, 211.
10. C. Hadfield, *The Canal Age*, David and Charles, Newton Abbot (1968), p. 150.
11. Ibid., p. 209.
12. E. T. Patterson, *Radical Leicester: A History of Leicester 1780–1850*, Leicester University Press, Leicester (1954), p. 40.
13. *Berrow's Worcester Journal* (5 November 1795).
14. T. S. Ashton, *The Industrial Revolution 1760–1830*, Oxford University Press, London (1948), p. 236.
15. H. R. de Salis, *Bradshaw's Canals and Navigable Rivers of England and Wales*, London (1928).
16. G. Head, *A Home Tour through the Manufacturing Districts of England in the Summer of 1835*, London (1836), p. 8.
17. Ibid., p. 11.
18. F. E. Hyde, *Liverpool and the Mersey: the development of a port 1700–1970*, David and Charles, Newton Abbot (1971), p. 56.
19. Ibid., p. 30.
20. H. J. Dyos and D. H. Aldcroft, *British Transport: an economic survey from the seventeenth century to the twentieth*, Leicester University Press, Leicester (1969), p. 103.
21. C. Hadfield and G. Biddle, *The Canals of North West England*, David and Charles, Newton Abbot (1970), pp. 210, 428.
22. Ibid., p. 90.
23. Duckham, *The Yorkshire Ouse*, David and Charles, Newton Abbot (1967), pp. 73–6.
24. D. Holland, *Bawtry and the Idle River Trade*, Doncaster Museum Publications 31 (1964), p. 17.
25. C. Hadfield and G. Biddle, op. cit., p. 193.
26. Ibid., p. 195;
    R. Thames, *The Transport Revolution in the Nineteenth Century: a documentary approach*, Oxford University Press, London (1971), Vol. 2, p. 50.
27. E. T. Patterson, op. cit., p. 29.
28. Ibid., p. 30.
29. Ibid., p. 40.
30. M. J. Wise, (ed.) *Birmingham and Its Regional Setting*, Association for the Advancement of Science, Birmingham (1950), p. 184.
31. W. T. Jackman, *The Development of Transportation in Modern England*, Cambridge University Press, Cambridge (1962), p. 370.
32. M. J. Wise and B. L. C. Johnson, 'The Changing Regional Pattern in the Eighteenth

2. THE IMPACT OF CANALS ON EXISTING SETTLEMENTS   37

Century', in *Birmingham and its Regional Setting*, ed. by M. J. Wise, Association for the Advancement of Science, Birmingham (1950).

33. F. de Saint-Fond, 'Impressions of Birmingham (1784)', in D. B. Horn and M. A. Ransome, *English Historical Documents 1714–1783*, Eyre and Spottiswoode, London (1957), pp. 473–4.

34. P. Barfoot and J. Wilkes, *Universal British Directory of Trade and Commerce*, Stalker, London (1791), Vol. 2, p. 201.

3

The Creation of Settlements by Canals

Wherever a large-scale activity is geographically concentrated so as to give a localised basis for mass employment, a town or at least the semblance of a town is created.

A. Smailes

As a stimulator of regional specialization, seaport growth, and industrial expansion, and as a converter of inland towns into minor ports, the canal was unrivalled during the Industrial Revolution. Yet canals were not simply stimulators of pre-existing settlements and activities; they were also responsible for the creation of settlements and activities quite new to the British scene. The canal system played a major role in the remaking of the landscape of Britain after 1760.[1] Features long known, but previously restricted to navigable rivers, were spread throughout the country. Wharves, locks, towpaths, and water-side limekilns, smithies, warehouses and pubs became as familiar to dwellers in the interior as to inhabitants of regions with ancient river navigations.

Completely new features, however, were to be found on the canals alone. About twenty inclined planes were built for carrying boats between two sections of canal meeting at different levels. Several boat-lifts were provided for the same purpose. Major aqueducts were constructed, notably in the more difficult terrain of the west, as on the Peak Forest, Lancaster, Forth and Clyde, and Shropshire Union canals. Reservoirs were made for the regulation of water supplies. Over forty miles of canal tunnel were cut, the longest single bore being Standedge, near Huddersfield, where the canal originally disappeared for 5,456 yd under the Pennines. A variety of dwellings were provided for canal workers: at locks, lockhouses for lock-keepers; along the canal, houses for maintenance staff and bridge-keepers; at junctions, toll-houses, and at wharves, housing for wharfingers, boatmen, and porters.

Urban Genesis: The Context

Only rarely did any of the above dwelling clusters become a settlement of significant size. At certain points along the canals, however, larger settlements did appear, almost always at places where a good deal of transhipping took place between canal vessels and other transport media. Canal-created settlements are thus a particular type of the large group of villages and towns brought into being by the needs of transportation routes at break of bulk positions.

The important role of transport lines in the process of urban genesis and growth has long been appreciated. Human activity swings between the two poles of movement and settlement; where movement comes to a halt, either permanently or temporarily, settlement may result.[2] Colin Clark, in his significantly titled paper 'Transport: Maker and Breaker of Cities', emphasizes this point.[3] Keslake, dealing with early road transport, and Weber, with nineteenth century cities, are among a large number of scholars who have illustrated the value of route junctions as sites for urban development.[4] When the junction is between two different media, the provision of a necessary minimum of installations at the transhipping point becomes almost obligatory. It is certainly mandatory when goods are to be transferred between water transport and land media. Innumerable examples of towns on creeks, on coastlines, and at bridgeheads testify to the generative capacity of such breakpoints throughout the world.

Timbuktu, at the southern margin of the Sahara Desert, serves to illustrate the general features of breakpoint urban development.[5] In Europe and North America the town has popularly been regarded as the epitome of remoteness. Yet the development of Timbuktu is related largely to its accessibility and strategic location with regard to ancient traffic routes. Time out of mind the southbound products of the Barbary Coast and the northbound wealth of the tropics have been exchanged in the district. Timbuktu's function as a major exchange point is directly related to its position at the meeting of land and water, at the point where the river Niger penetrates the Sahara most deeply. The entrepot city is connected with the Niger by a tidal slough or canal to its river port of Kabara. Equally remote, and yet equally centrally-placed within a communications system, the Canadian town of Tuktoyaktuk grew up at the point where the flat-bottomed vessels of the Mackenzie river met ocean-going ships unable to penetrate the Mackenzie delta.

Such cases emphasize that the use of such breakpoints is defined not only by nature but also by the level of technology available.[6] Once such a key breakpoint has been recognized, however, commercial transactions, and with them a settlement, can hardly fail to develop. Richard Meier has concisely explained the process of urban development at such breakpoints:

> 'Commerce is founded upon a series of transactions between buyers and sellers, each of whom benefits . . . The standard transaction requires a short period of time for negotiation, and is consequently restricted to one locale. Once an interregional market place has come to be recognised, shiploads and caravans of products must be redistributed over a short period of time. At this scale of operations it is evident that both buyer and seller require services in the form of transport, warehousing, banking, accounting, security, etc. . . . Artisans will set up their shops at sites calculated to capture a share of the [profit] . . . At linkage points in communications systems . . . change encourages change in the vicinity of a communications focus, and activity is piled upon activity in a small amount of space.'[7]

The result is a town devoted principally to transport, transhipping, and ancillary activities.

In the remote past such conditions must have been frequent, and especially so along waterways. Mumford assures us that 'the rise of the city is contemporaneous with improvements in navigation'.[8] A Canadian example confirms the persistence of the role of navigations in the genesis, development, and decline of settlements.[9] Before the construction of the first Welland Canal in the early nineteenth century, movement between lakes Erie and Ontario involved navigation of the Niagara river and frequent portages. Nevertheless, the towns of Chippawa, Queenston and Niagara emerged along the line, with St Catharines nearby. The canal, however, was routed through St Catharines, and thus the growth of the three river settlements was severely curtailed. While St Catharines expanded in response to canal traffic, the first Welland Canal and its subsequent realignments brought into being no less than eight new settlements. Between Port Dalhousie on Lake Ontario and Port Colborne on Lake Erie the towns of Merritton, Thorold, Dunnville, Allanburg, Port Robinson, Welland, and Wainfleet were laid out along the canal and its water-supply feeder.

Canal-created Settlements in Britain

In Britain the Canal Age was equally prolific in the creation of settlements where none had been before. Several points provided potential locations for canal-generated villages and towns. Such settlements could emerge at the canal head, or inland terminus, at junctions with other canals, at strategic points en route, and at the junction of the canal with a natural waterbody such as a non-tidal river, a tideway, or the sea.

Canal Head Settlements

Inland terminal settlements often took on a distinct character; that at Worsley has already been described. Perhaps the simplest case of the canal head as a settlement location is that of the Cassington Canal.[10] A private cut made by the Duke of Marlborough in the 1790s, the canal joined the village of Cassington to the Thames near the outfall of the Evenlode. Barely half a mile in length, by 1801 it was provided with a river entrance lock and a wharf at the head of navigation. By 1802 two limekilns were in the process of construction, and two years later a wharfinger's house had been built, soon to become the 'Barge Inn'. With a traffic in coal, salt, and groceries, the wharf became a second and separate focus for the village of Cassington, population 374 in 1801. It was so important that in 1823 the tenant of the wharf was assessed £2 for poor rates, whereas the local miller paid only £1 10s. A somewhat more important inland terminus grew up at Bugsworth, near Buxton, on the Peak Forest Canal. At this point the canal ended in several interchange basins connected to the Peak Forest tramway. Here a typical small canal settlement grew up, consisting of essentials only: inns; smithy; stables; repair workshops; limekilns; a wharfinger's office; post office; church; and cottages.

The canal head of most flourishing navigations was, of course, within an existing inland settlement. In some cases, however, the canal failed to reach its projected terminus; both the Pocklington and Market Weighton canals stopped short of their urban objectives. Goods carried by road to and from Market Weighton and Pocklington had to be transhipped at the respective canal heads, thus requiring the laying out of public wharves and coal yards, and the erection of warehouses.[11] Such settlements were, however, insignificant in size terms, and in general canals were not responsible for the creation of large independent urban entities at their inland termini.

Canal Junction Settlements

Small villages, such as Preston Brook, Aldersley Junction, Hurleston Junction and Fradley Junction sprang up where one canal met another. Typically, only small hamlets emerged at these locations, their buildings perhaps including a toll house, a boat yard and sheds, a warehouse, a public house, and some cottages. Fradley Junction, where the Coventry Canal meets the Trent and Mersey, is typical in that it is totally canal-oriented, having little relationship with the local road network or even with the mother village of Fradley. Port Dundas, Glasgow, at the junction of the Forth and Clyde and Monkland canals, is exceptional in its considerable size and accretion of industry in the shape of iron foundries and distilleries. Unlike most canal junctions, it was located adjacent to an already thriving city.

Canalside Settlements

A local resource, or the meeting of a road or tramway with the canal, was often the occasion for settlement generation. Although unable to support more than a few buildings at its head, the Market Weighton Canal called into existence the appropriately named village of Newport at the point where it was crossed by the road from Hull to the West Riding of Yorkshire. Stimulated by the rising demand for bricks in growing urban centres, local entrepreneurs were encouraged to exploit canalside clay deposits. Though the canal began to earn tolls from the carriage of general merchandise in 1776, the trade of the town of Market Weighton could hardly have supported the navigation. Indeed, the movement of Newport's brick and tile production became the raison d'etre of the canal. By 1823 the township contained seven brick and tile manufacturers and was producing annually about 1,700,000 tiles and two million bricks.

Much larger settlements grew up alongside canals in response to the many advantages of industrial location on the canal bank. The Potteries, never really inured to the transportation of their delicate wares along the abominable roads, were revitalized by the passing of the Act for the Trent and Mersey Canal in 1766. 'It is impossible to express the Joy that appeared throughout the Potteries, in the Neighbourhood of Newcastle, on Receipt of this important News—for nothing but an Inland Navigation can ever put this Manufactory on an Equality with their Foreign Competitors'.[12] Contemporary maps indicate that, though the canal did not enter all the Pottery towns, many soon put out new roads to its banks.

Wedgwood, a prime mover in both pottery manufacture and canal promotion, built a huge canalside factory which was provided with its own wharves. As cottages were built for the workmen the village of Etruria sprang up; characteristic of the times, the master potter constructed a large mansion for himself on higher ground overlooking works, workers, and canal. John Wesley, passing through the area in 1781, was so astonished at the changes wrought in its urban landscape that he exclaimed: 'How is the whole face of this country changed in about twenty years. Since which, inhabitants have continually flowed in from every side. Hence the wilderness is literally become a fruitful field. Houses, villages, towns have sprung up; and the country not more improved than the people'.[13] Canals having provided the catalysing influence promoting 'social amelioration and industrial efficiency' in an area formerly 'too remote from the seats of commerce', they were also indirectly responsible for a wave of urban growth sufficient to swallow up the separate identities of canal-generated settlements such as Etruria. The end result was in sight as early as 1785, for the fourteen distinct pottery towns and villages had even then begun to coalesce into 'seven miles of buildings all joined'.[14]

A more isolated, and thus more obvious, example of a canal-generated industrial settlement grew up in South Lancashire where the townships of Windle, Sutton, Eccleston and Parr met at a road junction graced by a chapel-of-ease known as St Helens. In the early eighteenth century this was an area of mixed farming broken by barren stretches of heathland. Some employment was also provided by the small-scale mining of coal, sand, and fireclay, and by the domestic cloth industry. The arrival of the Sankey Brook Navigation in 1757, however, wrought a complete transformation which eventually resulted in the rise of the new industrial town of St Helens.[15]

As soon as the canal reached Parr local coalowners inaugurated a trade with Liverpool and the Cheshire salt region which soon led to their preeminence in the commercial affairs of the district. Coal magnates were directly responsible for the growth of St Helens and of the smaller colliery townships which eventually coalesced with it:

'It is with great pleasure we give the inhabitants of Liverpool, and the country, the earliest notice, that the mines of J. Mackay, Esquire, are in most extensive opening, will be compleated this year, and that Sankey Navigation is now bringing up to the new ones in his own land. We are told by the gentleman's agent . . . that no part of the Kingdom will be better supplied for coals than this town and neighbourhood, they now being in such condition as to get immense quantities, that colliers are their only want, and the encouragement given them there is great, that the proximity of the town of St Helens, together with the extent and probable durability of the mines, renders it so inviting a situation for Colliers and their families to settle in that he makes no doubt (when once known) that they will have great plenty of men . . . His master, for the convenience of his people, has now built, and is still building, a considerable number of comfortable houses. . . .[16]

Such abundance of coal, now so readily transported, attracted industrial establishments to the St Helens district. In 1771, the same year that Mackay was soliciting colliers, a Warrington company was in negotiation for the establishment of a copper works, rival to an existing Liverpool plant, near the abundant coal supplies of Parr and Ashton townships. Supplied with coal at a discount via a railroad from the Sankey Brook Navigation, the Stanley Works operated at a great advantage over its Liverpool rival. Further, Mackay was able to attract the Parys Mine Company to his estates in 1779, leasing it land along the Ravenhead branch of the Sankey Canal. An equally good customer for his coal was the British Cast Plate Glass Company, which he had attracted to Ravenhead in 1773. As these primary coal and canal-using industries expanded, secondary manufacturing and services, such as the brewery industry, were stimulated.

At first individual companies were obliged, like Mackay, to provide housing for their work people. The Parys Company, for example, built cottages and took over the 'Navigation Inn', which then became a canalside place of entertainment for copper workers. A fairly enlightened employer, the company also provided newspapers, helped organize sick clubs and burial clubs, and instituted a policy of providing free medical attention. Some of this company paternalism was rendered unnecessary as the town of St Helens grew to be the focus of the new mining and manufacturing district.[17] In 1763 the village contained fewer than ninety houses and was frequently known as Hardshaw rather than St Helens. By the first decade of the next century the former name was forgotten and the place had come to be regarded as a 'country town'. The first completely new street was laid out in the 1790s; by 1805 two long rows of buildings flanked the road running between the two major foci of growth, the chapel and the canal.

During the period 1801–21 the population of the four townships increased from 7,573 to 10,603; at the latter date St Helens proper contained about 4,000 inhabitants. Three years later the first St Helens Building Society was formed, and in 1831 the population had risen to about 6,000. By the end of the Canal Age the character of St Helens had been defined, that of an urban-industrial complex based on canal transport and specializing in copper, glass, chemicals, and associated trades. In the 1830s the town still contained country boarding schools, and the devastating smoke from alkali works had yet to kill off trees and crops in the vicinity. All this was to change after an Act of 1830 provided St Helens with a railway to the Mersey at Widnes. The railway, which brought the port of Widnes into being, accelerated the changes brought about by the Sankey Brook Navigation.

River and Coast Terminal Settlements

Besides stimulating the growth of new towns and villages at inland terminal points and along their routes, canals also created settlements at their river or coast terminals. The Forth and Clyde Canal, for example, brought into being the small settlement of Bowling (1775) at its point of entry into the Clyde estuary. In a similar fashion Port Tennant arose near Swansea. The completion of the Carlisle Canal to the Solway Firth at Fisher's Cross, near Bowness, resulted in 1823 in the formation of a terminal settlement known as Port Carlisle. Near the canal's terminal basin and lock a neat two storey Georgian terrace was laid out with a uniform eaves line and fenestration, and elaborate door cases. Though later superseded by Silloth as Carlisle's outport, the village grew to comprise about fifty houses.

Similar settlements were set up at canal-river terminals in more interior locations. These varied from a few houses erected at Trent Lock, the outfall of the Erewash Canal into the Trent, to substantial towns such as Stourport at the junction of the Staffordshire and Worcestershire Canal with the Severn. Most canal-river terminals remained small, however. A number of such settlements occur along the Trent, but few

C

have grown beyond village size. Keadby, for example, grew with the coal trade along the Stainforth and Keadby Canal between Don and Trent, and Torksey, at the junction of the Trent and the Roman Foss-dyke Navigation, may claim to be one of the oldest canal ports in existence.

The sudden rise and slow decline of these small canal ports may be illustrated by the example of Weighton Lock. At the point of entry of the Market Weighton Canal into the Humber the canal company in the late eighteenth century built a well-proportioned house for its officers, together with some cottages. By the turn of the century the demand from market boats plying to and from Hull had led to the opening of both an inn and a shop. Brickyards were begun, and thus the Lock added its contribution to the expansion of Hull and other towns. Like many canal settlements, the Lock was hampered in its growth by the lack of a made-up road connecting it to land-based villages and towns. Although this was not of great importance in the Canal Age, it was thrown into focus by the opening in 1840 of the Hull to Selby rail line, which passed within three miles of the hamlet. When Market Weighton was in turn connected by rail to Hull (1865), as well as to York (1847), Weighton Lock became yet another casualty of the Railway Age. Market boats had ceased to call at the Lock by the late 1860s, the last local brickmaker is recorded in 1872, and both inn and shop had disappeared from the directories by the 1880s.[18] Two houses survive today where there were a dozen at the opening of the century.

Coalport, just downstream from Coalbrookdale on the Severn, is a better-known case. Here the Shropshire Canal arrived in 1791, and was carried down the valley side 207ft in a distance of 305 yd by means of an inclined plane; it then ran parallel with the river bank for some distance before terminating in Coalport Harbour. Inclined planes, rising and falling with the height of the Severn, were used to transfer goods between canal tub-boats and river vessels. As Coalport became the outlet for the Shropshire coal mines and ironworks, a brisk export trade was conducted in coal and pig, bar and sheet iron. An early nineteenth century observer noted: 'standing upon Coalport Bridge I have counted seventy barges standing at Coalport Wharf, some laden and others loading with coal and iron'.[19] Industry was attracted, and the Coalport China works moved from Caughley to a position alongside both canal and Severn, to be followed by a chain and wire rope works. A 'tar tunnel' was driven into the local coal measures, and during the nineteenth century petroleum was exported 'on a large scale under the name of Betton's British Oil'.[20]

Locational Decision-making

Most canal ports at canal-river junction positions have either remained small or have actually declined in size. A few, however, have grown to considerable proportions and remain viable urban communities in the latter half of the twentieth century. In great measure this success has been due to adaptability, coupled with the strategic location of these canal ports, which were originally founded at points of intervening opportunity, usually a tideway location, between interior mining and manufacturing regions and estuarial seaports. In this connexion it is manifestly important to investigate the decision-making process which led to the selection of a particular location for the canal port nucleus. This involves an attempt to understand the reasons for the decision, taken by the canal company or individual owner, to adopt a particular canal route from among a number of possible lines. It is this process which determined the river terminus of the canal and thus the site of the port which grew up there.

The reasons for the initial promotion of a canal generally included a major terminal objective, which roughly determined the canal's direction. Once this was clear, and bearing in mind the interrelated twin desires for shortness and cheapness, the precise alignment of the route was related to the physical and cultural features of the landscape through which the canal was to pass. Factors influencing route decision-making included: the techniques available, varying both through time and with the engineer employed; the availability of capital; the state of contemporary mapping and understanding of the landscape; and the need to join together as many traffic-generating points as possible. The specific landscape elements which influenced route alignment may be divided into three groups:

Positive or 'Pull' Elements

Attractive, favourable forces played a part in guiding the course of the canal. Apart from the major river, estuary, or seaport, almost always the primary objective of the longer canals, these forces included complementary waterways, connexion with which might prove advantageous, and certain fixed points such as towns, factories, and mines, especially those of the canal promoters.

Negative or 'Push' Elements

Repellant, unfavourable forces deflected the canal from an otherwise suitable path. Rival canal schemes and the estates of powerful landowners were important here. Drainage systems of little use as navigations, and their accompanying marshes, were other obstacles to the construction of a sound, inexpensive canal.

Contingent Variables

The quantity, quality, or availability of these were critical factors in route decision-making; they could be either positive or negative according to the local situation. Water supplies were of paramount importance, as was the availability of land. Geology exerted an influence mainly through physiography, for it was canal excavation which first gave widespread access to geological data, which remained poorly understood until long after the Canal Age. Relief, in fact, looming large in the minds of canal planners, was the major influential element in early route-making. Chance, including innumerable errors, may have altered the intended line, as in the fictional case of Squire Haggard who, coveting his neighbour's income from the sale of land for canal-building, in a nocturnal expedition altered the marking pegs to secure a semicircular detour through his estate.

Once the terminal point had been reached, basic installations usually appeared on the scene with some rapidity. A certain minimum of facilities was required, such as a lock keeper's cottage. Elsewhere docks might be interposed between canal and river, wharves and warehouses built, and the nucleus of a town begun. In terms of layout such towns generally conform to one of two types. Adaptive breakpoint towns grew up 'naturally', that is, their shape and component parts were determined by a multitude of decisions made by a variety of persons. Consequently the history of their development is often impossible to trace in any detail. In other cases, however, the need to provide a major transhipping facility, such as a dock, initially involved a single decision made by an individual or company at a single point in time. If the entrepreneur went on to provide dock installations and perhaps some housing, a planned town may have resulted. The layout of such a town may differ markedly from that of an adaptive settlement. In general it will be more regular; 'of necessity . . . a pioneering town in a strange place will have a simple plan . . . which can be easily laid out'.[21] Such decisions to create towns, or at least the nuclei of future towns, are not rare. One of many such ports in North America is Buffalo, which was soon joined by the Erie Canal: 'Buffalo Creek Harbour was begun, carried on, and completed principally by three private individuals . . . Over the grave of Samuel Wilkinson, which faces the harbour, is chiselled: "Urbem condidit" '.[22] It is with the creation of such ports at the tideway terminals of major canals that the bulk of this volume is concerned.

Canal-created River Ports

It is clear that canals *sui generis* had the capacity to stimulate the growth of inland ports at points of origin, at river and other terminals, and at any desired loading station en route. In order to study in some depth the genesis and development of canal-created ports, this investigation will be restricted to a small number of settlements sufficiently large to have developed considerable urban differentiation and port growth since their inception. Arbitrary limits have therefore been set. To qualify for inclusion a town must, by 1971, have attained the status at least of urban district, together with a population minimum of 10,000; there should be evidence of the existence of a dock system of some size. These criteria effectively exclude all settlements created by canals at canal head, canalside, or canal junction locations, together with small river terminals such as Port Carlisle and Coalport, and thus restrict the study wholly to those ports created at the junction of a major canal with a navigable river.

To stress the importance of the latter point, a reminder of the overall nature of Britain's Canal Age inland navigation system is needed:

'We can envisage the waterway system of Britain as a network of canals and rivers joining together the principal towns, and linking sources of raw materials with industrial areas. Some of the traffic on it was purely internal . . . Much, however, had arrived at a port by coasting or foreign-trading vessel, or was destined for shipment from a port. This trade passed to and from the ports at the edges of the web, where the navigable waterways ended and tidal water began.'[23]

It is just at these points of transhipment 'at the edges of the web' that the most striking examples of the canal-created river port, partaking of the character of both canal port and river port, grew up as links in the chain between interior industrial centres and outer seaports.

A further criterion concerns the nature of port origin. To qualify for inclusion a town, or at least the initial port terminal, involving a fairly elaborate dockland with associated buildings, must have been created *ex nihilo* in a near-vacant landscape for the express purpose of goods or passenger transhipment between canal and river. In brief, we are concerned with 'mushroom towns' which, springing up suddenly, appeared new and strange to contemporary travellers. A few excerpts from Head's description of Goole will serve to express this notion:

> 'The town of Goole has been forced into existance by the rich and powerful Aire and Calder [Navigation] Company . . . the town is actually built upon the Canal, the basin being close to the Docks . . . in most modern maps the town is not laid down. Yet there it stands on the banks of the [Yorkshire] Ouse . . . a small village risen to the dignity and importance of a considerable shipping port; and at the same time the very boys that play at marbles in the streets call to mind the digging of its foundations.'[24]

The English settlements satisfying these several criteria are: Runcorn, Cheshire, founded in 1771–6 by the Duke of Bridgewater at the terminus of the Bridgewater Canal; Stourport, Worcestershire, founded in 1771 by the Staffordshire and Worcestershire Canal Company; Ellesmere Port, Cheshire, created in 1795 by the Ellesmere Canal Company and rejuvenated in 1835 by the Birmingham and Liverpool Junction Canal; and, of course, Goole, West Yorkshire, laid out in 1826 as the terminus of the Aire and Calder Navigation's new cut from Ferrybridge and Knottingley. The distribution of these towns (Fig. 4) closely reflects the organization of the Canal Cross, connecting elevated interior manufacturing districts on coalfield sites with major rivers and estuaries carved as far inland as the New Red Sandstone belt.

This study, hopefully, demonstrates that these towns, created by similar forces in analogous positions within a short time-span, constitute an initial type. It also attempts to discover how far they were able to retain their original similarities through the vicissitudes of the Canal, Rail and Motor ages. Urban history is generally lacking in comparative studies. In this case comparison is achieved by the selection of representative elements of study, common to all the ports. Before the 1840s, certain themes must be investigated for each port. The nature of the pre-canal landscape, the process of decision-making whereby a specific canal route, and thus a specific terminal, was chosen, and the structure and operation of the initial river terminal port are important.

Even at this early stage the potential for landscape change at the four

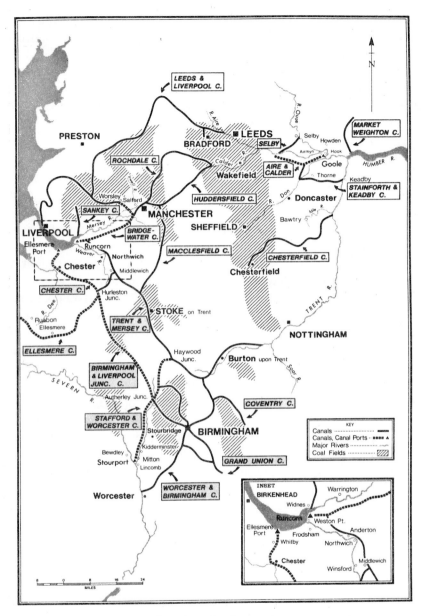

FIG. 4. Location of major canal ports.

termini was varied, and by no means great. A canal may lock directly into the river, or via a tidal basin or wet dock, or both, interposed between canal and river. Only the canal to Stourport reached its terminus as a narrow canal, incapable of taking vessels of over 7ft beam, and thus demanding a wharf or dock for the transhipment of goods to larger river vessels. Even this need, however, was reduced by the construction of horse towing paths which enabled narrow boats to go down the Severn as far as Gloucester and Sharpness. The three other canals were broad waterways of sufficient size to permit barges of 14ft beam to penetrate both canal and river. For them a dock for the transhipment of goods moving between seaport and interior was not a necessity, though the shortness of Ellesmere Port's wide canal promoted transhipping at that point.

Yet in all four cases a wet dock system was created, together with associated Canal Age trade, industrial, and urban developments. Company paternalism, and some frontier town characteristics, might be expected in such new settlements. Competition from other waterways was possible, and as the canal frequently superseded older river ports, and was to be superseded in its turn by the railways, the process of port replacement on each river system must be investigated.

The invention of the steam engine, and later, of the internal combustion engine, might be expected to have had grave repercussions on the trade, dock, urban and industrial development of the canal-created river ports. The fluctuations of canal and port traffic, changes in the canal line and its terminal dock system, and company paternalism with it concrete expressions, are considered as a single complex. Around the communications nexus represented by the company nucleus, the growth of the non-company sector of the town, including utilities and amenities, housing, industry, and administration, form a separate but related study. Trade and population fluctuations provide a background of chance, cause and effect.

3. Notes

1. W. G. Hoskins, *The Making of the English Landscape*, Hodder & Stoughton, London (1955).
2. L. Mumford, *The City in History*, Harcourt, Brace and World, New York (1961), p. 13.

3.   C. Clark, 'Transport: Maker and Breaker of Cities', *Town Planning Review* 28 (1958), 237–50.

4.   T. Keslake, 'What is a Town?', *Journal of the Royal Archaeological Society of Great Britain and Ireland*, 34 (1877) 199–211;
     A. F. Weber, *The Growth of Cities in the Nineteenth Century*, (1899).

5.   H. Miner, *The Primitive City of Timbuctoo*, Doubleday, New York (1965).

6.   C. Sjoberg, *The Pre-industrial City, Past and Present*, Free Press, Glencoe, Ill. (1960).

7.   R. L. Meier, *A Communications Theory of Urban Growth*, M.I.T. Press, Cambridge, Mass. (1962), pp. 37, 43.

8.   L. Mumford, op. cit., p. 88.

9.   J. N. Jackson, *The Canadian City*, McGraw-Hill Ryerson, Toronto (1973), pp. 38–41.

10. H. Compton and K. Belsten, 'The Cassington Canal', *Journal of the Railway and Canal Historical Society*, 12 (1966), 53–8.

11. B. F. Duckham, *The Inland Waterways of East Yorkshire 1700–1900*, East Yorkshire Local History Series No. 29, York (1972), pp. 40, 64.

12. *Aris' Birmingham Gazette* (28 April 1766).

13. W. T. Jackman, *The Development of Transportation in Modern England*, Cambridge University Press, Cambridge (1962), p. 366.

14. J. Aikin, *A Description of the Country from Thirty to Forty Miles Around Manchester*, Stockdale, London (1795), 516.

15. T. C. Barker and J. R. Harris, *A Merseyside Town in the Industrial Revolution: St Helens 1750–1900*, Cass, London (1954).

16. Ibid., p. 44.

17. Ibid., p. 168.

18. E. M. Reader, *Broomfleet and Faxfleet: two townships through two thousand years*, Sessions, York (1972), pp. 40–1, 44, 55.

19. J. Randall, *The Severn Valley*, Randall, Madeley (1882), p. 300.

20. *Idem., Handbook to the Severn Valley Railway*, Madeley (1863), p. 26.

21. S. E. Rasmussen, *Towns and Buildings*, (revised ed.), M.I.T. Press, Cambridge, Mass. (1969), p. 8.

22. J. M. Welch, 'The City of Buffalo', *Harper's New Monthly Magazine*, 71 (1885), 193–216.

23. C. Hadfield, *British Canals: an illustrated history*, David and Charles, Newton Abbot (1969) 4th ed., p. 138.

24. G. Head, *A Home Tour through the Manufacturing Districts of England in the Summer of 1835*, London (1836), pp. 226, 229.

The Genesis
and Development
of Canal Ports

Not houses finely roofed nor the stones of walls well-
builded, nay, nor canals and dockyards make a city, but
men able to use their opportunity.

Alcaeus of Lesbos, *c.* 600 B.C.

4
Runcorn in the Canal Age

An Act to enable the Most Noble Francis Duke of Bridgewater, to make a
navigable Cut or Canal from Longford Bridge in the township of Stretford in
the County Palatine of Lancashire, to the River Mersey, at a Place called the
Hempstones, in the Township of Halton in the County of Chester.

(2 Geo. III, c. 11; 1762)

Runcorn Before The Canal

Of the four rural areas untouched as yet by the transport revolution,
Runcorn had the best claim to some form of status as a settlement. The
pre-canal village occupied the northern slope of Runcorn Hill, the
northernmost end of a series of longitudinally trending ridges, forming a
rounded promontory between the converging rivers Mersey and Weaver.
Lying immediately opposite a smaller sandstone cape thrust out into the
Mersey from the Lancashire shore, this arrangement has given rise to a
marked constriction in the Mersey valley known as Runcorn Gap. At this
point the wide areas of floodplain which escort both Mersey and Weaver
to the sea contract to form only a narrow strip below the mass of Runcorn
Hill.

Runcorn Gap, the paramount physical feature of the area, was early
exploited by travelling man. It is possible that the Romans, with their
base on Halton Hill, used Runcorn as a shipping place.[1] During the
conquest of the Danelaw, Runcorn became the site of one of a series of
fortresses erected by the Mercian princess Ethelfleda. Sited on Castle
Rock, close to the shore, it was in a superb position to dominate the
boundary river. The first church was probably coeval with the castle, for
an extensive Runcorn parish existed long before the second Baron Halton
sought salvation in 1133 by founding at Runcorn a house of the Canons
Regular of the Order of St Augustine.

The focus of local activity, however, was soon to desert Saxon Runcorn for Norman Halton, for only ten years after its foundation the priory was removed to Norton in the shadow of Halton Castle. After the Dissolution the priory was taken by the Brooke family as a private residence, an act which had important repercussions in the age of canal building.

Although Runcorn appears as a wooded and wasted area in Domesday Book, some evidence of commerce and industry, in the shape of fishing and milling, is available for early medieval times. The gap was not ignored, for in the twelfth century the sixth Baron Halton established the first ferry between Runcorn and the marshy Widnes promontory. Though unable to compete with established crossings upstream, the ferry was of local utility. By this time Runcorn was becoming a place of resort for shipping, there being references to 'the Porte of Runcorn' for 1378 and 1409.[2] Some of the visiting vessels were seagoing, and in the fifteenth century there were connexions with Beaumaris and Dublin. Indeed, in 1481 the mayor of Dublin was commanded to proclaim that every Irish merchant ship charged with goods for Runcorn or any other place in Cheshire should first call at the official quays in Chester.[3] At this time the Mersey, though leading to an embryo textile zone, was hardly able to encroach on the primacy of the Dee which, however, led only into the Welsh hills. Mersey shipping remained negligible until the eighteenth century; while small vessels served Cheshire via the Mersey and Weaver when tides permitted, they were in no way obliged to tranship at Runcorn.

By the late seventeenth century the Runcorn district had become, at least in commercial terms, more remote than it had been in medieval times. With a rudimentary parish administration and with local transport little improved, the villages of Higher and Lower Runcorn pursued their own way of life, hardly disturbed by the world outside. Other settlements in the region had grown to proportionately greater importance, notably Manchester and Liverpool. A cul-de-sac whose only outlet was a frequently interrupted ferry, Runcorn was bypassed by the roads running from Warrington to Chester and into the Wirral. Such isolation is difficult to conceive until one realizes that Cheshire roads were 'some of the most detestable roads in England . . . so worn and rugged that it is hardly safe much less easy to pass over them'.[4] Because of lack of demand, a local turnpike crossing the Chester–Warrington road and terminating at the Runcorn ferry was not feasible before the coming of the Bridgewater Canal.

The ferry itself achieved some degree of fame, 'The Ballad of Will the Ferryman, a water eclogue' appearing in 1758.[5] But local circulation was not intense; agricultural produce was carted to the markets of Halton and Frodsham, though some was shipped across the ferry and thence to Liverpool or Warrington. With its predominantly clay soils the district supported pastoral rather than arable pursuits, with some emphasis on the production of the famed Cheshire cheese. Extensive areas of heath and moss varied the economy. In addition, the fine freestone of Runcorn Hill was extensively quarried, though the largest quarries lay in the adjacent township of Weston. Both townships sent stone to Liverpool, shipping assuming greater importance in the early eighteenth century after the passing of Acts in 1720 for the improvement of Mersey, Irwell and Weaver. Weaver vessels, however, mainly concerned with the salt trade, had little cause to round the headland to Runcorn, where there were tidal difficulties, while the bulk of Mersey shipping also passed it by.

Thus the Runcorn which received the canal, though having some long-standing links with transportation and commerce, was still a remote and lonely Merseyside village. Although near the junction of two rivers on which trade was fast increasing in response to the silting of the Dee, Runcorn had no significant share in the trading activities of the time. To a large extent, Runcorn before the canal clearly answers to the epithet 'obscure village' so frequently applied by nineteenth-century writers bent on emphasizing the vast changes wrought in the landscape by the Industrial Revolution. By the mid-eighteenth century:

'Once the site of a stronghold of strategical importance, the home of a powerful ecclesiastical fraternity, and the head of an extensive parish, Runcorn was . . . shorn of its glories. The peculiar geographical position of the township placed it far out of the reach of the great highways, and outside its own limits the hamlet was little known.'[6]

The Decision-making Context

Throughout the eighteenth century travellers continually stressed the ebullient growth of Liverpool, soon far to exceed Chester in size. Defoe was amazed at its dynamism: 'It visibly encreases both in wealth, people, business and buildings. What it may grow to in time, I know not'.[7] This blossoming was contingent upon developments in both hinterland and foreland. The new imports, sugar, tobacco and cotton, stimulated manufacturing both in Liverpool and Manchester, and with the growth of textile production and the extraction of coal and salt, speeded the accretion of capital and the development of organizational techniques. 'The eighteenth century's success story', Liverpool received a great stimulus from the demands of its hinterland, and such was this stimulus that the average annual tonnage of shipping entering the port increased nearly two and one half times between 1716 and 1765.[8]

Inland navigation was one of a rash of new enterprises which came into being as the pace of economic activity quickened, the North-West being the scene of the earliest developments in this field. Liverpool merchants had full cognizance of the need to improve facilities. Their first dock Act of 1710 demanded a complementary opening up of the hinterland, and three projects were put in hand simultaneously. Cheap coal was expected to reach Liverpool via the river Douglas, an Act for the improvement of which was passed in 1720, while inland commerce and the salt trade in particular was to be furthered by the Weaver and Mersey and Irwell improvement Acts of 1721. The Mersey and Irwell Navigation (MIN) set out to cheapen transport and give better access to the east coast, the Wakefield head of the Aire and Calder Navigation (AC) being only 28 miles from Manchester. A further addition to this web of water routes came in the 1750s when coal, salt and port interests united to obtain an Act to make the Sankey Brook navigable from St Helens to the Mersey. A canal parallel to the brook was opened in 1757 and by 1770 nearly 100,000 tons, mostly coal, were annually passing down to the Mersey.

These early achievements add perspective to Brindley's engineering career. It is necessary to relate the canals which brought Runcorn into being to what had gone before. At this time goods moving across the Pennines could reach Leeds, Wakefield and Manchester by water, packhorse trains traversing the intervening moors. Coastal goods reached Manchester either from Liverpool or via the AC which advertised the east coast route as 'the quickest, fastest and cheapest way'.[9]

A canal from Mersey to Trent through the Midland Gap, skirting the Pennines rather than attempting to cross them, seemed a suitable choice for those wishing to establish uninterrupted water transport between Liverpool and Hull. Between 1755 and 1760 three surveys, allegedly on behalf of Liverpool Corporation and certainly supported by Staffordshire gentlemen, notably Lord Gower, confirmed the feasibility of a Trent–Mersey link.[10] Agitation for this canal came mainly from the

North Staffordshire potters who depended entirely on road transport, Burslem being at least 20 miles from the nearest navigable points on the Weaver, Trent and Severn. To and from these three estuaries the pottery area supported an annual traffic of the order of 12,000 tons. It is significant that potters predominate in the list of Trent and Mersey Canal (TM) subscribers, which included many famous names of the Industrial Revolution.

While this agitation was going on the Duke of Bridgewater was executing a canal to carry coal from Worsley to Manchester. The links between these two very different schemes were manifest in the persons of James Brindley and John Gilbert, sometime employees of Lord Gower. Gilbert, a mining engineer, entered the duke's service in about 1753 and probably brought about the unlikely partnership of Brindley and Bridgewater. The duke, as Earl Gower's brother-in-law, had been exposed to the latter's championing of canals. Thus the 'canal triumvirate' of the duke, Gilbert, and Brindley was well equipped for a ready interchange of ideas concerning inland navigation. Titled coal-owners were a common eighteenth-century phenomenon, and their desire to extend their markets was a great stimulus to early canal promotion. A grand tour had acquainted the duke with the engineering marvels of Southern Europe; thus, when confronted by the twin problems of flooded mines and inadequate land and river carriage, he could with some assurance turn to the canal as a means of overcoming both difficulties, though the Worsley–Manchester coal canal was only the latest in a series of such endeavours.

The first Act (32 Geo. II, c. 2; 1759) was for a canal which bifurcated on leaving Worsley; one branch was to proceed directly to Salford, the other to effect a Mersey connexion at Hollins Ferry. The work soon ran into difficulties and Brindley advised a change of route. The Hollins Ferry branch, moreover, had depended upon the cooperation of the MIN, which could not be assured.[11] Brindley's plan, however, dispensed with a river connexion and took the line across the Irwell at Barton, not to Salford but to Manchester itself. As soon as the much reviled Barton aqueduct was proved watertight the river company, which had allegedly refused to carry the duke's coal for less than 3s 4d per ton from Barton to Manchester, offered the same service at 6d. Fortunately for the future of Manchester and Runcorn the duke had by this time become adamant in his desire to create an alternative to the river monopoly.

The exact date on which the triumvirate fixed upon the idea of

connecting Manchester and Liverpool is not clear. The idea may have
been in embryo in the Hollins Ferry branch; before this Act had been
passed the duke had purchased land at Liverpool for subsequent dock
construction. The omission of this scheme from the second Act (33 Geo.
II, c. 2; 1760) is strange, though it may have been left out in order to
avoid stirring up too weighty an opposition at any one time. Egerton
believed that an interurban canal was the duke's object from the
beginning; the coal canal, supported by the duke's own adage: 'a
navigation should have coals at the heels of it', was always subordinate to
the desire to reap toll income, 'the Great, Commercial, Productive,
Beneficial, Consideration of Tonnage' from a Liverpool–Manchester
canal.[12] Facts are lacking to confirm or deny this theory, but it is clear
that though the first canal had provided an outlet for Worsley coal, the
interurban through traffic was as much impeded as ever.

    At mid-century only an annual 2,000 tons of goods moved by land
between Manchester and Liverpool at £2 per ton, and no coach ran
between the towns until 1767. In fact 150 packhorses left Manchester
each week for the traditional outlets of Bewdley and Bridgnorth on the
Severn. The MIN thus claimed a virtual monopoly of the interurban
bulk traffic. Though charging only 12s a ton for freight, toll included, the
company was alienating traders by the flagrant abuse of power; delays,
losses, and spoilage were frequent. Unfortunately, there is little written
evidence providing a favourable view of the MIN operations. Young
summed up the pro-duke opinion of the MIN: 'an unsure navigation for
inland boats, not to say a dangerous one . . . the carriage of goods can
never be half so cheap and regular as upon a canal'.[13] His early difficulties
with the river company, together with low coal profits which would not
speedily recoup his outlay, encouraged the duke to attempt to capture the
interurban trade and create his own monopoly. His opposition to the
MIN became explicit with his proposal for a branch canal from the
Manchester line to meet the Mersey at Hempstones Point above Runcorn
Gap.

    Opposition to this scheme was greater than the duke had previously
experienced. Ruinous compensation had to be paid for land along the
route. On the passing of the duke's third Act (2 Geo. III, c. 11; 1762),
authorizing the Hempstones cut, the MIN offered a substantial reduction
in charges to parties who would enter into contracts with it. The duke
thereupon enlisted public opinion in his support by his much publicized
aim of resisting 'every Attempt to Monopolise the Carriage, or lay any
unreasonable Restraint upon Trade'.[14] More practically, the duke began

to purchase shares in a MIN competitor, the Salford Quay Company. By 1771 he controlled 138 of a total 200, and had temporarily quelled the opposition.

The long gap between the Act and the completion of the canal in 1776 was not wholly due to disputes over land. While advancing his canal through Cheshire, the duke was also taking part in a controversy over Earl Gower's Trent–Mersey scheme, which was being harried by several rival projects. The scheme had been conceived as having three arms; a branch was to meet the Severn at Bewdley while the Mersey line was to end at Runcorn Gap, but Sir Richard Whitworth, a rival projector, though agreeing in principle, was insistent that the north-western terminus should be at Winsford on the Weaver.[15]

Two factions quickly arose. Opposing the Whitworth scheme, Bridgewater and Gower agreed that the TM should not itself terminate at Runcorn Gap, but should in fact join the duke's canal some distance before that point. Yet a third group, largely backed by Liverpool Corporation, wanted a direct link to Liverpool by means of an aqueduct over the Mersey at Runcorn Gap. Suggested earlier by Brindley, this idea was rejected by the duke on the grounds of difficulty and expense.

The progress of the struggle to secure the western terminus of the TM is highly relevant to the future of Runcorn. Though Josiah Wedgwood had envisaged a tentative terminus near the Weaver mouth, he was later entertained by the duke and Lord Gower who declared against the link. Despite the Weaver trustees' inducements the TM promoters, at a meeting on 30 December 1765, made clear that they had no intention of joining the Weaver. As the proposed line was to parallel the Weaver for some distance, the apprehensive trustees began to support rival schemes. A grandiose Trent–Mersey–Severn link, independent of Whitworth's, was evidently a bluff. A more serious proposal involved a canal which was to leave Manchester and, passing through Stockport and Macclesfield, reach the Weaver at Witton Brook. Not only would the Witton Brook canal rival the duke's as an inter-urban link, it would also surround his canal and cut it off from contact with the TM.[16] With so much at stake, a stream of partisan pamphlets followed.[17] One of them assured industrial Cheshire that the duke would make a more efficient branch canal from Stockport to Sale Moor on his trunk line. An eloquent rejoinder, however, accused the duke of attempting to create a monopoly. At the same time, a pamphlet probably written by Whitworth emphasized the difficulties the TM line would have to face over water supply, tunnelling, and lack of traffic, there being 'only one manufacture, which lies at

Burslem, called the Pottery Manufacture' on the line. Rehearsing his own Weaver–Trent link, Whitworth denounced the proposed junction of the TM and Bridgewater canals as contrary to the public interest, making the valid point that TM narrow boats would necessitate cargo transhipment between that canal and Liverpool. His own canal, which was to take vessels of 12ft beam, would enable through traffic to penetrate both canal and coastal waters.

Even more valid was Whitworth's argument concerning the organization of the proposed Canal Cross between Mersey, Trent, Thames and Severn. Such a plan, he believed, was too great an undertaking for private enterprise and should rather be a matter for the government which alone possessed the necessary funds and organizational skills. This concept, which would have saved so much trouble in later years had it been carried out, was too far ahead of its time. A retaliatory pamphlet denies self-interest on the part of the TM promoters, stating: 'The object of this design is not local, it is not confined to a few Towns or Counties'. A Weaver terminus would occasion damage and delays as boats waited for tides, the Weaver being full of shallows and unable to carry even the produce of Cheshire. Proposed Cheshire canal links with the TM were equally discounted as mere projects, whereas the Bridgewater Canal was already under construction. Although the Weaver route would have shortened the distance to Liverpool, a crushing argument concerned access to Manchester. The distance from Northwich, 32 miles by the TM, would via the Weaver be at least 48, and would also require a disproportionately greater time to cover. Besides having to wait for tides in order to round Runcorn headland, a vessel in the Weaver would have to be 'carried down a Sort of navigable Steps, Seventy Five Feet, to descend into the Mersey, and then be mounted up another Series of Steps Seventy Nine Feet High to come to the Duke of Bridgewater's Canal'.

Opposition began to weaken. Petitions for the TM and Whitworth's scheme, and for the Duke of Bridgewater's and the Witton Brook canals, were all received by Parliament between January and March 1766.[18] The outcome of these two separate but interrelated battles would decide the fate of Runcorn village. Supporting petitions mostly favoured the TM scheme and its proposed Bridgewater junction as 'a more perfect navigation'. While Wedgwood opined that the TM would result in 'a Saving of Three Fourths of the Expence of Carriage', a petition from the merchants of Stafford succinctly put the case against the Weaver connexion: 'the Navigation of the said River Weaver is frequently obstructed by Floods, neap or low Tides, so as to render the Carriage upon it very uncertain and precarious. Merchants . . . frequently choose to have their Goods conveyed by Land, at a very great Expence, rather than by the said Navigation'. These highly partisan statements apparently carried a good deal of weight.

As Gilbert's brother was made chairman of the committee considering the TM Bill, it made rapid headway, receiving the Royal Assent on 14 May 1766 (6 Geo. III, c. 96) to the chagrin of the Weaver trustees. Clause 84 of the Act stated that the canal should join the Bridgewater at Preston Brook, the united trunk thence proceeding to Runcorn Gap, a plan which 'would render both the said Navigations more convenient and complete and be of great Advantage than if the said Navigation of the said Duke of Bridgewater had terminated at the Hempstones'. In 1766 also the duke's Stockport branch was authorized (6 Geo. III, c. 19) and the Witton Brook Bill eased out of the Lords. The Stockport branch may have been a bluff for it was never begun, the hopes of the towns south of Manchester being sacrificed to the duke's all-consuming desire to be 'the largest dealer and carrier in Europe'.[19]

The general alignment of the duke's canal was not in dispute. Committed to the south side of the Mersey by his earlier desire to reach Manchester rather than Salford, the interurban line was obliged to turn westwards. A line north of the Mersey would have involved extra length, the crossing of the Sankey Canal, and extensive cutting through mosses. The duke's finances in 1762–6 being in a parlous state, the shortest line was undoubtedly the best, though the Runcorn Gap terminus was sufficiently better than that at Hempstones to warrant the extra length.

An assessment of decision-making must take into account Brindley's engineering techniques. Though capable of constructing aqueducts which were the wonder of Britain, he is said to have had a distinct aversion for locks. His ideal canal consisted of a single deadwater level carried as far as possible, with lockage concentrated at the termini. Such long summit levels acted as reservoirs, partially obviating the problems which were to bedevil many later, locked canals, but which could only be achieved by avoiding cuttings and following hillside contours. The technique of cut and fill, now an engineering commonplace, was unknown to Brindley. A pragmatist, he trained his canals along hillside slopes, this method requiring artificial embankments only on the offside. The circuity involved in contour-following was not considered a disadvantage in the early industrial age, for though sinuous, such canals were somewhat shorter and traffic on them much speedier than on contemporary rivers.

As no records report the decisions made by the proprietors, the duke's financial situation and Brindley's techniques must be bases of conjecture. Hempstones would not have been a good terminus. It was in fact a compromise between the original Hollins Ferry scheme and the ideal, an aqueduct carrying the canal directly to Liverpool. Not only was the tidal situation adverse and excavation in marshland difficult, but lockage down to the point might have involved separate locks with intervening pounds. But to continue much beyond Hempstones was to restrict the choice of Mersey entry. To end the canal upstream of the gap would be to subject it to the same tidal difficulties; to continue much below, towards the barrier imposed by the Weaver, would incur extra expense without corresponding benefit. Consequently, the canal was planned to join the Mersey at Runcorn, a short distance below the gap at a point where a fairly steep slope to the Mersey enabled Brindley to concentrate his locks into a staircase.

The construction of Britain's first large-scale deadwater canal went forward on three fronts: into the Worsley mines; towards Manchester; and towards Runcorn. The coal canal was only 10 miles in length; the interurban line was to be at least 24 and involved crossing the morass of Sale Moor. Despite continual difficulties the duke insisted on a 4ft 6in deep waterway capable of taking barges of 14ft beam. This is evidence of the courage and determination of one whose future was staked on an unprecedented enterprise the success of which was in no way assured. The TM was restricted to the 7ft gauge because of its greater length (93 miles) and considerations of speed, cost, and water supplies.

One of the duke's major obstacles was lack of ready cash. By 1792, when he was £27,707 in debt, the phrase 'land sale' had become a frequent occurrence in the day books.[20] Coal profits were negligible at this time, reaching only £4,802 as late as 1775. Some relief was obtained in 1765, however, when the duke borrowed £25,000 from his bankers on the security of his Worsley estate. His debt by this time had reached £60,879.

Malley has traced the progress of the canal across Cheshire.[21] As sections were opened, warehouses sprang up and working boats were put on the canal to gather what trade they could. The early sections had 'the appearance of a great navigable river rather than a canal cut at the expense of a single person'.[22] From 1770 to 1771 the final section to

Runcorn and the TM junction were completed, the whole of 1772 being occupied in constructing the locks at Runcorn.[23] While the canal proper was almost wholly in use by 1771, the lock staircase was not opened until 1 January 1773, occasioning great rejoicing when 'the *Heart of Oak* a Vessel of Fifty Tons Burden from Liverpool, belonging to the Duke, passed through . . . Upwards of 600 of His Grace's workmen were entertained upon the Lock banks with an Ox roasted whole, and plenty of good Liquor'.[24] Most significant for the future of the small village near the canal terminus, however, were the two final toasts:

'Prosperity to Trade and Navigation.
Prosperity to the Town of Runcorn'.[25]

The Initial Terminal

The canal port of Runcorn took its name from the parish and township in which it grew up. The Duke of Bridgewater had envisaged this spot as his Mersey terminus since at least 1766, but was unable to realize his ambition for a further decade. Sir Richard Brooke had recently spent some £20,000 on rebuilding Norton Priory and laying out its gardens. Questioning every land valuation made by the duke's surveyors, he rallied the Old Quay Navigation (MIN) and other opponents of the duke in an effort to prevent the canal from crossing Norton Park.[26] The baronet was clearly playing for time, hoping that by holding out he could discourage the duke, whose total debt had swollen to £133,219 by 1771 and £229,213 five years later.

As the canal came to an end west of Norton, leaving the short Runcorn–Astmoor section without hinterland connexion, the *Heart of Oak's* entry into the canal in 1773 could only have been a publicity gesture. From 1771 at least, through traffic was obliged to tranship twice. Goods were carried by river between Liverpool and Bank Quay (Warrington), while goods moving to and from Manchester by canal were unloaded at Stockton Heath. Between these points the duke ran a cartage service from 1771 to 1776. By 1774, however, small parcels of land gained from Sir Richard Brooke had enabled the Bridgewater Canal to push a little further into his estate, so that additional carts could be run between Norton and Astmoor. Clerks and porters were now required at four places besides the planned termini and intervening towns. The cost of the service was heavy, and the day books of the duke's agents record large sums disbursed 'for carting Goods, Wages to Flat Crews, Incidents viz. Cartage . . . by Sir Richard Brooke's where the Navigation is not yet made'.[27]

Commercial men, recognizing the advantages afforded by the functioning parts of the canal, soon rose in a body to demand an end to the inconvenience. Encouraged, the duke then played his trump card and appealed to Parliament against Sir Richard. Isolated by public opinion and physically out-flanked by the canal, the latter bowed to the inevitable. Brindley's principle of keeping the canal on a single level had posthumously prevailed; by 21 March 1776 the one-mile link was complete. The relief of the Manchester merchants at this final removal of the brake on trade and mobility was such that they boarded the inaugural boats and provided 'a grand Entertainment [for] all ranks of People'.[28]

The duke's canal was one of the success stories of the eighteenth century. People of fashion flocked to see its wonders and the occasional death of a person on such a 'Journey of Pleasure' provided news items for the local press.[29] More valuable information reached the public through less ephemeral works; Raffald's *Manchester Directory* (1772) and contemporary issues of the *Annual Register* and *Gentleman's Magazine* carried stories of the Duke's operations.[30] Newspaper advertisements frequently mentioned the presence of the canal as a means of increasing the attractiveness of property, and it is clear from the day books that the canal port rapidly sprang into life once the vital connexion had been secured.

Entering the township from the east, the canal passed between Higher and Lower Runcorn to meet the Mersey at a lonely spot well beyond the church. Smiles and Malley observe that the duke had to pay dearly for land purchased under the compulsory powers of his Act.[31] But the scanty evidence consists of erratic day book entries, the usual formula for which, 'Paid £x for Land Purchased for the Navigation', is of little use in the absence of further detail. Much land was acquired in the period 1771–8, but was not paid for until 1781–90. No accurate information on the extent of the Bridgewater estate at Runcorn is available, but it is clear that the multiplicity of landowners with whom the duke had to deal was in complete contrast to the ownership structure in Norton, where the Brookes had full sway.[32]

Ten broad locks, built in staircase pairs, were required to reach the Mersey about 90ft below canal level. Their design was attributed to 'the amazing Abilities and indefatigable Industries of Mr John Gilbert . . .

with the assistance of the late very ingenious Mr Brindley'.[33] Vessels of 50 tons could negotiate the lock staircase into the small upper basin connecting it to the canal summit level. Though Brindley had recommended drystone walls for the locks, the duke insisted on brick walls ribbed with stone and 'pounded' at the back, a practice which, though cheap, was to prove successful.[34] At the lower end of the staircase a small tidal dock was built to facilitate the entry and egress of vessels. Large stone walls and piers were necessary to protect its entrance from violent Mersey tides, and a reference to 'making a Cut in the Tideway at Runcorn', with an accompanying breakwater of sunken hulks, denotes an attempt to improve the basin's approaches.[35] A warehouse and other buildings were finished in 1775.

No elaborate plans were made by the canal triumvirate for the settlement adjacent to the Runcorn works (Fig. 5). Though the day books frequently refer to brick-making and the carrying of lime to Runcorn, local clay facilitated brick and tile production at Runcorn itself, and pottery works using the same material persisted into the nineteenth century. Further, the adjacent quarries provided large quantities of sandstone at quarry-head prices. Besides its use in the terminal dockworks, Runcorn freestone was used in quantity along the canal.

Only a few scattered references record the measures taken by the duke to house his permanent employees at Runcorn. His Worsley housing schemes are, in comparison, well known. At the Mersey terminus, 'the vast works . . . occasioned a great influx of workmen, and the consequent building of a number of dwelling-houses, inns, shops, etc.'[36] The day books record the building of houses in 1772 and the erection of 'several new Dwelling Houses at Runcorn' in 1776.[37] Some of these dwellings remain as two short rows flanking the remains of the upper basin (Top Locks). The steep fall to the Mersey precluded much building adjacent to the lock staircase, restricting it to the level areas at Top Locks and near the Mersey shore.

At the latter level, early Runcorn's most impressive structure arose. The duke's *hôtel*, Bridgewater House, erected to enable him to supervise the construction of the locks in 1772, was used thereafter on his frequent visits to his port. An imposing structure of red brick ornamented with stone ribbing, and facing inland, the fine three-storey Georgian house was reached by a coach road laid out on the north side of the locks. The duke's energetic presence was soon to confirm the embryo port as the new focus of activity in Runcorn township.

Trade and Port Development

From the 1770s the duke's canal built up a thriving trade in TM goods, notably iron and pottery wares. On the trunk line to Manchester, where both the MIN and the duke's line used the tidal Mersey for almost half their journey from Liverpool, rate cutting provided new traffic for each. The interurban flow included cotton, wool, sugar, grain and timber upstream, return cargoes consisting largely of coal, stone and manufactured goods. Runcorn itself was the generator of a steady traffic in local stone and potatoes.

Market and passenger boats soon began to ply towards Manchester, and by 1776 special fast passenger boats had reached Runcorn. A large number of boats were built at Bangor-on-Dee between 1765 and 1775, while others were constructed at Worsley and, later, at Runcorn.[38] In 1787 wages were paid at Runcorn to the crews of 18 canal lighters and 37 flats working between the new port and Liverpool, and in 1795 the duke registered 37 coal boats and 44 lighters. By the turn of the century supplementary Liverpool vessels had to be hired to accommodate the influx of trade, and every tide saw up to 43 flats, each of 35 to 60 tons burden, leaving Runcorn for Liverpool.[39] By 1803, when the duke's death necessitated an inventory of the stock and the setting up of the Bridgewater trustees, a formidable fleet had been built up.[40] The coaling squadron, with eight specialized vessel types, accounted for about two thirds of the aggregate of 363 vessels, and 46 canal lighters were complemented by 60 Mersey flats. The names of the latter summarize the broad scope of the duke's endeavours, ranging from his landed estates (*Ellesmere*), his port estates (*Liverpool*), and his growing external connexions (*Dantzic*), through a parade of personal and industrial virtues (*Robust, Enterprize, Diligent*), to his ambitions as a paragon of commerce (*Success, Goliath*).

The preponderance of coal boats was not reflected in their financial contribution to the duke's success. In 1779 both colliery and navigation were providing equal revenues, but thereafter colliery receipts approximated to only 35–40 per cent of navigation returns. In terms of profits the latter's contribution was nearly four times as large. Navigation profits, stimulated by the development of Runcorn, doubled and redoubled in the periods 1780–4, 1784–96, and 1796–1802. In the climactic period 1780–90, after thirty years of unremitting effort, the accumulated debt reached the daunting peak of £346,806. It was not to go higher, for 1789 was the first year in which profits exceeded the interest on the debt.

Of the specialized trades, Worsley coal rarely reached Runcorn, largely on account of the duke's inability to supply more than a part of the demands of Manchester. Passengers also avoided the new town at first, for no regular packet services ran between Runcorn and Liverpool in the early years. As a goods transhipment point, however, Runcorn flourished. As traffic increased in volume, special rates were granted to encourage the TM trade, inroads being made even into the Weaver Navigation's monopoly of the carriage of Cheshire rock salt. The salt trade gives some indication of the restricted role of early Runcorn. Of the 11–16,000 tons moved annually in the period 1780–90, almost the whole was transhipped into flats for Liverpool. Only small amounts left Runcorn for Ireland and other places by coasting vessels.[41] As at this time the depth of the channel off Runcorn locks was only 7ft, compared with as many fathoms at Liverpool, coasters were rare visitors to the canal port. 'Vessels of the burden of 120 tons have recently discharged clay from Poole and Exeter, and flintstones from London at Runcorn, but as it frequently occasioned much delay by missing the channel and grounding . . . for a whole neap, the masters in general prefer delivering their cargoes at Liverpool which are afterwards carried up by the flat bottomed vessels'.[42]

It was partly in order to encourage coasting traffic that attention again turned to the state of the Mersey channel. The cut through the marshes of the headland, which in the 1770s separated Runcorn Island from the mainland, was widened to form a substantial 'Gut in the tideway'. But sand bars had reformed at the lock outlet by 1798, and work proceeded for a decade thereafter in an attempt to raise a sufficiently large 'Bur Bank in the River at Runcorn to get a deep to the Lock Gates'.[43] On arrival at the latter, vessels could use a tidal basin excavated about 1780 to ease congestion among vessels waiting to ascend the locks. Later in the century the duke purchased more land at Runcorn, rebuilt the warehouse, and ordered further boats. The basin was enlarged, and the completion of a new dock with several arms and two locks provided a second point of entry into the Mersey after 1791. Subsequently, the docks were extended, a new warehouse and graving dock built, and the wharves extended. By 1801 a further dock was being excavated.

Competition by Water and Rail After 1800

1803, the date of the duke's death, saw the complete reorganization of
Bridgewater affairs. It appears that the Bridgewater trustees, headed by
R. H. Bradshaw as canal superintendent, established a new commercial
climate. A doubling of the freight rates in 1800 had led to a short term 16
per cent increase in profits, and the accumulated debt, halved over
twenty years by the cautious duke, was reduced by 75 per cent in the two
years 1804–5, and entirely wiped out the following year.

At this entrepreneurial watershed, and in the midst of a maelstrom of
ducal activity whose ever-widening circles were changing the economic
and social life of an entire region, the Bridgewater estate at Runcorn was
flanked by rival canal and dock developments. Already a waterway
nexus, the tidewater entry-point of the Sankey, Bridgewater, TM,
Weaver, and MIN navigations, the area's position as a transhipment
node was further emphasized by the activities of the two latter waterways.
The MIN wished to enhance its competitive ability vis-a-vis the duke's
canal on which vessels proceeded more 'easily, safely, progressively,
surely, equally, regularly, certainly, by given times, in nearly straight
lines'.[44] It is not surprising therefore, to find that the MIN actively
considered a canal from Latchford above Warrington to the Hempstones
as early as 1783. Begun in 1799, it was completed in the year of the
duke's death. In 1804, the following year, it was extended to a point
about one mile above the duke's locks, just short of Runcorn Gap. Here a
basin, with a river lock, was excavated, and a rival Runcorn canal port
established.

This was a relatively advantageous position at first, for in that area the
Mersey channel lay along the Lancashire shore, thus compelling vessels
bound for the duke's locks to approach their destination from the north,
via the Runcorn Island cut, which tended to silt up. But by the late 1820s
the channel had moved to the Cheshire shore, to the delight of the
Bridgewater trustees and the severe discomfiture of the Old Quay
directors. In 1830 the latter attempted to divert the channel back to the
north shore by removing some rocks on the Lancashire side, but this was
unsuccessful. As the duke's trustees refused them the right to use the
Runcorn Island cut until 1842, the rival port at Runcorn Gap was hard
pressed. This atmosphere of competitive improvement was exacerbated
by users of the navigations; the MIN, for example, was told in 1803 'by
some considerable Freighters that the inattention and irregularity at the

Quay in Liverpool would compel them to send their Goods by the Duke's Canal if the evil was not speedily remedied'.[45]

At about the same time as the MIN was cutting its Runcorn–Latchford canal, the Weaver Navigation was engaged in an exactly analogous plan. Carriers and salt proprietors were concerned to extend the navigation from Frodsham to a deepwater outlet at Weston Point, below Runcorn Gap. Avoiding the tortuous Weaver mouth, the canal was completed in 1810 with a small basin and sea-lock at Weston Point. Piers were added in 1817–20, and by this time the employment of a harbour-master and lock-keeper attested to the success of the measure in promoting traffic. With the close juxtaposition of three canal ports at Runcorn Gap, a clash of interests was inevitable. The Weaver vied with the duke's canal as an outlet for the heavy traffic of the TM. The MIN paralleled the Bridgewater line, and soon after the completion of its dock at Runcorn a Runcorn–Manchester packet service was begun and a price war initiated with the duke's trustees.[46]

Under the stimulus of such competition the Runcorn area was revitalized. Mutally encouraged by rumours of each others' plans, and by a more or less united opposition to the interference of Liverpool in Runcorn Gap affairs, all three canal bodies were moved to extend their works. In the 1830s and forties the Weaver trustees extended the dock at Weston Point, built stables, warehouses, and dwellings, created sea walls, and provided a 'Weaver Hotel'.[47] Moreover, sensible of the 'national wave of concern for the spiritual state of the working class', they prohibited Sunday work and, in a fit of benevolent paternalism, provided their workers with churches and schools at a number of places.[48] At Weston Point a church was built by 1841, together with a parsonage and school. Minister, schoolmaster, boilerman and even the choir were on the company payroll.

Meanwhile, the MIN was improving its position. In the twenties it still could not rival the Bridgewater line. In a list of thirty-six Liverpool carriers 'by land and water', sixteen had offices adjacent to the duke's Liverpool dock, only one being located by the Old Quay wharf.[49] Head compared the MIN unfavourably with its powerful rival on all counts, especially with regard to its 'humbler task of crawling along the Mersey and . . . Irwell'.[50] Nevertheless, the duke's trustees were concerned about the MIN's extension of its Runcorn port works. Despite opposition from Liverpool, which objected to the new works as a danger to navigation, the MIN began excavation in 1822 and by 1829 had completed a large new dock with a second lock parallel to the first.[51] Much larger than the latter, which could pass only about twenty vessels on an average tide, the new tide-lock was designed to take up to 120 craft per tide.

In 1825 the duke's locks could take up to sixty craft per tide, but were in an advanced state of dilapidation. Moreover, the engineer Sutcliffe had visited Runcorn a decade earlier, and while observing the 'numerous and lofty warehouses, extensive wharfs, docks, and basins' to be 'more like storehouses and conveniences for a royal navy, than auxiliaries for a canal', he regarded the lock staircase as badly placed and wasteful of water.[52] So great an object of admiration forty years before, the lock staircase was replaced by a second flight in the period 1825–8. Leaving the original flight below the top staircase pair, which was later doubled, the new flight descended diagonally to the second tidal basin, which was suitably enlarged, and was connected in to the existing dock complex (Fig. 5). With large intermediary basins and access to the Mersey somewhat lower than the first flight, the new staircase proved much more efficient than the former; a faster transfer time between river and canal helped improve the Bridgewater system's flagging popularity. South of the new line of locks, Francis Dock was completed in the early 1840s, and was later to be connected with the Weaver's Weston Point canal.

With the completion of these new works, the duke's Runcorn canal port was fully refurbished for the prosecution of a vital waterborne trade, and was able to hold its own despite the inroads of the rival canal ports established by the Weaver and the MIN. Two other movements, however, had already been set in motion. Both planned to limit, if not entirely to supersede, the importance of Runcorn as a shipping place. The Mersey Conservancy scheme came on the scene in 1829. While not explicitly opposed, it went wholly unsupported by a strong canal lobby which also resisted Liverpool's attempts to impose further dock dues on ships bypassing the seaport on their way upstream to the canal ports.[53] In recognition of the growing importance of minor Mersey creeks, a customs house had been established in Runcorn before 1822.[54] The fight against Liverpool's monopoly of foreign trade was temporarily rewarded in 1847 when Runcorn was appointed an independent bonding port.[55]

The other movement was more formidable. As early as 1822 local navigations were alerted to the threat of a railway between Liverpool and Manchester. Merchants of the two cities proposed, by means of such a railway, to reduce the intercity distance to 33 miles, compared with about 48 by both Bridgewater and MIN lines. Bradshaw, sensible of the likely diversion from water of the estimated 1,300 tons of goods passing daily between the two cities, 'expressed himself decidedly hostile to the projected

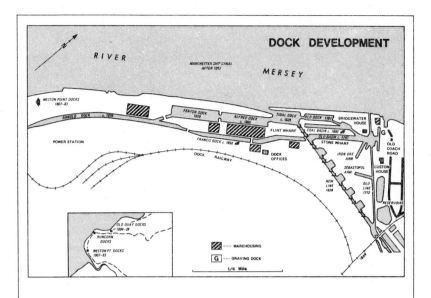

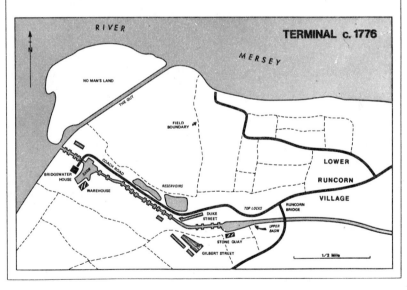

Fig. 5. The port of Runcorn.

Rail Road', and for the next two years united with the MIN in opposition.[56] To counteract this, the railway offered the Marquis of Stafford, principal beneficiary of the duke's canal, 1,000 shares in the venture and the power to appoint three directors to the board. The acceptance of this offer paved the way for the completion of the railway in 1830. This was followed by a virulent rate war, in which Bradshaw cut rates by up to 30 per cent. Though persuaded to give up the post of superintendent in 1834, Bradshaw had tarnished the image of the canal system and seen his profits reduced by five-sixths in the period 1824–34.

Although fear of railway competition had thrown Bradshaw and the MIN into temporary alliance in 1831, the subsequent years saw renewed waterway rivalries, with the MIN following Bradshaw in a spiral of rate reductions. An agreement between the railways and the Bridgewater trustees in 1840, together with a necessary improvement of the MIN line which could not be afforded, precipitated a crisis. Faced with involved agreements with railways, carriers, and the duke's trustees, the Old Quay was pleased to sell out to the latter in 1844.[57] The same year saw an agreement with the Ellesmere and Chester Canal Company by which the trustees took over the whole flat and tug service between Liverpool and Ellesmere Port. The two canal lines had long been in competition, which had been rendered more violent by the completion, in 1843, of a substantial dock and warehouse at the canal port of Ellesmere Port (described in detail in Chapter 6). Further, in 1845 an agreement was reached with the Liverpool and Manchester Railway (LMR) whereby the combined Bridgewater and MIN lines were to be allocated two-thirds of the interurban traffic. The waterways consistently exceeded this allocation.[58] Finally, in 1847 the trustees extended their operations to include freightage between Liverpool and the new railhead at Birkenhead. Though the Birkenhead and Ellesmere Port trades never proved really profitable, and the combined Bridgewater and MIN service still supplied about 70 per cent of the profits of the whole concern,[59] the extension of the trustees' control over a great part of the lower Mersey traffic provided a sure foundation for further development.

Urban Development

Very little can be gleaned respecting urban growth before 1800. The duke's account books occasionally refer to house construction, largely an extension of the buildings flanking the lock staircases at Top Locks. The major burst of building activity, however, took place after the turn of the century and further away from the docks. In 1801 Runcorn contained only 320 dwellings. Over 100 of these comprised the Top Locks group together with a number of small brick terraces erected between Top Locks and the ferry. With the few cottages on the restricted area of level land near the tidal locks, the original nuclei of Higher and Lower Runcorn made up the total.

The expansion of housing, which more than quadrupled in the period 1802–31 and had increased eightfold by 1851, was the result of a vast influx of people to the new canal port. Runcorn's population rose by over 45 per cent in each of the three census decades up to 1831. Land tax assessments reveal that whereas Runcorn in 1780 had two large landowners only, one of whom was the duke, by 1830 a variety of taxable industrial enterprises had appeared, together with shops and several rows of houses built by workmen's building societies. Indeed, Fowler noted that in the twenties the town 'had risen more rapidly than at any former period . . . On the same spot where formerly cattle were accustomed to graze, may now be seen a row of neat-looking cottages, or a line of more elevated and extended buildings'.[60] New construction, largely of brick though with a fair amount of Runcorn stone, mainly grew up around Lower Runcorn village, situated a little to the east of both Top Locks and the ferry. From this early nucleus, building extended along three paths, later High, Church, and Bridge streets, which provided the basic structure determining further urban development. In 1829 none of these streets boasted a continuous building frontage, but by mid-century this was becoming a reality. Beyond, in the fields alongside the Bridgewater Canal, small manufactories and humble house rows were erected and unimaginatively named by local industrialists and speculators. Small independent settlements also arose around the tide-water terminals of the MIN and Weston Point canals.

Of the factors contributing to this expansion, the role of Runcorn as a resort was not unimportant. In 1795 interest in the locks was held responsible for the arrival of 'parties of pleasure from the country round'. This initial attraction led to Runcorn's becoming 'a place of some resort for salt-water bathing . . . the agreeable situation and the good air of the place . . . are useful auxiliaries to the effects of the bath'.[61] By 1811 the activity was sufficient to warrant the publication of a short guide book,[62] and by 1834 the compendious *Visitors' Guide* styled Runcorn 'The Montpellier of England'.[63] In 1822 riverside baths had been erected, to be followed nine years later by the handsome

Belvedere Terrace, erected on the waterfront specifically for visitors. Neither air nor river was long to remain unpolluted. Until the thirties bathing and industry grew side by side; by 1850 Runcorn was committed to the latter and bathers had moved on to more genteel shores. The first industries were based upon agriculture; a brewery, a tanyard and two soap and resin works had by 1821 appeared on the canal side above Top Locks. In that year nearly half the town's rateable value comprised industrial and commercial undertakings. But as the Bridgewater estate accounted for 86 per cent of this proportion, and the MIN a further 4 per cent, it is clear that industry proper was still poorly established.[64]

Within a decade the Bridgewater Canal had asserted itself as the prime focus of an expanding industrial sector. In the 1830s seven small shipyards were operating, and quarrying activity had been extended because of cheapened water carriage. The soap works, seeking cheaper sites and fewer restrictions than in Liverpool, were extended to manufacture turpentine, vitriol and alkalis. In the same decade two further tanneries, an acid works, a malting-house, timber yards, slate works and a steam mill arose. Most of these were extended or had found new competitors by 1851, at which time the trustees' estate still accounted for two-thirds of the commercial portion of a rateable value seven times greater than in 1801.[65] By mid-century Runcorn was an industrial going concern; the chemical industry, which still dominates the town, had become firmly established. This intrusion of 'chemical nuisances', however, was not unopposed. Frequent extensions of the soapworks, culminating in the erection of two rival chimneys which dominate contemporary prints (Fig. 6), provoked certain residents beyond endurance. Supporters of a campaign to keep Runcorn clean invoked divine wrath and that of local landowners in defence of their 'healthy little village', but to no avail.[66] The pleas of this environmental protest group went unnoticed as the landed gentry quietly removed and Runcorn began to experience the evils of unrestricted alkali production, long before the establishment of the first works across the ferry at Widnes in 1847.

As public houses and small shops were being established as a complement to industry and the established church, the first nonconformists on the scene erected a Wesleyan chapel in 1807. A spate of interdenominational rivalry followed, with the establishment of chapels by Huntingtonians (1818), Welsh Calvinists (1829), Congregationalists (1829), Independents (1835), Primitives (1838), Baptists, and finally Catholics (1846). A floating chapel on the

Fig. 6. Runcorn from Widnes Ferry, c. 1850, with the Old Quay docks to the left and the tall chimneys of chemical works along the Bridgewater Canal dominating the port.

Bridgewater Canal competed with a mariners' chapel near the Old Quay docks. The established church was forced to enlarge its original edifice, and to erect a second in 1838. Most sects also established schools, and until the forties Runcorn, like contemporary St Helens, possessed a number of boarding schools for the progeny of Liverpool merchants.[67]

On this more secular level, the 1820s saw the establishment of a number of social organizations and popular charities. 'Aquatic excursions' were a favourite treat, and local rivalries centred round the MIN's *Eclipse* and the trustees' *Bridgewater* steam packets which had competed on the Liverpool–Runcorn run since the early days of steam. But, as if symbolizing the separate existence of town organization free of canal control, the townsfolk established a bridewell (1808) and a weekly market and twice-yearly fair (1811). A town hall was built in 1831 in the centre of Lower Runcorn village, but the land was provided by the Bridgewater trustees. The Board of Health, established in the same year, demonstrates the balance of power in the town. While the board itself was composed of influential chemical manufacturers, building contractors, and shipyard owners, the necessary hospital was provided gratis by the trustees. The MIN had much less influence; it gave up its gas plant in 1837 when the Runcorn Gas Light Company was formed. Within ten years gas was being supplied to Weston village, Weston Point docks, nearby Halton, and the new Widnes docks, as well as to the two dock systems in Runcorn proper.[68] By this time Runcorn was the obvious centre of activity of the Runcorn Gap area. Moreover, with 160,000 tons of goods transhipped from coasters for the interior in 1845, it was evidently capable of remaining prosperous as a canal-based settlement, despite the Stephensons' claim that ten years after the opening of the LMR the Bridgewater Canal would be choked with rushes.

4. Notes

1. C. Nickson, *A History of Runcorn*, Mackie, London (1887), p. 6.
2. Ibid., p. 26.
3. C. N. Parkinson, *The Rise of the Port of Liverpool*, Liverpool University Press, Liverpool (1952), p. 29.
4. Cole (1775) quoted in D. Sylvester and G. Nulty, *The Historical Atlas of Cheshire*, Cheshire Community Council, Chester (1958), p. 55.

5. *Gentleman's Magazine* (June 1758).
6. C. Nickson, op. cit., p. 153.
7. D. Defoe, *A Tour Through the Whole Island of Great Britain*, Dent, London (1962), Vol. 2, p. 256.
8. R. Davis, *The Rise of the English Shipping Industry in the Seventeenth and Eighteenth Centuries*, Macmillan, London (1962), p. 37.
9. *Manchester Mercury* (24 July 1753).
10. J. Aikin, *A Description of the Country from Thirty to Forty Miles Around Manchester*, Stockdale, London (1795), p. 117.
11. C. Hadfield and G. Biddle, *The Canals of North West England*, David and Charles, Newton Abbot (1970), pp. 20–1, 23.
12. F. H. Egerton, *The First and Second Parts of a Letter to the Parisians*, Didot, Paris (1820), p. 36.
13. A. Young, *A Six Months Tour through the North of England*, London (1770), p. 287.
14. *Manchester Mercury* (1 April, 2 May 1762).
15. R. Whitworth, *The Advantages of Inland Navigation*, Baldwin, London (1766), p. 7.
16. BM, 213, i. 5 (95).
17. BM, 213, i. 5 (93–4, 96–7).
18. *JHC* (January–May 1766).
19. W. H. Chaloner, 'Charles Roe of Macclesfield (1715–18): An Eighteenth Century Industrialist', *Transactions, Lancashire and Cheshire Antiquarian Society*, 63 (1953) 52–86.
20. Bridgewater day books: Northamptonshire CRO: EB 1459–64; Lancashire CRO: BW/C 2/4 D (1, 2, 5).
21. E. Malley, *The Financial Administration of the Bridgewater Estate 1780–1800*, unpublished MA thesis, University of Manchester (1929), p. 17.
22. A. Young, op. cit., p. 282.
23. Northamptonshire CRO: EB 1461, p. 22.
24. *Manchester Mercury* (5 January 1773).
25. H. Malet, *The Canal Duke*, David and Charles, Dawlish (1961), p. 98.
26. Ibid., p. 121.
27. Northamptonshire CRO: EB 1460 (1774).
28. *Williamson's Liverpool Advertiser* (29 March 1776).
29. *Chester Courant* (7 May 1771).
30. *Annual Register* (1773), XVI 65, XIX 127; *Gentleman's Magazine* January 1776.
31. S. Smiles, *Lives of the Engineers*, Vol. 1 (1862), p. 378; E. Malley, op. cit., p. 214.
32. Northamptonshire CRO: EB 1460, 62 (1770–90).
33. *Manchester Mercury* (4 January 1773).
34. F. H. Egerton, op. cit., p. 65.
35. Northamptonshire CRO: EB 1460 (1773).
36. J. Aikin, op. cit., p. 417.
37. Northamptonshire CRO: EB 1460 (1776).
38. Northamptonshire CRO: EB 1461.
39. F. H. Egerton, op. cit., p. 38, note 43.
40. Northamptonshire CRO: EB 1464 (1803).
41. Northamptonshire CRO: EB 1460 (1779).

42. R. C. Jarvis (ed.) 'A Custom Letter Book of the Port of Liverpool 1711–1813', *Chetham Society*, Third Series 6 (1954), 126.
43. Northampton CRO: EB 1461.
44. F. H. Egerton, op. cit., p. 40.
45. MIN, 2 (6 April 1803).
46. MIN, 2 (6 February 1805), (6 August 1806); MIN, 4 (3 July 1822).
47. Cheshire CRO: deposited plan 85 (1828).
48. C. Hadfield and G. Biddle, op. cit., p. 139.
49. E. Baines, *History, Directory, and Gazetteer of the County Palatine of Lancashire* Vol. 1, (1824), p. 464.
50. G. Head, *A Home Tour through the Manufacturing Districts of England in the Summer of 1835*, London (1836), p. 5.
51. MIN, 4 (2 December 1826).
52. J. Sutcliffe, *A Treatise on Canals and Reservoirs*, Rochdale (1816), p. 128.
53. MIN, 5 (9 December 1829); MIN, 6 (4 June 1836).
54. J. Pigot, *The New Commercial Directory*, Manchester (1822), p. 22.
55. F. C. Mather, *After the Canal Duke*, Clarendon Press, Oxford (1970), p. 258.
56. MIN, 4 (5 February 1823).
57. MIN, 7 (13 January 1844).
58. F. G. Mather, op. cit., p. 190.
59. Lancashire CRO: BW/C 2/4 (3) (1844).
60. G. Fowler, *Visitor's Guide to Runcorn and its Vicinity*, Walker, Runcorn (1834), p. 21.
61. J. Aikin, op. cit., p. 417.
62. J. Greswell, *An Account of Runcorn and its Environs*, Runcorn (1811).
63. G. Fowler, op. cit., p. 22.
64. C. Nickson, op. cit., p. 163.
65. Ibid., p. 167.
66. *Liverpool Mercury* (20 April 1838).
67. T. C. Barker and J. R. Harris, *A Merseyside Town in the Industrial Revolution: St Helens 1750–1900*, Cass, London (1954).
68. C. Nickson, op. cit., p. 185.

5

Stourport in the Canal Age

An Act for making and maintaining a navigable Cut or Canal, from the River Severn, between Bewdley and Titton Brook, in the County of Worcester, to cross the River Trent, at or near Heywood Mill, in the County of Stafford, and to communicate with a Canal intended to be made between the said River and the River Mersey.

(6 Geo. III, c. 97; 1766)

Stourport Before The Canal

A tract of rolling country defined by the rivers Severn and Stour, which meet at Stourmouth some four miles below both Bewdley on the former and Kidderminster on the latter river, provided the setting for the canal port of Stourport. Near Stourmouth the settlements of Upper and Lower Mitton stood on the Stour's right bank. A mill had been in existence in Domesday times, and was later joined by other corn and fulling mills which sought to benefit from the power provided by the Stour.

Navigation was an integral part of local life. The Severn had been navigable 'time out of mind' in the sixteenth century; in the following century small boats could get up to Welshpool and larger vessels reach Shrewsbury, the highest of the larger river ports. During the growth of West Midlands industry in the seventeenth and eighteenth centuries the Severn played a part in regional economic development equal at least to that played by the railways in the succeeding century. Coal was the chief commodity carried in bulk, if not in value, the Shropshire mines being at first capable of supplying the whole area served by the Severn and its tributaries. 'These rivers appear to have carried almost the entire trade of the district through which they flowed; their navigation was an indispensable factor in the commerce of the west'.[1]

About four miles upriver from Stourmouth the town of Bewdley played a major part in the organization of trade between the Midlands and the outer world. A town 'not antiently famous',[2] Bewdley seems to have become important in the sixteenth century by virtue of its position, its bridge, and its proximity to the oakwoods of the Wyre Forest which provided timber suitable for boatbuilding. The focus of packhorse routes, Bewdley also functioned as a breakpoint at which large cargoes were discharged into vessels of lesser draught for upstream distribution. Merchants from Bristol, then second only to London as a seaport, established depots in the town and dealt with packhorse trains from as far afield as Manchester and Sheffield. In Bewdley's heyday even the sun shone with especial favour on the town, so that 'a man cannot wish to see a towne better . . . with the sun from the east, the whole town glittereth, as it were of gold'.[3]

Of the Severn tributaries, a number were of sufficient importance to merit improvement in Restoration times. A local man, Andrew Yarranton of Astley, 'that typical projector of a much-projecting age', was instrumental in obtaining a private Act in 1662 to make navigable the rivers Stour and Salwarpe. The chief impetus for this venture lay in the desire of the Staffordshire coal owners to compete in the Severn market on equal terms with waterborne Shropshire coal. This was reaching settlements less than 20 miles from the Staffordshire mines, land carriage from the latter quickly increasing the retail price until competition was well-nigh impossible. Coal movement itself served to increase the difficulties of land carriage in a kind of vicious circle; Plot in 1686 records that the roads of the coal district were worn by coal waggons into almost impassable ruts.[4] This being the case, and despite the opposition of Shropshire interests, Yarranton, in his own words, 'fell on, and made [the Stour] completely navigable from Stourbridge to Kidderminster; and carried down many hundred tons of coales, and laid out near one thousand pounds, and there it was obstructed for want of money'.[5]

Kidderminster first received coal by water in 1665. By this time the town was a flourishing manufacturing centre, concentrating particularly on cloth-making. Begun in the thirteenth century, the cloth trade assumed even greater importance with increasing specialization. In 1735 the first carpet factory was established, herald of a host of such mills which contained 1700 looms by 1772.[6]

It was perhaps unfortunate for Kidderminster that the lowest 4 miles of the Stour remained unimproved, although the river was used by Severn trows for part of the distance. Navigation on the Stour, however, was of minor importance in the early eighteenth century compared with power provision. Before the substitution of coal for charcoal and the rise of steam power the pattern of West Midland industry was primarily related to water power, the major centres of iron production lying on the streams flowing centrifugally from the Midland Plateau rather than on the plateau itself. A comprehensive list of works operating in 1717 indicates a dozen or more forges on the Stour in Staffordshire and Worcestershire.[7]

Because of the demand from the forges of this neighbourhood the Severn carried England's heaviest traffic in pig iron, mainly from the blast furnaces of the Forest of Dean. 'At the beginning of the eighteenth century a single partnership controlled seventy per cent of the output of the Forest . . . and annually despatched some 1,000 tons of tough pig iron to forges on the Worcestershire Stour, via Bewdley and its embryonic rival at the confluence of Stour and Severn'.[8] The reference to Stourport is unfortunate; the port had scarcely been conceived in the early eighteenth century. But the immense traffic in high-quality pig iron which penetrated as best it could along the partially-improved Stour is not in question and the significance of the Severn to the iron trade can hardly be exaggerated. The accounts of Wilden Forge, less than two miles from Stourmouth, bear out the comparative cheapness of water carriage. Land transport of pig from Halesowen to Wilden, a mere 12 miles, cost 7s per ton in 1692, whereas the 80 miles of water from Redbrook on the Wye were covered for the same sum. Again, the cost of sending iron rods to Bristol by river was only half that of land carriage to Birmingham, only 20 miles away.[9] In the late eighteenth century Nash estimated that the Stour, less than 24 miles long, supported a greater number of works than any other English river of the same length.[10] There is no evidence of a transhipment point at the confluence of Stour and Severn before the construction of Stourport, but Nash reports vessels mooring nearby in order to take advantage of the refreshment offered by the Stourmouth Inn.

This Severnside tavern lay some distance from the village of Lower Mitton. The latter was dominated by the towns of Bewdley and Kidderminster, respectively the seats of commerce and manufacture, and neither more than four miles away. Although to some extent drawn into the lives of these larger communities, Mitton in the mid-eighteenth century preserved a great measure of social and economic autonomy through the possession of its own mill, inn and church. A turnpike road led through the village to the Severn at Ferry House, from which point passengers were ferried to the further bank. Except for three lowlying dwellings, one of which was the Stourmouth Inn, the houses of the village intermittently lined the sides of a curved street at about 100ft above sea level, the church lying somewhat aloof on higher ground for easy access from the still higher hamlet of Upper Mitton.

It is likely that mixed farming was the chief occupation of these villages. Diversity of employment was provided by ironworks, mill, and ferry, and the village's forty or so buildings were able to support a few fundamental services. The picture is essentially one of a quiet agrarian hamlet, disturbed occasionally by the rattle of a carriage down to the ferry, itself only one of many and probably little used in comparison with Bewdley Bridge. The immense Severn traffic by-passed Lower Mitton as it did many another riverside hamlet, though the Stour valley iron traffic may have provided occasional employment and a welcome change from the tedium of agrarian village life.

Early nineteenth century writers, seeking to emphasize the contrast between the area before and after the arrival of the Staffordshire and Worcestershire Canal (STW) almost all have recourse to the phrase 'barren sandy heath' in describing the riparian zone on which Stourport was built. Such a concept was dear to the hearts of generations raised on Samuel Smiles, and despite the fact that Stourport arose in enclosed meadowland, it was opined in the 1820s that: 'scarcely more than fifty years ago, the site which it now occupies was a sandy, barren, unprofitable heath, with only a few scattered cottages, exhibiting a picture of desolation and poverty'.[11]

The Decision-making Context

Bristol, though losing ground to Liverpool, was still the second city of England, exercising quasi-metropolitan functions throughout the eighteenth century.[12] Standing at the nexus of a web of road and water communications it was the commercial capital of the West, its inland and coasting traffic including domination of Britain's iron trade, of which the Severn was the major highway. However, though the Bridgewater Canal was the result of agitation by both seaport and industrializing hinterland, in the Midlands it was the inland merchants and traders who were the chief protagonists in the struggle to bring about a canal connexion with the Severn. Above Bristol the Severn's vast traffic supported several smaller ports, notably Gloucester, Tewkesbury, Worcester and Bewdley. Although shallows, fords and other obstructions were frequent, the river was the goal of numerous packhorse trains and the canals which followed them. Goods were transferred from land carriage to the Severn as early in the journey as possible, and the river was probably the busiest of its size in Europe, except for the Meuse.[13]

Transport was of vital importance to West Midlands industrialists, who in the first half of the eighteenth century had initiated a series of road improvements. Responding to the growth of industry and the relative efficiency of transport on the Severn, agitation for improved inland water access to that river had become frequent by the middle of the century. Lying almost equidistant from Weaver, Trent and Severn, the West Midlands was the obvious source of early demands for a canal connexion between the three rivers to give access by water to Liverpool, Hull and Bristol. Though Congreve's Severn–Trent scheme of 1717 came to nothing, the idea was not forgotten, being revived on a larger scale by Wedgwood in connexion with his plans for a Trent–Mersey canal.[14] Rather more emphasis was given to the Severn link by Whitworth, but the route he advocated had a completely different orientation.[15] His canal was to run from the Severn near Shrewsbury to Burton-on-Trent, a branch leaving at Great Bridgeford for the Weaver at Winsford. The line's shortness and cheapness were, however, offset by major disadvantages. Passing through neither the pottery district nor the West Midlands, entering the Severn too high up for adequate navigation, and terminating in the Weaver under the control of another body, the scheme succumbed to the more obvious viability of the TM. Other attempts to forge a Severn connexion were no more than tentative suggestions.[16]

James Brindley had envisaged the TM as the 'Grand Trunk', England's central aorta from which would spring smaller traffic arteries, the whole forming a cross-like pattern connecting the four great estuaries. The scheme was to be furthered by the passing of Acts in 1768–9 for the construction of the Coventry and Oxford canals from the Midlands hub to the Thames. The projected Severn connexion was left to separate promoters after TM supporters had made it clear that they would not build it. Thereupon, a group of businessmen led by James Perry of Wolverhampton immediately made plans for the Trent–Severn junction.[17] Despite the agitation for Whitworth's scheme, Perry, designating Brindley as surveyor, decided to promote a Bill early in 1766.

Perry told the Parliamentary committee considering his application that the Stour iron trade must greatly benefit from a canal which would reduce the prevailing land carriage rates from 8s to 1s 9d per ton.[18] Most of the landowners involved had already given their consent to the proposed route. Significantly, the persons given leave to prepare the Bill included several active promoters of the complementary TM scheme, and both lines received the Royal Assent on the same day, 14 May 1766.

It was clear to the Trent-Severn canal promoters that Whitworth's line would be of no use to Wolverhampton, the town providing the active nucleus of their subscribers. In planning their general line they were unequivocally in favour of the river valleys of the Penk, Smestow and Stour. As Congreve had recognized fifty years earlier, these valleys provided the most readily accessible axis of communication between the Severn and Trent which would also pass near Wolverhampton. The demands of the latter, perched almost on the critical watershed dominating these valleys, themselves surrounded by long stretches of difficult hill country, fully endorsed the strategy. The canal thus adopted the optimum route in terms of length, engineering difficulty, and economic viability. Its final length of a little over 46 miles was only half that of the TM, and with fewer engineering works and less opposition the Trent–Severn link was finished long before its contemporary.

Brindley was responsible for setting out the line, though his assistants, Simcock and the elder Dadford, bore the brunt of the work. Adherence to contouring principles was, naturally, marked; the canal hugged the valley sides with embankments only on the offside, the most economic means of construction in terms of quantity of earth moved and the primitive implements then in use. Brindley, however, was unable to repeat his Bridgewater success and built his first locks on this canal. 'The undertaking was thought wonderfully bold, and the attempts of Yarranton, joined to the great extent of the undertaking, the sandy spongy nature of the ground, the high banks necessary to prevent the inundation of the Stour at the new canal, furnished its opponents, if not with sound arguments, at least with very specious topics for opposition and laughter'.[19] All these supposed obstacles were overcome by the experienced engineer.

The canal's junction with the Severn was of especial interest to the town of Bewdley. No transport historian can have failed to have encountered the story of Bewdley's suicide, a supposed example of the fate of conservative towns which, rejecting transport innovations, succumbed to fossilization.[20] As it is critical to the determination of the Severn terminus of the canal, the story must be considered in detail from the points of view of engineering feasibility and the available documentary evidence.

At the Severn end, the last fixed point on the canal route, according to the Act, was to be the thriving textile centre of Kidderminster. The Severn outfall, however, was described vaguely as 'between Bewdley and Titton Brook', a distance of about six miles. Assuming that the engineers and promoters had debated the possibilities of Bewdley versus the junction of Stour and Severn (Stourmouth) as the terminus, the advantages of each can be assessed, bearing in mind the exigencies of local topography and the adequacy of contemporary maps. Bewdley's main claim lay in its status as a thriving riverport fed by established long-distance packhorse routes and in its well developed shipping and forwarding infrastructure.

Stourmouth had every other advantage. A canal leaving Kidderminster for Bewdley would have had to lock up from about 100ft above sea level to 250ft, and then down again to the Severn at Wribbenhall, over the block of hills separating Stour and Severn. On reaching Wribbenhall, difficulty would have been experienced in constructing a canal basin in the steep Severn bank. To continue down the Stour Valley, however, was both easy and cheap, for a sandstone shelf following the 100ft contour on the right wall of the valley was an ideal track for a Brindleyan contour canal, and avoided the swampy alluvium of the valley floor. Moreover, whereas the Bewdley line would have disturbed an established park, the Stour line not only avoided the parks set on high ground above the valley but also linked up a number of active Stour forges. Further, once it had crossed the Stour at Kidderminster, probably to avoid the town by following the relatively straight sandstone shelf, the canal's junction with the Severn was fairly well fixed at a point about 100yd above the Stour confluence. Had the canal kept to the left bank, it would have been restricted to a narrower belt between the river and the prohibitive 100ft contour. Wilden Ironworks and left-bank tributaries would also have had to be avoided, while following the sandstone shelf might have involved cutting through Hartlebury Common to meet the Severn near Lincomb, notorious for its shallows.

If Brindley did choose Bewdley first, as is alleged, it is clear that unless his engineering concepts had radically altered in this midland milieu, this choice was not based on a close examination of the terrain, and was likely to be altered substantially on closer inspection. Bewdley, therefore, was unlikely to become the canal terminus in the first place, let alone be given a chance to reject the offer. The documentary evidence for the rejection must now be examined. One of the story's earliest appearances was in

1799, little more than thirty years after the event: 'Brindley proposed making the bason at Wribbenhall and consequently requested the assistance of the inhabitants of Bewdley for its completion. Unfortunately the scheme was rejected, and, I am credibly informed, with less politeness than the offer merited'.[21] The tale of rejection was taken up by a number of later writers and by 1883 a local antiquarian was insisting that the inhabitants of Bewdley had actually petitioned against the canal.[22] Today the legend is perpetuated in both popular and academic literature.[23]

Confusion seems to have arisen over a petition made by Bewdley and its rejection of a canal. The citizens of Bewdley made at least two petitions in this critical period, presenting them to the House of Commons on 15 February 1766. The second petition opposed Whitworth's Severn–Trent–Weaver canal as a danger to the Trent–Mersey and Trent–Severn proposals. The text makes much of the obstructions in the Severn above Bewdley and states: 'The Petitioners conceive, that . . . Birmingham, Wolverhampton, Walsall, Stourbridge, Kidderminster, Bewdley and Dudley, and places adjacent . . . cannot receive the least benefit from the said intended Navigation'.[24] The people of Bewdley were neither oblivious nor hostile to canals, but were only too aware of their probable benefits. This awareness is evident in the petition presented immediately before the one outlined above, at a time when the Trent–Severn line was much in the news, but its exact route probably not decided. A preliminary petition from Wolverhampton had stated that in view of the intended cutting of the TM Canal, 'in order to extend the Navigation aforesaid, . . . it is practicable to make a Navigable Canal from or near Bewdley . . . through Kidderminster' to the Trent. This proposition was supported by petitions from Walsall, Stourbridge, Kidderminster, Dudley and Bewdley, all favouring a 'Bewdley Canal' and 'setting forth, that the Petitioners apprehend . . . such a Canal will be of great Public Utility'.[25]

The Bewdley petitioners in each case consisted of 'The Bailiff, Justices, Aldermen, Capital Burgesses, Merchants, Gentlemen, Clergy and Tradesmen of the Borough'. It is almost inconceivable that there could have been 'leading men' capable of 'petitioning against the canal'.[26] Bewdley was founded on trade, and its merchants and shippers would hardly have been likely to have let such a golden opportunity slip their grasp. It is probable that the Trent–Severn line, later the STW Canal, was at first planned extremely haphazardly with either no explicit Severn terminus or with Bewdley as a tentative suggestion based on small-scale maps uncorrected by local survey. As late as 20 March 1766 the Commons committee reporting on the canal quoted Brindley as placing the Severn terminus 'at or near Bewdley'. The canal was known throughout its parliamentary passage as the 'Bewdley Canal', and even the Act failed to specify an exact terminus. But within one month of Bewdley's petitions to Parliament, and only four days after the report of 20 March, the Wolverhampton promoters had decided to reroute the canal to meet the Severn 'at or near a Place called Stour's Mouth'.[27]

Finance was apparently not a great problem and little strong opposition was encountered. Construction made steady progress, though as late as April 1768 Brindley was recalled to resurvey the route to the Grand Trunk, further evidence of the lack of careful route planning and of the *ad hoc* basis on which early canals were built.[28] It is probable that the completion of the Compton–Severn section and with it the initiation of traffic from Wolverhampton was the primary object of the projectors; when this section was completed the navvies were moved to the less important section towards the Trent. August 1770 saw Brindley summoned yet again from his Grand Trunk and Bridgewater schemes, and in November the canal was reported 'finished and completely navigable from Compton to the River Severn'.[29] At the same time advertisements to this effect were ordered to be inserted in newspapers, but none appeared until 28 March of the following year. The TM junction, however, was postponed throughout 1771, and the whole canal was not announced as completely navigable until May 1772.[30]

The Initial Terminal

The Staffordshire and Worcestershire Canal Company had envisaged a small Severnside terminal port from the beginning. Stourmouth, the original name, was first changed to Newport, the more definite nomenclature of Stourport being fixed upon at the time of the opening of the Compton–Severn section in 1771.

Completed almost simultaneously with the Bridgewater Canal, the STW's achievement was almost completely over-shadowed by the duke's venture. The local press made little mention of the waterway, devoting more space to the contemporary but far less important Droitwich Canal. The Severn was still unbridged at Stourport, and newspaper references to transriverine townships completely ignored the new port.[31]

Nor did significant details appear in regional or national directories until the nineteenth century. Unlike Runcorn with its long established place-name, the area in which Stourport was planted remained a blank space on county maps as late as the 1780s. By 1787 Cary had noted a 'New Canal' and the name 'Stourport', although he shows no evidence of buildings except at Lower Mitton. Three years later, though depicted as a separate settlement, Stourport had been misplaced on the right bank of the Severn.[32] Smith's *New Map of Worcester* (1801) was little better for it placed the port in the position of Lower Mitton while failing to show the canal terminal. Not until the work of Greenwood in the 1820s was Stourport accurately represented by the private cartographers.[33]

The effects of the new canal, however, were of great local importance. Passing to the east of Lower Mitton chapel, the canal was immediately presented with an obstacle. To continue directly to the Severn would have involved excavating along the line of Lower Mitton's village street. Between chapel and village, therefore, an S bend was inserted in the line; on coming out of the bend the canal was able to lock down to the Severn a little way above Ferry House (Fig. 7).

The company purchased only the minimum area of land necessary for its plans. It was extremely anxious, however, to gain possession of riparian land at Lower Mitton, and surveyors were instructed to measure the necessary terminal plots in November 1768, fields further inland being surveyed in 1769.[34] Two Severnside fields, which together comprised a little over seven acres, were purchased in the latter year. As the rest of the company estate consisted of a narrow strip little wider than was necessary for the canal and associated spoil dumps, these seven acres comprised the entire site available for the new port.

The two fields were specifically purchased 'for the Bason', a single dock being completed in 1771. To avoid entering unpurchased land the double broad lock to the Severn, incorporating a small intermediary basin, was made from the south-west corner of the dock, although the canal entered the north-east corner (Fig. 7). Quays were levelled around the dock perimeter, and two small graving docks made for the use of Severn trows locking up into the basin. The amount of traffic which flocked to the first dock, however, was so great that the company was obliged to excavate another. Two strips of land were purchased 'for the enlargement of the Canal Basin' in 1773, though the work was held up by difficulties experienced in gaining control of all the required land. By 1776 narrow river locks leading to the proposed second dock were under construction.

Within five years of the canal's completion cranes and other dock

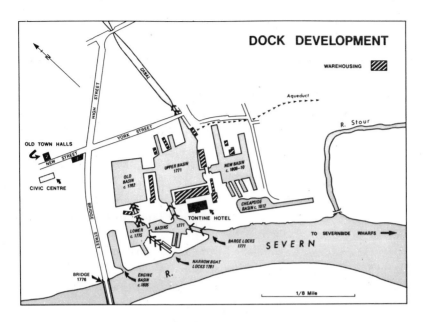

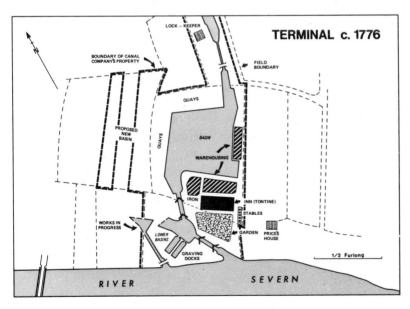

FIG. 7. The port of Stourport.

furniture had been installed. The Long Warehouse was erected on the eastern side of the first dock, the whole of the southern side being taken up with the Iron Warehouse and its one-storey neighbour, designed 'for the storage of Goods of the greatest Value and such as are most liable to Damage'.[35]

Only the initial installations were previously planned. The company built a limited amount of accommodation for both goods and people at first, extending it as the need arose. Initially bricks were shipped down the canal from a farm near Kidderminster. In 1769, however, a two acre Severnside field was purchased, 'the whole of it for a Brick Kiln'.[36] From this a large quantity of dark red bricks issued; tiles were also produced, and before the introduction of Welsh slate later in the century all the buildings of Stourport were tiled.

A remarkable print, published in March 1776 and dedicated to the STW proprietors, gives a vivid impression of the initial terminus (Fig. 8). Set alongside the well-wooded Stour, the basin exhibited a scene of great activity. Trows found the river impeded above the port by a new stone and brick bridge erected in 1773–5. Superseding the 'inconvenient . . . dangerous and uncertain' ferry it enabled the Kidderminster–Tenbury turnpike to be rerouted through Stourport, adding to the importance of the new settlement.[37] The bridge was not erected without opposition; in 1774 forty-seven citizens of Bewdley petitioned a local landowner to oppose the measure.[38] Their grounds for opposition were numerous. Believing Bewdley Bridge to be sufficient for the traffic, they stated that another bridge would lead to the desertion of existing turnpikes, obstruct the movements of river craft, and increase the numbers of the poor. The main object, however, was to prevent at all costs the growth of Stourport. Having failed to attract the canal terminal, Bewdley realized that its trade was likely to decline. Its remaining function was as a local market centre, drawing largely from the western side of the Severn. A bridge, the necessary condition for the creation of a rival market centre at Stourport, would serve to hasten the older town's demise.

Apart from pre-existing and dockland structures Stourport's early buildings were few. A temporary watch-house placed near the upper locks in 1775 was replaced by two cottages 'under one roof' for the residence of lock-keeper and wharfinger. Though the excavators could be

FIG. 8. The Stourport terminus of the Staffordshire and Worcestershire Canal, 1776. A new bridge, locks, Severn trows, docks, warehousing, and the Tontine Inn testify to the changes wrought by the canal in the formerly placid rural scene (compare Fig. 7).

accommodated in huts, there were at least six permanent employees at
Stourport in 1772. Further housing was still under consideration in 1774,
but clearly some provision had to be made for visitors and the higher
grades of employee. To this end the company erected an hotel of colossal
dimensions. Three storeys high and seven windows wide on its Severn
face, the Tontine had three large wings at the rear. A garden was laid out
on land sloping down to the Severn, and two stables added. The great
brick structure was occupied by 1773, and in the following year a 'chaise
house' was erected close by.[39]

Symbol of the STW's determination to build up a flourishing trade at
Stourport, the hotel's bulk dominated the whole settlement. Its majestic
command of the waterfront was calculated to impress the most hardened
waterman. However, the port at once attracted independent
entrepreneurs. The minute books make frequent reference to Ames, Bird,
and York among others who rented quayage from the company. Aaron
York was responsible for one of Stourport's first private dwellings, for in
1776 he was given leave to wheel bricks for housebuilding over the
company's wharf on payment of 6d for the privilege.[40]

There is no evidence that Brindley, who lacked architectural
pretensions, played any part in the layout of the terminal; the company
apparently relied on the elder Dadford. But the small port envisaged by
the former had by 1776 become a vital, compact unit. The focus of Severn
craft, canal narrow boats, and road traffic, the canal town was already
taking the first steps towards its future role as the most important inland
port in the West.

Port Development, 1772–1816

Unlike Runcorn, Stourport had only a brief career as a resort, and its
distance upriver from Bristol and Gloucester gave no opportunity for the
establishment of a packet service. Nevertheless, throughout the 1770s
Stourport was 'the resort of People of Fashion in Worcester and the
adjacent Counties . . . Scarcely a Day passes but several Parties of Ladies
and Gentlemen come here in their Carriages. Regattas . . . are not
unusual'.[41] This function probably died towards the end of the century
with the upsurge of commerce.

Generating little traffic along its own line, the canal's initial prosperity
was bound up with its position as the strategic link between Trent,
Severn, and connecting canals. The junction of the Birmingham, Dudley,

and Stourbridge canals with the STW, in its first decade, soon converted Stourport into a busy commercial hub. The only through water route between the Midlands and the Severn for twenty years, providing Birmingham with its most convenient links with Liverpool, Bristol, and even London, the STW thrived on the transit trade. Locally, the canal raised the market value of fruit and promoted hop-growing. Regionally, it aided the dissemination of Staffordshire coal, the manufactured iron ware, pottery and glass of the Midlands, Stourbridge clay and Lancashire baled goods, while produce from both the upper and lower Severn reached Midlands markets through Stourport.

The stream of traffic emanating from connecting navigations soon necessitated the provision of further dock space at Stourport. A second pair of river locks were led up to a second upper basin completed in 1781. An engine and aqueduct, used for abstracting water from the Stour for the basins, soon proved inadequate, and the Engine Basin, opening into the Severn, was completed about 1805.[42]

At least nine warehouses graced the two docks by 1795, and throughout the next twenty years trade remained buoyant. Although a number of dock arms were built for individual carriers, a score of whom had offices at the port, traffic had again outgrown dock facilities by the turn of the century. In 1804 a plan was proposed for a third dock, which was to have a separate upper canal lock and a lateral link with the original upper basin. The latter was to be provided with a second canal lock and yet a third set of river locks.[43] Such an intricate system, with three canal locks leading into the Severn via three upper and two lower basins and three river locks, would have provided Stourport with a remarkable dock complex.

Unfortunately, only the lateral cut was made, leaving the new basin as a cul-de-sac. On the latter's completion in 1810, a further dock was decided upon. The restricted nature of the estate, hedged in by buildings, was responsible for the narrow length of Cheapside Basin; excavated in 1810–12, this latest dock also lacked direct connexion with the Severn. Though the cul-de-sac of a cul-de-sac, its dock space proved valuable in easing contemporary congestion, with its concrete expression in the apparently ceaseless growth of warehousing well into the 1820s.

At the turn of the century, Stourport's major built-up area consisted of the seventeen acre dock estate, of which the two docks existing in 1800 covered nearly five acres. Though iron, clay and grain warehouses surrounded the first dock on three sides, the preponderant open wharfage and stacking grounds were almost wholly given over to coalyards. The focus of activity was undoubtedly the Tontine Inn with its adjacent counting houses.

Beyond the STW pale, the town moulded itself around the dock estate. Following York's lead, several speculative builders had arrived by the early 1780s when York Street was laid out fronting the docks. John Wesley dismissed Stourport, in 1781, as 'a small well-built village'. Returning in 1788 he remarked: 'Where twenty years ago there was but one house; now there are two or three streets, and as the trade increases it will probably grow into a considerable town'. In 1790 he found 'Stourport . . . twice as large as two years ago'. Indeed, when the original bridge was destroyed by floods in 1795, it was estimated that the population had risen from about a dozen in the 1760s and 600 in 1773 to almost 1300, a twofold increase in little over two decades.[44]

Although from company records it appears that the STW owned little housing, a comparison of extant canal buildings and nearby housing, confirmed by detailed architectural analysis, indicates that much of the early building was done by STW workmen.[45] Buildings surrounding the estate are almost uniformly of local brick and plain tile, with brickwork, gable ends, and bonding identical with canal-side buildings and found nowhere else in Stourport. Diversity in building style came with the speculators. In York Street the canal carriers' mansions erected in the 1780s possess vast vaulted brick cellars with access to the wharves. Almost all the dwellings of this period were of three storeys, increasingly roofed with slate, and with extensive cellarage.

This war-time period of intense activity was accompanied by a boom in share values. Between 1785 and 1806 annual dividends leapt almost threefold, reaching a peak in the period 1812–15. This was the zenith of STW prosperity. Moreover, the Stour ironworks, despite new coalfield growths, survived by using canal-borne coal. In the 1830s the valley still boasted five active works below Kidderminster, one of which had been located on the canal bend above Stourport as early as 1789.[46] It rapidly became famous for its castings and tinned holloware when acquired by the energetic Baldwins of Wilden Forge.

Momentum carried the boom into the early 1820s, when Stourport appeared 'a neat bustling mercantile town . . . a lively little seaport', principal link between Midland narrow boats and the 60 ton trows of the West.[47] The establishment of regular hop and general markets, bank, post office, and other facilities, was complemented by 'the early association of industry and elegance' in the shape of a 'dancing assembly'. Set in the midst of trees and pastures, Stourport appeared in the early nineteenth century 'a complete Maritime town in the very heart of the kingdom, which . . . seems . . . a new creation. Its houses are mostly on a good scale, its streets comfortable, full of shops and thronged with people; whilst an air even of elegance pervades it'.[48]

The Effects of Competition, 1816–45

Conscious of its position as a vital link in the national canal network, the STW spent much money and energy in encouraging the construction or improvement of water links. Although originally expressing some interest in the ill-fated Leominster Canal, the STW, with metropolitan markets in mind, was far more interested in the Thames and Severn Canal (TS). Involved in this development as early as 1774, James Perry was the moving spirit behind both STW and TS.[49] But hardly had the opening of the latter in 1789 provided Birmingham with its first water link with London, than the Fazeley–Oxford line, shorter by 42 miles, was completed. As an interurban route this completely superseded the TS, so that the STW's plan for coal sales in the lower Thames region was stillborn.

Active interest in the vital Severn waterway proved no more useful. The company's promotion of horse towpaths was no substitute for improvement of the channel, which Telford in 1796 showed to be too shallow for considerable periods; 'there were not two months in which barges could be navigated, even down the river, with a freight that was equal to defray the expenses of working them'.[50] Exasperated by widespread opposition to other improvement schemes, the STW obtained an Act (30 Geo. III, c. 75; 1790) for the improvement of the Severn to Diglis, near Worcester. Erecting jetties to increase the scour, the company was indicted for damaging the river, and was forced to remove them.[51]

While connecting navigations failed to live up to expectations, rival navigations were vigorous. Within thirteen years of the opening of the STW a rival line proposed, by connecting Stourbridge with Diglis, to divert the northern and Midlands trades from Stourport. Its promoters asserted that craft of 5 to 15 tons burden could not reach Stourport for half the year and that the port 'from its entering the Severn in so improper a place . . . has been found totally inadequate'.[52] Realizing that all hinged upon Severn improvement, the STW in its anxiety even considered 'the practicability of making a canal passable for Severn Vessels' between Stourport and Worcester.[53]

Though the rival Bill was defeated in 1786, the move to make Worcester the main outlet for the Midlands soon reappeared in a different guise. The Worcester and Birmingham Canal (WB), authorized in 1791, was the first fully to brave the obstacle of the Birmingham Plateau. In a flurry of partisan pamphleteering the time-consuming lockage of the WB was weighed against its reduction of the Birmingham–Diglis distance by about 30 per cent.[54] The WB's advantages over the STW were considerable; opened in 1816, it permanently captured much of the latter's traffic.

With the completion of the WB, STW revenue plunged sharply and the effects reverberated throughout Stourport. In the decade 1812–21 the population scarcely rose; many male workers left the town. Only nineteen houses were built. A spate of toll reductions quickly became a flood. A system of drawbacks and bounties on tolls became ever more complicated as connecting navigations followed suit. Through rates could no longer be determined in advance for 'each company was busy adjusting its own tolls in the light of others' actions, which in turn were caused by their own in an endless regress'.[55]

In 1825, less than a decade after the WB had partially superseded the Wolverhampton–Stourport section of the STW, the projected Birmingham and Liverpool Junction Canal (BLJ), leaving the STW at Autherley for Nantwich, threatened to withdraw traffic from the Wolverhampton–TM section. When the new artery opened in 1835, the STW decided to impose a toll of 1s per ton on goods crossing its line between the Birmingham and BLJ canals. The latter, however, proposed an aqueduct to cross the STW and withdrew its Bill only on the STW's reduction of the toll to 4d. Water became a major problem. The 23,450 tons of goods crossing the STW in the first eight months of 1835 used nearly 10 million cu ft of STW water, so that 'to keep the Trade afloat' the company was obliged to purchase water and to construct new reservoirs.[56]

With traffic diminishing on both sections of its line, the STW attempted to recoup its losses by reverting to its early interest in forging new links. In the 1820s a number of minor tramways were built between the canal and collieries, the phase culminating in the opening of the Hatherton Branch Canal in 1842. At the other end of the line, mounting criticism of the Severn had resulted in the completion in 1827 of the Gloucester and Berkeley Ship Canal (GB). A projected extension to

Worcester, conceived in the Canal Mania, was revived in 1825, though nothing was done. The GB, however, benefited the Severn river ports by improving connexions with their estuarial counterparts. In 1814 the Severn's first steam packet had begun a Gloucester to Worcester run, and by 1830 steam tugs were making the same trip.[57] There was renewed agitation for improvement above Worcester. While threatened by the BLJ overpass, the STW in 1836 was supporting a proposed Severn Navigation Company which wished to provide by means of locks a depth of 12ft to Worcester and 6ft to Stourport, sufficient to allow vessels of 100 tons up to the latter. This scheme recognized the existence of a sharp break of slope at Worcester, above which double the hauling strength per ton was necessary.[58]

Such was the variety of opposed interests, the scheme ground to a halt. When it was revealed that a lock would not be made at Diglis the STW petitioned successfully against the improvement Bill. A Severn Improvement Association then gained momentum, and in 1842 the Severn Improvement Commission, headed by Lord Hatherton of the STW, gained power to provide a depth of 7ft to Stourport. By 1845 the locks were opened, the highest being at Lincomb, a little below Stourport. After dredging it was reported that the river had attained a depth of 6ft in all seasons. Almost immediately, however, complaints were made that the depth was not being maintained. By 1851 it had fallen to 3ft 6in and with it traffic and revenue.

Complementing the STW's reliance on such a poor waterway, railway competition was to provide what later appeared to be Stourport's death blow. Though connecting with the exemplary BLJ, which had stimulated a reconstruction of the Birmingham Canal on modern lines, the STW line had never been improved. Consequently Midlands traders found rail carriage a great attraction. Although the STW's original raison d'etre had been superseded by the opening of a Birmingham–Gloucester railway in 1840, the STW remained largely concerned with waterway rivalries. Its real fears were still rooted in the past: 'if the Company is to retain its present Trade, some reduction in their Tonnage Dues must soon take place, otherwise Rival Canal Companies will ingross the whole Trade for the West of England, and once diverted, it will be very difficult to regain'.[59]

To the south, however, despite the continuing shipment of about 70,000 tons of coal per year from both Stourport and Worcester, traffic moved onto rail. The effect of this, and of the post-1835 transfer of northern traffic to the BLJ and the Grand Junction Railway (GJR), together with the increasing unsuitability of the Severn as vessels increased in size, caused a marked fall in STW revenue. The company attributed this to depression, strikes, and lockouts in Staffordshire, but the real causes were deeper and more lasting.[60]

This loss of trade was accompanied by a slackening of urban growth in Stourport; indeed, the town registered a small decline in population in the decade 1832–41. References to the 'poor of Stourport' began to appear in the company minutes. The Cheapside Basin stacking grounds, laid out only 26 years before, were let off as garden plots in 1838.[61] The massive Tontine was subdivided, and by 1842 contained twenty separate dwellings besides the original inn.

An increase in industrial employment partially compensated for the decline of the carrying trade. Industrial establishments, including a vinegar brewery and a foundry, had been established in canalside locations before 1800. In 1828 the STW discovered that two local carriers had extended the Kidderminster carpet industry to Stourport by setting up looms in warehouses rented from the company.[62] Freed from the restrictions of Kidderminster, the industry expanded; in 1847 a third carpet and worsted mill was established near the Stour, the water of which had a reputation for dye-striking. By the early 1820s cheap sites near the canal bend had been acquired for foundry extensions and for the erection of a tanyard and a gasworks. House-building by these industrialists was the prime cause of Stourport's continued growth. Much of this construction followed the early building pattern, the uniformity of brickwork, window type and eaves line producing a pleasant unpretentious unity of character in the streets surrounding the STW dockland.

Even in the later 1840s, however, the town remained dominated by the canal company. The canal and docks directly or indirectly remained the well-spring of the economy. Absolute control was exercised over the dock estate. Privately-built warehouses were bought up by the STW, which also provided counting houses for carriers using the canal. At first only Stourport residents were allowed to rent dock and wharf space, and employees and others were often summarily given notice to quit or directed where to live and where to hold their markets.

Authoritarian control, however, had its benefits. The STW supervised the market, provided a slaughterhouse, regularly repaired its houses, and allowed the Baldwins to extend gas lighting to the town. Financial help was given to several worthy causes, including a new market hall (1833), the enlargement of Lower Mitton church (1834), National schools

(1840s), and the provision of a police station (1841). Although refusing the request of the local incumbent to prohibit Sunday navigation, the company offered him its 'mite towards the Expense of establishing a Library at Stourport and for purchasing Books treating on the profanation of the Sabbath'. In 1812 the company had responded somewhat more willingly to the repeated requests of residents for a town clock by erecting a handsome chronometer on the Iron Warehouse. Centrally situated in the dock estate and visible from all the major streets, the clock symbolized the dependence of Stourport upon the Staffordshire and Worcestershire Canal Company.

5. Notes

1. T. S. Willan, 'River Navigation and the Trade of the Severn Valley 1600–1750', *Economic History Review*, 8 (1938), 68–79.
2. Habington, quoted in W. H. B. Court, *The Rise of the Midland Industries 1600–1838*, Oxford University Press, London (1938), p. 6.
3. Leland, quoted in T. Harral, *Picturesque Views of the Severn*, Whittaker, London, Vol. 1 (1824), p. 282.
4. Plot, quoted in M. J. Wise and B. L. C. Johnson, 'The Changing Regional Pattern in the Eighteenth Century', in *Birmingham and its Regional Setting*, ed. by M. J. Wise, Association for the Advancement of Science, Birmingham (1950), p. 167.
5. A. Yarranton, *England's Improvement by Land and Sea*, Everingham, London (1677), p. 66.
6. J. R. Burton, *A History of Kidderminster*, Stock, London (1890), p. 171.
7. B. L. C. Johnson, 'The Charcoal Iron Industry in the early Eighteenth Century', *Geographical Journal*, 117 (1951), 167–77.
8. Ibid., p. 169.
9. M. J. Wise and B. L. C. Johnson, op. cit., p. 170.
10. T. R. Nash, *Collections for the History and Antiquities of Worcestershire*, Payne, London Vol. 2 (1782).
11. T. Harral, op. cit., Vol. 2, p. 1.
12. W. E. Minchinton, 'Bristol—Metropolis of the West in the Eighteenth Century', *Transactions, Royal Historical Society* Fifth Series 4 (1954), 69–89.
13. W. G. East, 'The Severn Waterway in the Eighteenth and Nineteenth Centuries', in L. D. Stamp and S. W. Wooldridge, *London Essays in Geography*, University of London Press, London (1951).
14. C. Hadfield, *The Canals of the West Midlands*, David and Charles, Newton Abbot (1966), p. 21.
15. R. Whitworth, *The Advantages of Inland Navigation*, Baldwin, London (1766), *passim*.

16. T. S. Willan, 'The Navigation of the River Weaver in the Eighteenth Century', *Chetham Society*, New Series 3 (1951).

17. *Aris' Birmingham Gazette* (28 January, 24 March 1766).

18. *JHC* (20 March 1766).

19. T. R. Nash, *Supplement to the Collections*, Payne, London (1799), p. 47.

20. J. D. Porteous, 'Bewdley's Suicide: a Reassessment', *Journal of the Railway and Canal Historical Society*, 13 (1967), 44–6.

21. T. R. Nash, *Supplement* . . . , op. cit., p. 47.

22. J. R. Burton, *A History of Bewdley*, Reeves, London (1883), p. 15.

23. e.g. J. Simmons, *Transport*, Studio Vista, London (1962), p. 34.

24. *JHC* (15 February 1766).

25. *JHC* (15 February 1766).

26. see F. C. Laird, *A Topographical and Historical Description of the County of Worcester*, Sherwood, London (1818);
    J. R. Burton, *A History of Bewdley*, op. cit., p. 15.

27. *Berrow's Worcester Journal* (27 March 1776).

28. STW 1/1 (5 April 1776).

29. STW 1/1 (6 November 1770).

30. *Berrow's Worcester Journal* (28 March 1771, 4 June 1772).

31. e.g. *Berrow's Worcester Journal* (3 July 1766, 28 March 1771, 5 March 1772).

32. J. Cary, 'A Map of Worcestershire, from the Best Authorities' (1787, 89); 'Worcestershire' in *England Delineated*, (1790).

33. C. Greenwood, 'The County of Worcester' in *Worcestershire Delineated*, C. and J. Greenwood, London (1822).

34. BWB Wolverhampton: land purchase book 1, pp. 83–4.

35. STW 1/1 (15 June 1775).

36. STW 1/1 (5 April 1768).

37. *Berrow's Worcester Journal* (15 September 1775).

38. Worcestershire CRO: (3198) 705 135/22, 'Petition of the Borough and Inhabitants of Bewdley to D. Zachary' (1774).

39. STW 1/1 (29 December 1773).

40. STW 1/1 (19 December 1776).

41. *Berrow's Worcester Journal* (14 September 1775).

42. STW 1/2 (20 October 1803).

43. STW 1/4 (24–6 July 1806).

44. John Wesley, quoted in W. T. Jackman, *The Development of Transportation in Modern England*, Cambridge University Press, Cambridge (1962), p. 366; and J. R. Burton, *A History of Kidderminster*, op. cit., p. 138.

45. T. W. L. Cooper, *An Historical Survey of Housing in Stourport-on-Severn 1770–1870*, unpublished thesis, School of Architecture, Birmingham College of Art (1966).

46. *Worcestershire* (Victoria County Histories) Vol. 2 (1906), p. 269.

47. T. Harral, op. cit., p. 3.

48. F. C. Laird, op. cit., p. 248.

49. STW 1/1 (17 May 1774).

50. J. Plymley, *A General View of the Agriculture of Shropshire*, Nicol, London (1803), p. 286.

51. T. R. Nash, *Supplement* . . . , op. cit., p. 7.

52. BM 712 C. 40 (1) 'Observations on the Intended Worcester Canal' (1785).

53. STW 1/1 (26 December 1785).
54. BM 8776 s45 'The General Utility of Inland Navigation' (1791); BM 4e 13 I 187.
55. C. Hadfield, *The Canals of the West Midlands*, op. cit., p. 129.
56. STW 1/5 (27 October 1830); (3, 15 September 1835).
57. *Berrow's Worcester Journal* (7 August 1814).
58. W. G. East, op. cit., p. 99.
59. STW 1/6 (2 May 1839).
60. STW 1/6 (5 January 1843).
61. STW 1/6 (4 October 1838).
62. STW 1/5 (4 September 1828).

6

Ellesmere Port in the Canal Age

An Act for making and maintaining a Navigable Canal from the River
Severn at Shrewsbury in the County of Salop, to the River Mersey at or near
Netherpool in the County of Chester.

(33 Geo. III, c. 91; 1793)

Ellesmere Port Before The Canal

The canal town of Ellesmere Port was planted in the Wirral
Peninsula of Cheshire, defined on two sides by the Mersey and Dee.
Though the settlements of the peninsula are largely restricted to
sandstone outcrops, the site of the future town was dominated by an
undulating boulder clay plateau stretching north from Chester and
falling uniformly and gradually to a narrow Mersey floodplain of
the same material, now occupied by the Manchester Ship Canal.
Estuarial encroachments were a common phenomenon, periodic floods
in medieval times rendering hundreds of acres unfit for
cultivation. Floods rendering the marshland untenable, almost all
settlements were perched upon higher ground inland. Though most
were located on sandstone, the south-east corner of the Wirral
Hundred had a number of clayland settlements, most of them
occupying strategic positions on the embryonic road network.
Netherpool, for example, was protected by the Rivacre Brook and the
Mersey on a site where the latter's rocky shore provided a landing
place and where the river, at its widest but shallowest, was
favourable at low water. Only Whitby, in whose township the
Ellesmere Canal was to reach the Mersey, had none of these
advantages.

The emphasis on roads reflects the unimportance of river traffic on the south Mersey shore. Until the rise of Liverpool the Dee was the chief commercial estuary of the region. Unlike much-frequented Chester, the Wirral remained *terra incognita* until the late eighteenth century. 'The earliest itinerants avoided it. Leland appears anxious to escape from it, and it is very questionable whether Camden ever visited Wirral at all'.[1] Yet after the Dissolution a number of wealthy families were in part supported by the townships surrounding Whitby. Stanney Hall housed the Bunburys, the Stanleys dominated Hooton and Childer Thornton from Hooton Hall, while the Pooles inhabited Poole Hall, the only dwelling in remote Netherpool.

Whitby, lying six miles from Chester on a minor road, shared the relatively sparse population and unremarkable history of the south Mersey shore. Though a single alehouse had been established in 1561, in the seventeenth century Whitby, Overpool and Netherpool were of minor importance in comparison with Stoke and the Stanney townships. The commercial and military traffic to Ireland via the Wirral had little effect on this corner of the peninsula.

By the early eighteenth century, however, the Wirral was undergoing a major reorientation of economic activity. The decline of Chester as a trading port was reflected in the burgeoning of the port of Liverpool, and with it the regularization of ferries between the south Mersey shore and Lancashire. An increasing number of passengers travelled via regular coach services to the Liverpool ferries, especially after the turnpiking of four roads under the first Wirral turnpike Act of 1787. Such was the demand, coaches were running three times weekly between Chester and Woodside Ferry as early as 1762.[2] This traffic in some measure stimulated the growth of such villages as the Suttons, whose cores exhibit a considerable amount of eighteenth-century building. However, as the northerly ferries were by far the most frequented, the Whitby area benefited little from the quickening pace of activity. Off the main roads isolated villages, linked by tortuous muddy tracks, had altered little in aspect since Defoe at the beginning of the century had declared: 'This isthmus has not one market town on it'.[3] Settlements communicated infrequently, intense local rivalries being expressed in traditional rhymes:

'In Stoke there are but few good folk,
In Stanney hardly any . . .'

The agricultural base was not particularly good. It is clear from the Stoke parish registers that the inhabitants of Whitby hamlet were predominantly farmers and their labourers, although a fisherman was recorded in 1787. The population of Whitby township immediately before the arrival of the canal in 1795 cannot be calculated exactly. At a time when Ellesmere Port contained at the most three dwellings, the 1801 Census accords Whitby 170 residents, consisting of twenty-nine families in as many dwellings. Prior to the canal, these inhabitants were wholly resident in the compact hamlet, which was grouped around the inn, smithy and hall. John Grace, a local landowner, lived in the hall, though most of the township had passed into the hands of the Grosvenor family, ultimately dukes of Westminster, in the early part of the century.

Near the Mersey no buildings of any kind existed prior to the planting of Ellesmere Port. Indeed, seventeenth-and eighteenth-century maps reveal the persistence of a pattern which had been fixed in Domesday times; this small riparian zone was a permanent negative area, surrounded by an arc of small hamlets.[4] The village of Ince and the farm which had succeeded Stanlaw Abbey lay close to the Mersey on the east, but were established on relatively secure outcrops of Bunter Sandstone. To the west only Poole Hall stood near the river, a once-proud mansion 'quite desolated and in decay and the Gardens all neglected and a Wilderness'.[5] Between Poole Hall, the site of Stanlaw Abbey, and Ince a causeway known in part as Poole's Wharf persisted in the early eighteenth century as a narrow track, though repeated estuarial incursions had swept it away by 1750. Only narrow tracks approached the area, which was so desolate that even the advent of the canal failed to improve it beyond the immediate point of impact. Though in Ormerod's day Ellesmere Port had 'assumed the appearance of a petty port' its former situation had not been equal to that of Little Sutton, described in 1819 as 'an inconsiderable village . . . destitute of anything to attract the eye'.[6]

The Decision-making Context

Defoe's prediction that Liverpool and Bristol could coexist as trading equals proved unfounded within the century, for Liverpool steadily usurped its rival's hinterland by means of a ramifying web of inland waterway connexions.[7] By 1790 Brindley's dream had become reality; a great St Andrews Cross of canals connected England's major commercial estuaries. On this framework many miles of minor canals were being hung. None of these, however, had penetrated Shropshire or the Marches o any extent; here land carriage on inadequate roads was inevitable for raffic endeavouring to reach Dee and Severn. Thus agitation for the Ellesmere Canal came, as its name suggests, from the landlocked interior rather than from the outer seaport.

The Chester Canal, completed in 1779 in the post-Bridgewater rash of peculation, ran forlornly from Nantwich to Chester to meet the ncreasingly deserted and silted Dee. Created in the hope of preventing he diversion of trade from Chester to Liverpool by the TM, the latter lealt the death blow almost at once by preventing the proposed Middlewich Branch of the Chester Canal from joining its line. Deserted by its shareholders, besieged by creditors, burdened with debt and with hardly any traffic, the company had £21 7s 5½d in hand by 1788. When he Ellesmere Canal came on the scene its northern counterpart was all out moribund.

Undeterred by this example and fired with the idea of revitalizing local industry and serving agriculture by the better distribution of coal, slate, ime and general goods, three gentlemen met 'soon after the conclusion of the American War' to discuss a scheme for linking the Mersey with the Dee and Severn, and thus providing themselves with a variety of outlets. The main objective was stillwater access to a major estuary for the industrializing Wrexham–Ruabon area.

During a national wave of canal interest, soon to burgeon as the Canal Mania, a meeting held at Ellesmere, Shropshire, on 31 August 1791 set up a committee which included the mayors of Liverpool, Chester and Shrewsbury.[8] The latter, no longer a major riverport, was much in favour of the venture, but was to benefit least. Though William Jessop's first report on the various routes proposed emphasized the magnitude of the task, the scheme was brought before the public in September 1792, 'a year of unbounding prosperity'.[9] Little opposition was encountered. Landed proprietors, often local MPs, flocked to support the scheme and it was largely to please these that the many small branches, so characteristic of the Ellesmere Canal, were planned.

The Bill, presented to the House on 25 February 1793, was assisted in its passage by petitions from the upper Severn towns and from the Chester Canal, which saw the new venture as a chance to revitalize their declining trades. Possibly because the committee discussing the almost unopposed Bill was headed by Kynaston Powell, one of its chief promoters, the Bill made a very quick passage through both Houses, receiving the Royal Assent on 30 April 1793.

The promoters of the Dee–Severn line had originally intended the

E

canal to run from Chester along the eastern side of the Dee, thus avoiding the difficult western hill country.[10] At a meeting in late 1791 Joseph Turner, a Whitchurch engineer, suggested a much easier alternative route from the inland terminus of the Chester Canal at Nantwich through Whitchurch, to the west.[11] Though surveyed, this line was abandoned in favour of Jessop's plans.

In 1792 Jessop decided on yet a third route, which had the merit of pleasing the promoters in that the main line was to be taken west of the Dee through Wrexham and Ruabon. Had this line materialized it would have been one of the most costly lines ever built for it involved lengthy lock staircases, nearly four miles of tunnelling, and several difficult aqueducts. Jessop's views prevailed at first, despite the appointment of Thomas Telford as 'General Agent, Surveyor, Engineer, Architect and Overlooker of the Canal'.[12] When subscriptions opened on 10 September, however, the rebuffed eastern canal group opened a rival subscription. The supporters of the western canal at once determined to crush this rival, to the extent of supporting Turner's earlier plan for joining the Whitchurch Branch to the Chester Canal, thus surrounding the proposed eastern canal and rendering it useless. After negotiations, a compromise was decided upon. Twin trunk lines were to be made in the shape of the former western line and the Whitchurch–Chester line, uniting at Chester with the Dee–Mersey Wirral line 'as the head of both streams'.[13] It is ironical that despite this show of force the western canal supporters had within a few years to concede the superiority of an eastern line.

Two salient features were common to all four plans. The object of the trunk line was to connect Shrewsbury on the Severn with Chester on the Dee, while from Chester a wide canal was to meet the Mersey at Poole's Wharf.[14] The Netherpool district lay almost due north of Chester and was thus the Mersey outfall of the shortest route between Chester and that river. It is not clear whether the surveyors realized that at this place the Mersey channel lay close inshore, and because of the Gowy outflow and the tidal scour around Pool Rocks was not subject to periodic dearths of water as were the channels at Runcorn and Frodsham. While the Shrewsbury connexion was only a secondary consideration it was obvious to the promoters that a Mersey terminus would be of far greater benefit than a Dee connexion only; they were able to profit by the example of the Chester Canal. In fact the Wirral line was to be the real outlet for the 115 mile project, giving unimpeded access to Liverpool via the free Mersey estuary. This objective was hardly in dispute, for as early as 1791 it had been so indicated and mapped by Joseph Turner.[15]

Planning the Wirral line through 'the flat Wirral Peninsula' was not as straightforward as some writers suggest.[16] Clearly the straightest line possible, with the least lockage, was necessary for this major outlet. The surveyors, however, found themselves thwarted in this endeavour by the wide backbone of the Wirral Plateau, trending southeast–northwest directly across the path of their canal. Fortunately, the general trend of ridge and valley which caused so much difficulty to the Leeds and Liverpool Canal was broken between Backford and Stoke by the narrow Broxton valley. Its sides defined by sandstone outcrops in an almost unrelieved landscape of boulder clay, this dry valley was the only major break in the ridge of low hills running from Helsby to north Wirral. By leading the canal through this gap at a level nowhere exceeding 50ft above sea-level it was possible to cross the physical barrier presented by the Wirral Plateau without recourse to lockage. The company's instructions in 1791 were: 'From the Chester Canal Bason the proposed Canal to proceed . . . locking up as high as conveniently may be; so as to carry the canal on a level through the Backford valley near Wervin to the River Mersey near Stanlow House and Poole Hall being a distance of ten miles'.[17] The canal plunged through the Broxton valley alluvium to reach the more congenial boulder clays on the far side. On emerging near Stoke, however, the route was aimed directly at the marshy Gowy valley. The surveyors were thus compelled to reorient their line immediately after leaving the Broxton valley, and provided an almost right-angled bend just east of Stoke. Ease and cost of lockless excavation being generally proportional to distance, the canal was then carried as close as possible to the marshland edge to meet the Mersey not in Netherpool but in Whitby township.

Financial support, at least for the Wirral line, was at first no problem; the Ellesmere Canal was promoted at the height of the mania. When the subscription was opened in 1792 the chairman was overwhelmed by 'the paroxysm of commercial ardour . . . The books were opened about noon, and ere sun set a million of money was confided to the care of the Committee'.[18] The Earl of Bridgewater, the Canal Duke's successor and soon to become the chairman of the Ellesmere Canal Company, took a full 9 per cent of the shares, no doubt expecting the canal to benefit his extensive estates near Whitchurch and Ellesmere.[19]

While part of the Llanymynech Branch was being cut to meet the proposed Montgomeryshire Canal, the Mersey–Dee line was in progress. The company showed foresight in cutting the Wirral line first, for not only was it relatively easy to construct but it was also the vital estuarial link, capable of supporting immediately a remunerative traffic between Chester and the Mersey and thus helping to finance more arduous construction in the hinterland. According to Jessop, all the proposed trunk lines had specified, as early as 1791, that the Wirral line should be built to take boats of 14ft beam, although the remainder of the canal was built solely on narrow gauge lines.[20]

The exact date of completion is not known. An 'elegant passage boat' was launched into the canal at Chester on 8 June 1795 but the passenger service was not begun until 1 July.[21] The three locks into the Mersey were not finished until early 1796. There is no record of a celebration; the initiation of goods traffic was quietly made by the familiar string of coal boats, which reached Chester from the Mersey in February 1796.[22]

The Initial Terminal

The broad Wirral line, specifically constructed to enable Mersey vessels to reach Chester, was less an attempt to revitalize the ancient port than to use its social capital as a basis for a transhipment point between the broad and narrow sections of the Ellesmere Canal; but basic installations were soon found to be necessary at the Mersey outfall in the area known as Stanley House, apparently a confusion of the local place-names Stanlow and Stanney with the land-owning Stanley family. The terminal was designated Ellesmere Port by the company as early as 1795.[23] Unlike their counterparts in Lower Mitton, however, the local inhabitants refused to acquiesce and referred to the new settlement as Whitby Wharf or Whitby Locks. The local and regional names were used side by side as late as the 1860s when the railway station was named Whitby Locks, and the name persisted in the term 'Locks goods' used into the twentieth century on Liverpool docks.

The completion of the Wirral line evoked little interest in the local press: in length it was only one twenty-third of the proposed canal; in the Canal Mania far more spectacular engineering feats were being accomplished; and finally, all attention was focused on Telford's brilliant Pontycysyllte and Chirk aqueducts at the other end of the line. Only company advertisements publicized the Wirral line in the Chester and Liverpool papers, though the Mersey terminus was mentioned neither in news nor in advertisements. Indeed, those newspapers which reported the commencement of traffic spoke only of Liverpool and Chester.[24] Though the canal was mentioned in several contemporary works, no national or regional directory acknowledged the new settlement until the mid-nineteenth century.[25]

Pre-canal maps show large blank spaces in the area of riverine Whitby, Burdett's original map (1777) being no exception.[26] The 1794 edition, however, anticipated the completion of the Wirral line by depicting a 'Junction of the Dee and Mersey'. Though the canal took its place on the map from this early date, its terminal was rarely named until the arrival of the Ordnance Survey.

The canal entered Whitby township some distance from the hamlet and only a half dozen meadows were involved. In March 1795 a company surveyor was ordered to value the land taken for the Wirral line but not yet paid for.[27] Apparently much land at the terminus was not acquired until after the completion of the canal, for contemporary minute books reveal the proprietors' vexation at the high prices demanded by Whitby landowners. These were so high that the company's agents were instructed to buy the smallest area possible, consistent with its plans.[28] Thus, like Stourport, Ellesmere Port was founded on a very restricted site, only certain parts of vital Merseyside fields being purchased from Earl Grosvenor. All told, the area on which the new port was built covered less than four acres.

The purchased portions of these fields were intended for dock construction. The descent to the Mersey, about 30ft, was accomplished by means of three broad locks which reached a tidal basin via three small side basins (Fig. 9). A stillwater dock at summit level was constructed rather as an appendix to this scheme in both scope and shape, the latter conditioned by the restrictive boundaries of the estate. Excavation in the marl was not difficult, and the spoil was dumped along the canal sides. Water deficiences were overcome by the erection of a 'fire engine', capable of transferring a 'lockful of water per hour' from the tidal to the upper dock.[29] The open space remaining was used as wharfage, though a small warehouse was ordered to be built in 1795. In the minutes of 1796 appears an order 'that the Wirral Line . . . be extended from the Bason at Whitby on the summit level in a direct line to the further Bason made upon the level of the River Mersey'.[30] The disadvantages of the cul-de-sac nature of the upper dock had quickly been appreciated, but though improvements were later made, this direct water link was never constructed.

Telford had been made responsible for planning all 'Bridges, Aqueducts, Tunnels, Locks, Reservoirs, Buildings, Wharfs and other Works' on the canal.[31] A recognized architect, his talents were given little

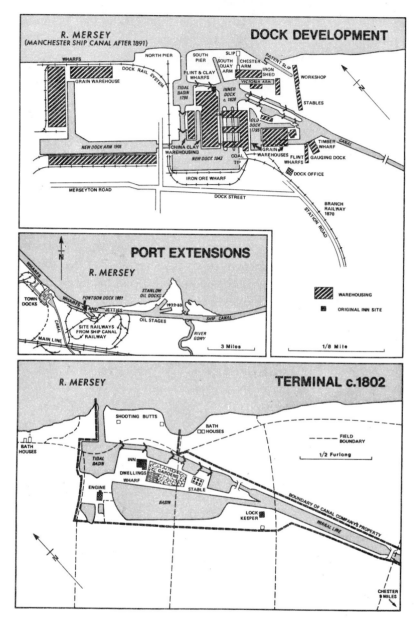

FIG. 9. The port of Ellesmere Port.

cope at Ellesmere Port in the face of limited supplies of both land and money. Local boulder clay facilitated brick-making, an activity which continues today. Nineteenth-century brickfields were located in Childer Thornton, Whitby Heath, Little Sutton and elsewhere, but the bricks used in the Port were probably made on the estate. Ponds located near the engine shed in 1802 may have been brickponds rather than pre-existing marlpits. Stone was easily imported via the Mersey, and used for pierheads to protect the entrance to the lower basin.

No building graced the site in 1795. The demands of passenger traffic, however, soon made imperative the construction of some form of accommodation at the terminal. Not wishing to extend its obligations, in early 1795 the company asked Whitby landowners if they were willing to provide suitable buildings, warehouses and wharfs. The landowners were not interested; by September Telford was seeking a contractor to carry out the construction of a public house and warehouse to the company's plans.[32] In the following year the proprietors planned to erect dwellings for canal workers, but no such dwellings had appeared in Ellesmere Port by 1802. As most of the line's business was transacted at Chester, regular employees at the Port were few.

On the slope between the locks and the upper basin a small inn was built with two small dwellings and stables nearby. A lockkeeper's cottage commanded the junction of canal, locks and dock. The tavern was reported complete in 1801 and the ground around it cleared and levelled 'so as to be clean and commodious for travellers'.[33] Reflecting the eighteenth-century craze for genteel outdoor activity, a number of shooting butts and bathing huts appeared on the Mersey shore. Set down in the wilderness, the Port at the turn of the century showed little sign of becoming the thriving community which arose in Victoria's reign. With only five separate structures built in as many years after the completion of the canal, the settlement confirms Mortimer's opinion of 1847 that 'a few years since, there was on the site . . . only one public house, three small cottages, a mere shed as a substitute for a warehouse, and one set of locks'.[34]

The Passenger Period, 1795–1835

Commercial goods traffic was not slow to appear on the Wirral line, although it did not quite fulfil the prospects originally envisaged by the proprietors. In 1791 Turner had prophesied a yearly 12,000 ton trade between Liverpool, Chester and Shrewsbury, mainly in coal, lime and 'merchant goods'.[35] The progress of construction above Chester however, effectively prevented the realization of this expectation. The Shrewsbury line was terminated at Weston in 1797, and all hopes of a direct Severn link were abandoned in 1818. Moreover, the main Ruabon–Chester line had been delayed and finally abandoned at a time of monetary crisis in the first decade of the new century.[36] Thus the original eastern and western lines were both found wanting, and the third alternative, a short cut from Whitchurch to the Chester Canal, was necessary if the Ellesmere Canal was not to remain in two discrete parts. Opened in 1805, the Whitchurch–Hurleston section gave the Wirral line a circuitous connexion with the rest of the canal. So tenuous was this link, however, that the proprietors abandoned their original aim of promoting interestuarial traffic and began to concentrate on moving agricultural commodities within the almost self-contained system. In comparison with this trade, traffic to and from the Mersey via the independent Chester Canal was quite subordinate in the early years.

The Wirral line accordingly began to develop a specialized function, inaugurated soon after its completion. A regular packet service between Chester and Ellesmere Port began on 1 July 1795, passengers being transferred to and from Liverpool packets at the latter port. The service rose rapidly in popularity, over 1700 persons being carried in the first month alone, no doubt at the expense of the Wirral coaches and northern ferries.[37] Canal packets ran at least until 1834, when Head noted that 'the indications of business were fewer than might be imagined . . . and the inland produce chiefly consisted of live fowls'.[38] The service may have continued until the opening of the Birkenhead railway in 1840. On the Mersey the company purchased a steam packet within a year of the arrival of the first steam vessel from the Clyde in 1815. Simultaneous efforts to introduce steam on the canal, however, proved disappointing in terms of time and bank damage.

Steam navigation, however, succeeded in furthering a facet of Ellesmere Port's economy quite different from the transhipping of passengers, cattle, and cargo. As early as 1795 the packet service and tavern were considered likely to render the settlement 'a desirable and fashionable resort, as well for the sea bather as for the less stationary traveller'.[39] From 1797 special pleasure boats appeared and in 1801 the inn 'with suitable apartments for the accommodation of sea bathers . . . and other genteel company' was advertised to be let. The existence in 1823 of 'baths for hot bathing, in fresh and salt water' indicates that a regular bathing season had been established.[40]

There is little evidence relating to other trades. The importance of the Chester Canal to the Ellesmere system was acknowledged in 1813 when the two companies amalgamated to form the United Company of Proprietors of the Ellesmere and Chester Canals (ECC). In conjunction with Mersey steam navigation and reduced tolls on iron ore this move may have encouraged traffic.[41] Successive toll reductions almost from the opening of the Wirral line had encouraged some trade, and regular carriers had established installations at Chester, where a new basin was constructed in 1809. In this period Ellesmere Port passed, but did not tranship, cargoes of timber, lead, iron, bricks, coal and general goods, largely towards Liverpool.

These activities had no great effect on the port. The facilities available at the turn of the century were evidently capable of supporting the traffic until the late 1820s. Indeed, in 1805 Telford had recommended that workmen employed at the locks should be dismissed, which probably accounts for part of the fall in population of Whitby township from 170 in 1801 to 75 in 1811. The negligent use of hastily built installations, however, had resulted in widespread damage by 1801. The quays, locks, piers and bridges were found to be in poor repair and the dock gates wholly 'destroyed and carried away', the latter allegedly due to the importunate demands of the crews of Mersey flats for entry at unsuitable states of the tide.[42]

By 1805, however, the Wirral line was attracting the gaze of speculators. Perhaps because it was developing Chester, the company was unwilling to provide further facilities at Ellesmere Port. Its contracts with speculators, usually specifying a time limit after which the ECC had the option of purchasing developed land, emphasized the company's preoccupation with the main body of the canal. Such contracts, however, were unlikely to attract long term developers and several schemes to provide shipyards, timber yards, workshops, cranes, and cottages on land leased from the ECC came to nothing. The first new buildings were not completed until 1817 when John Grace, recognizing the likely impact of steam navigation, built six cottages outside the ECC estate.[43] It was probably this event which stimulated the company to begin negotiations with the Marquis of Westminster for the purchase of further land.

However, except for a small shipyard begun by a Mr Hazledean in 1825 and later taken over by the company, and a wharf built by the

Marquis for his tenants, Ellesmere Port had changed little between the turn of the century and the late 1820s. Bathing and passenger transit required few facilities. A woodcut on a bathing handbill of 1823 shows a primitive steamer approaching a settlement of three buildings engulfed in shrubbery. A boundary hedge had been grown, the locks and pierhead had been renovated, and means found to prevent the inn garden from slipping into the tidal basin. Although recovering to 250 in 1821 with the arrival of steam and cottages, the township's population had again fallen to 234 by 1831. But it almost quadrupled in the period 1832–41 and had risen to 909 (617 of whom resided in the port) by 1851. Clearly a major revolution occurred in this period.

The Revolution in Trade After 1835

Turner's expectations of 1791 were partially fulfilled in an annual revenue varying until 1835 between £16,000 and £27,000, though the high cost of construction in the south prevented the declaration of high dividends. The ECC system, consisting of many small branches depending mainly on primary industries and with its trunk line leading from a promising position on the Mersey by a circuitous route into a largely agricultural hinterland, was seemingly not destined to be a vital artery of the Industrial Revolution. In 1817 even land carriage was regarded as a major threat, resulting in toll reductions, and the agricultural depression of 1822 came as a great blow.[44] Ellesmere Port would doubtless have remained a minor way-station with scarcely a dozen dwellings had proposals from another quarter not burst upon the scene in the 1820s.

In 1825 the parochial ECC was offered shares in the BLJ, a canal which was to revitalize the inland waterway connexion between Birmingham and Liverpool, and which has already been introduced in Chapter 5 in connexion with the STW. The Ellesmere company was quick to seize this opportunity to inject new life into its almost moribund system. The 41 mile BLJ line provided a more direct interurban link than the older TM, and gave Ellesmere Port a thriving industrial hinterland for the first time, albeit a hinterland shared by well established Runcorn. Encouraged, the ECC revived the old Chester Canal scheme for a branch to join the TM at Middlewich. The Bridgewater trustees had no objection to this, though they did charge a heavy compensation toll on all passing traffic. There had long been an intimate connexion between the two companies in the shape of the Earl of Bridgewater and in the early days thriving Runcorn looked paternally upon its tiny neighbour downstream. Accordingly, the Middlewich Branch, leaving the ECC line at Hurleston, was opened in 1833. It carried little traffic, however, until the junction, not far from Hurleston, was made between the ECC and BLJ lines on 2 March 1835.

Thanks to the plans of Telford, and to William Cubitt who carried out Telford's plans after the latter's death in 1834, 1835 proved to be a more significant date in the development of Ellesmere Port than the opening of the Wirral line in 1795. After forty years of stagnation, traffic began an upward turn. For example, the half year ending 30 June 1836 saw 14,246 tons of Staffordshire iron exported via Ellesmere Port, though nothing was said of iron ore imports which within two decades were to become a staple trade.[45] Great growth in the volume of port traffic was expected, for not only did the new canal give better access to the Midlands, Lancashire and Yorkshire, but also forged new links with the Severn and the Thames.

The BLJ, an external force, was thus responsible for fundamental changes in Ellesmere Port's physical form and economic functions in the 1830s. Anticipating the completion of the BLJ line, a series of warehouses, designed by Telford, was under construction in 1829. Constructed of brick and slate, these severely classical monuments to the canal trade dominated the central area of Ellesmere Port's dockland until the late 1960s (Fig. 10). To accommodate them, the old dock was partly infilled and truncated to less than half its original size, while the lower intermediary basin was enlarged to form an inner dock with several arms. One of these ran beneath the three wings of the central warehouse, providing a covered transhipping place. This warehouse was complemented by the construction of offices, a patent slip on the Mersey bank, several internal slips, and new wharfs, stables, and workshops.[46] Through this reconstruction the buildings of the original terminal had been entirely swept away in 1833 (Fig. 9).

Accommodation for people had to keep pace with that provided for vehicles and goods. Before company housing schemes were in full swing, it is likely that some ECC employees were temporarily housed in Whitby, trudging daily along the muddy path which was the sole road access to the port. In the 1830s the first planned streets appeared; the first new dwellings since Grace's Row of 1817 were the twelve cottages of Porters' Row built in 1833. Still inhabited in the 1960s, these brick and slate dwellings, built by William Rigby of Runcorn, provided the model for a further forty-one cottages which were erected in 1837–9 to form Union Street and Shropshire Row. Four more substantial houses were ordered in 1835 to accommodate ECC employees and merchants' clerks. By 1838, therefore, the company had provided at least sixty houses for its employees, and the total of dwellings in the township rose from 41 to 102 in the 1832–41 decade. Yet more were needed, for a high rate of overcrowding, with over eight persons per dwelling, prevailed in 1841.

Fig. 10. At Ellesmere Port in 1967 derelict barges front Telford's decaying warehouses with their undercover loading facilities (now demolished).

Several persons speculated in housing outside the estate after 1835. In the 1840s W. A. Provis, an ECC contractor, leased land from the Marquis of Westminster adjacent to Dock, Church and Pool (later, Queen) streets which were then being laid out. The first, as befitted the boundary between the ECC estate and the private developments beyond, was planned to be 40 yd wide, whereas the transverse Church Street was to be 12 yd only. By the mid-forties several speculators had built dwellings on the south side of Dock Street; a variety of building styles, contrasting sharply with the uniformity of style prevailing within the company estate, was given unity only by straight frontages and the bevelled corners of Church Street.

A single example illustrates the first weak stirrings of industry at

Ellesmere Port, the cramped nature of the company estate, and the willingness of the ECC to extend control over adjacent property. In 1832 one H. G. Dyar purchased a two acre plot between the ECC dock and the Mersey in order to excavate a private dock. Two years later the land was sold to J. L. Bruit, a Liverpool hide merchant who, encouraged by the bustle of new construction, purchased a further piece of land on the western side of the company estate. On this he built a house, two cottages, and a tannery. This was probably not an economic proposition, for within the year Bruit offered the development to the ECC. The latter had dock expansion in mind and, eager to extend its estate which was 'much confined round the edges of the proposed basin', the company bought the land, used the materials of the tannery in the erection of cottages on the same site (Shropshire Row), and placed its agent in the rather substantial house.[47] Thus the ECC was able to avoid the construction of housing on valuable wharfage space, leaving sufficient land in the original estate for dock expansion.

New installations enhanced the importance of the port's position on the Mersey. The ECC, having previously stirred only rarely to condemn estuarial abuses, began to take a new interest in the river. From 1836 the company cheapened its Mersey shipping operations by using its own steam tugs to tow unrigged, and therefore fully loaded, flats and timber floats.[48] In the same year a Liverpool Docks Bill, exempting shipping using Runcorn but not Ellesmere Port from the payment of seaport dues, was forced out. This threat, together with the advantages likely to accrue should the port be exempted, stimulated the ECC to create new dock space. In 1836 a sea lock and dock were ordered to be excavated, the spoil being used for brickmaking. Against a background of rising revenue, a set of narrow locks was also to be provided paralleling the old broad flight, the tidal basin repaired, and a sea wall begun. This opening of the port to coasters, it was hoped, would encourage the import of Irish livestock, Caernarvon slate, Cornish pottery materials, and even foreign produce, and relieve the ECC of providing expensive and cramped warehouse space in Liverpool. The doubling of revenue between 1832 and 1839 enabled the company to purchase new vessels, and by 1840 the ECC possessed thirty flats and timber floats and two steam tugs, and was envisioning the excavation of a timber dock at Liverpool.[49]

Four acres of land suitable for the new Ellesmere Port dock were purchased from the Marquis of Westminster, and Bruit's lockside lot was used for the new lock flight. In 1839 Provis' tender for the new dock was accepted, and work began under the direction of Cubitt. The 110 ft × 32 ft sea lock leading from the tidal basin, and the 435 ft × 139 ft dock were opened amidst great rejoicing in September 1843 (Fig. 11). Compared with the inauspicious opening of the canal in 1795 this was a veritable gala, celebrating the change in function of the settlement from a minor way-station to a port capable of taking seagoing vessels.[50] Significantly, the first ships to enter were, as had been hoped, from Ireland, from Bangor carrying slate, and from Ulverston carrying iron ore. In the same year, on the recommendation of Cubitt, transhipping between river and canal vessels was transferred to Ellesmere Port from Chester, thus saving wear and tear on the Wirral line. This action confirmed Ellesmere Port as a port in nature as well as in name. After the resolution of a conflict with the Marquis' tenants who, having free access to the quays, had covered the iron ore wharf with manure, traffic of all kinds began to increase. At once the ECC informed shareholders that, where once had been a few dwellings whose inhabitants were mainly engaged in facilitating the passage of vessels through the locks, a port had arisen and contained:

'nearly one hundred houses, an extensive range of first class Warehouses, a Noble Dock with Wharfs, Shipbuilders' Yards etc. occupying a space of about Twenty Acres, and other Buildings and Houses are constantly erecting.
There are frequently congregated at this spot as many as Sixty Vessels of all denominations, forming with the resident Population, from One Thousand to One Thousand Five Hundred Souls.'[51]

With a church and school nearly completed, the village was showing signs of advancement in both social and economic spheres.

In 1843 the ECC clearly believed that renewed prosperity was inevitable. Not a year had passed before this illusion was shattered. As early as 1842 it had been realized that the company's powers of canal carriage would not be of major benefit except on the Wirral line. Above Chester full loads were rarely available; delays while waiting for cargo gave the advantage to road carriage which was not confined to a roundabout route. 'From the want of this regularity the Commercial Trade of the canal has suffered much, the short distances by land operating both by their speed and punctuality'.[52]

Moreover, in 1843 a minor price war in the Mersey trade began with the Bridgewater trustees. The latter had dropped their paternalist mask as soon as the smaller port's facilities were improved to rival those at Runcorn. They drastically reduced tolls and charges, especially on iron and pottery materials, the growing staples of Ellesmere Port. In the

Fig. 11. Traditional scenes of enthusiasm at the opening of Ellesmere Port's New Dock, 1843.

following year, not long before their purchase of the MIN, the trustees undertook to rent the ECC's Liverpool–Ellesmere Port carrying trade. This arrangement was not terminated until 1852, and as the canal carrying trade had also been farmed out, the ECC was reduced to the position of rentier, interested only in dividends. These, however, were to rise no higher after the boom of 1837–49, and the company's revenue eventually became unable to cope even with the interest on its liabilities. The situation was worsened by the aggressive policy of the hostile TM which forced the ECC to follow suit in a spiral of toll reductions.

There were other Mersey problems. While the new dock was still under construction, Liverpool occasioned further alarm by reintroducing its Docks Bill, and the ECC was busy throughout 1840–1 trying to interest other navigations in opposing the proposed Mersey Conservancy. In the latter year the building of the sea wall drew the company's attention to several streams discharging into the Mersey east of Stanlow Point. To divert these through Stanlow would greatly assist 'in keeping Open and improving the low water Channel upon the maintenance of which the Existence of Ellesmere Port depends'.[53] Intermittent proposals for avoiding this shifting channel had early appeared, usually involving the extension of the canal past Ellesmere Port to a point further downstream. As early as 1796 an extension to Netherpool was proposed, and three years later a survey of a line to Bromborough was ordered.[54] Largely because of the opposition of the engineers Telford and Jessop, who preferred to use the Mersey as much as possible, nothing was done. Though the scheme was revived in 1825, it was again shelved because of the ECC's recent involvement with the BLJ. The stream diversion proposal was welcomed as an alternative to the shifting of the canal outlet downstream, but again, nothing was done. The vital importance of the scheme was underlined six years later, when the Mersey channel began to silt up.[55]

Problems were also arising in the hinterland. Railway competition was at work. The ECC, which had once supported the BLJ in warding off the original GJR proposal, was now forced to amalgamate with the new canal company to prevent its 'falling into hostile hands'.[56] The BLJ's lack of success, attributed to the intransigence of connecting waterways and the competition of the GJR, was reflected in heavy debt. As the two boards shared the same chairman, Lord Powis, and had many shareholders in common, no difficulty was experienced in obtaining an Act for the merger. But before the amalgamation was ratified a subcommittee was set up to consider the future of the ECC, and in particular the possibility of converting the line into a railway. In June 1845, at the height of the Railway Mania, it reported that 'The Company are now threatened with railways parallel to their Canal throughout its whole course . . . if the projected Railways be executed the traffic on the Canals will be seriously interfered with and the dividend . . . endangered'.[57] As the system of working boat trains had been used for some time on the BLJ, the value of rail carriage was readily appreciated. Furthermore, the company had considered railways as canal adjuncts since its inception, and a railway had partly taken the place of the original western line. Accordingly, the Railway Sub-committee recommended a wholesale conversion of the canal system into railways, though the Wirral line was to be preserved.

Acts were passed in 1846 for railway conversions of part of the ECC and BLJ lines. These Acts changed the name of the no doubt confused 'United Kingdom [sic] of Proprietors of the Ellesmere and Chester Canals' to the Shropshire Union Railway and Canal Company (SURC).[58] Hardly had the SURC tasted independence when the newly formed London and North Western Railway (LNWR), seeing it as a dangerous rival, offered to lease it from autumn 1846 at a favourable rate. The Act authorizing the lease passed in 1847, and a Shrewsbury to Stafford rail link was opened in 1849, almost sixty years after Shrewsbury petitions had helped to create, without subsequent reward, the Ellesmere Canal. Further railway construction, however, was prevented by the LNWR, and as the railway did not prove as successful as had been expected, the SURC directors decided to concentrate once more on improving the canal trade.[59]

Accordingly, fifty flats were ordered and the Bridgewater trustees were given notice to quit their operation of the Ellesmere Port–Liverpool run. SURC headquarters were removed to Chester after a temporary sojourn in Wolverhampton. Thus Ellesmere Port, created in the Canal Mania, found in the Railway Mania the promise of continued existence as a canal port under railway tutelage.

6. Notes

1. W. W. Mortimer, *The History of the Hundred of Wirral*, Whittaker, London (1847), p. ix.

2. E. H. Rideout, *The Growth of Wirral*, Bryant, Liverpool (1927), p. 30.
3. D. Defoe, *A Tour through the Whole Island of Great Britain*, Dent, London (1962), p. 68.
4. H. C. Darby and I. S. Maxwell, *The Domesday Geography of Northern England*, Cambridge University Press, Cambridge (1962), p. 360; D. Sylvester and G. Nulty, *The Historical Atlas of Cheshire*, Cheshire Community Council, Chester (1958), *passim*.
5. Quoted in T. A. Coward, *Cheshire Traditions and History*, Methuen, London (1932), p. 65.
6. G. Ormerod, *The History of the County Palatine and City of Chester*, Lockington, London, Vol. 2 (1819), p. 236.
7. D. Defoe, op. cit., p. 257.
8. ELC 1/4 (31 August 1791); C. Hadfield, *The Canals of the West Midlands*, David and Charles, Newton Abbot (1966), p. 167
9. ELC 1/4 (9 January 1792); 1/7 (26 November 1805).
10. J. Turner, *A Description of the Intended Canal from Shrewsbury to Liverpool and Chester*, (1791), p. 4.
11. ELC 1/4 (7 November 1791).
12. ELC 1/1 (23 September 1793).
13. ELC 1/4 (11 September, 25 October, 15–30 November 1792).
14. ELC 1/4 (28 June 1791); J. Turner, op. cit., p. 6.
15. J. Turner, op. cit., *passim*.
16. C. Hadfield, op. cit., p. 169; L. T. C. Rolt, *Thomas Telford*, Longmans, London (1958), p. 43.
17. ELC 1/4 (15 September 1791).
18. ELC 1/7 (26 November 1805).
19. E. A. Wilson, 'The Proprietors of the Ellesmere and Chester Canal', *Journal of Transport History*, 3 (1957), 52–4.
20. ELC 1/4 (15 September 1791).
21. *Chester Courant* (12 June 1795); *Gore's Liverpool General Advertiser* (9 July 1795).
22. *Nottingham Journal* (27 February 1796).
23. ELC 1/1 (21 December 1795).
24. *Billing's Liverpool Advertiser* (29 June 1795).
25. W. Wallace, *A History of Liverpool*, (1795), p. 20; T. Wedge, *A General View of the Agriculture of Cheshire*, (1794), p. 10.
26. J. Cary, 'Cheshire' (1771, 1789); J. Burdett, 'Cheshire' (1777).
27. ELC 1/1 (6 March 1795).
28. ELC 1/2 (10 February 1797).
29. ELC 1/2 (26 September 1796).
30. ELC 1/2 (23 June 1796).
31. ELC 1/1 (23 September 1795).
32. ELC 1/7 (7 May, 8 June, 9 September 1795).
33. Telford's report of 25 November 1801, quoted in T. W. Roberts, *The History and Development of Ellesmere Port from 1785*, unpublished ms., Ellesmere Port Public Library (1960), p. 24.

34. W. W. Mortimer, op. cit., p. 231.
35. J. Turner, op. cit., p. 15.
36. ELC 1/7 (2 November 1805); ECC 2 (26 February 1818).
37. *Chester Courant* (12 June 1795).
38. G. Head, *A Home Tour through the Manufacturing Districts of England in the Summer of 1835* London (1836), p. 61.
39. *Chester Courant* (12 June 1795).
40. *Gore's Liverpool General Advertiser* (30 July 1801).
41. ELC 1/3 (5 November 1812).
42. ELC 1/6 (May 1801); 1/7 (5 February 1805).
43. ECC 1/8 (4 December 1817).
44. ECC 1/4 (31 July 1817, 25 July 1822).
45. ECC 1/3 (11 August 1836).
46. Cubitt's report, ECC 1/3 (29 July 1841).
47. ECC 6 (29 August, 9 October 1837); BWB Leeds, Deed 563 (31 May 1834).
48. ECC 6 (6 December 1836).
49. ECC 1/3 (4 November 1836, 6 August 1840).
50. *Illustrated London News* (23 September 1843), p. 198.
51. ECC 1/5 (22 December 1843).
52. ECC 1/5 (25 August 1842).
53. ECC 1/5 (19 March 1841).
54. ELC 1/5 (30 November 1796); 1/2 (27 November 1799).
55. SURC 1/37 (4 August 1847).
56. Statement to the Board of Trade, SURC 4/1 (1845).
57. ECC 1/3 (12 June 1845).
58. ECC 1/9 (9 December 1845).
59. SURC 1/42 (4 December 1846, 14 September 1848); 1/37 (5 May 1848).

7
Goole in the Canal Age

An Act to enable the Undertakers of the Navigation of the rivers Aire and
Calder in the West Riding of the County of York to make a navigable Cut or
Canal from, or out of the said Navigation at Knottingley, to communicate
with the river Ouse near Goole . . .

(I Geo IV, c 39; 1820)

Goole Before the Canal

The district of Marshland lies in the extreme east of the West Riding of
Yorkshire and as its name suggests was once a marshy area at the nexus of
the many Humber tributaries. Estuarine transgression and extensive
marsh suggest a zone of subdued relief ranging in the Goole area from 8 to
20ft above sea level. The landscape is one of extreme flatness, somewhat
reminiscent of Holland in its sweeping distances and innumerable rivers
and dykes.

In this southern portion of the Vale of York the tidal rivers Ouse,
Wharfe, Derwent, Aire, Don and Trent meet near Goole to form the
Humber estuary. One of the major historical features of the surrounding
plain was the constant battle against encroaching waters. The recurrent
theme in Dugdale's *History of Imbanking and Drayning* is the failure of local
inhabitants to repair the banks without which their fields, if not their
hamlets, were in danger of inundation.[1] Among interminable lists of
lawsuits concerning local banks is the first authenticated mention of
Goole (1362), which at this time was little more than the junction of a
drain (goul) with the Ouse.

Drainage being the major regional problem, a system of ditches was in
existence as early as 1200 AD, emptying surface water into the Ouse

through cloughs or tidal valves. Large scale flood control, however, was hardly attempted until the seventeenth century, by which time the bankside settlers had consolidated their position against a rising sea level. To the south of Goole lay the worst drainage problem of all, the Royal Chase of Hatfield, where anastomosing Trent tributaries formed what amounted to an inland delta containing the river 'islands' of Axholme, Thorne and Hatfield. Long subject to depredations by peripheral settlements, the chase was deforested in 1626 when Cornelius Vermuyden, a Dutch engineer, was appointed to drain it.

His principle was to lead rivers round the flat areas and to speed their discharge by embanking, deepening, and shortening them. For this purpose the plexus of rivers was disentangled, the river Idle being led round to the south, the Don to the north. Originally the Don had two major distributaries, one running north-eastward to the Trent, the other flowing sluggishly northward to Turnbridge on the Aire. Both were used by Doncaster ships from an early date.[2] Vermuyden's plan was to divert the bulk of the Don waters, taking the increased volume of water along the Turnbridge Don's almost imperceptible fall. But townships were flooded, anti-Dutch feeling ran high, riots ensued, and petitions were sent to the authorities.

Minor improvements proving useless, in 1630 the Crown ordered the formation of a relief drain.[3] After much vacillation, two parallel drains were constructed, leaving the Turnbridge Don at right angles and proceeding eastwards to meet the Ouse in a sluicegate just north of the hamlet of Goole. The sluice was designed to obstruct the ingress of tides, York shipowners having complained that tides there flowed 2ft higher before the cutting of the drains. In the late seventeenth century, however, floods destroyed the Goole sluice, sweeping away the narrow bank between the drains to form the wide, straight, artificial channel still known as the Dutch River. This channel was to provide both a barrier to and a fixation-point on the Ouse for the Aire and Calder (AC) Canal, which arrived in the 1820s.

By this latter date agricultural improvement had profoundly altered the features of the district. Warping was the local *pièce de résistance*. Drains led Humber tides via sluices into embanked fields. Draining back slowly, the water left behind a finely laminated muddy deposit, producing a highly prized light-brown soil very suitable for potatoes. Though the major warping period ended in the mid-nineteenth century, the process was one of the chief agents which, though leaving Humberhead flat, rendered it far less stale and unprofitable than before.

A rich mixed farming economy operated, concentrating on stock, some cereals, potatoes, and other roots. Flax mills prospered. Fishing and fowling were still common. Goole township itself contained 450 persons in 1821, five years before the coming of the canal. Smaller than Airmyn, a river port since medieval times, Goole had recently eclipsed nearby Hook in terms of population. The nearby market towns of Howden (2,080 population in 1821), Thorne (2,713) and Selby (4,097), the latter two with major shipping interests, were all growing in size, especially Selby at the lowest Ouse bridge-point.

Set among these larger settlements Goole was an insignificant township distinguished only by its position straddling the Dutch River at its junction with the Ouse. Formerly merely a straggle of cottages, the settlement had been reoriented by the need for a bridge over the Dutch River. The hamlet nucleus consisted of a mill, three inns, and a number of farm houses with associated labourers' cottages. Copies of the Goole town books survive for the period 1723–1811. They record throughout the generally unremarkable details of hamlet life. In 1787 the chief concern was the eradication of moles, while in the early nineteenth century the building of a second new house was sufficiently revolutionary to bear detailed description. Contacts with the outside world were maintained by a regular carrier, and by occasional ships calling at Murham Staith. A local farmer recorded these vessels, which averaged no more than five calls per year in the period 1818–26. There is no indication that they loaded any cargo other than potatoes, most of which were carried to London.[4]

Though the mouth of the Dutch River was the infrequent anchorage of vessels negotiating the dangerous navigation of the Don between the coalfields of the Doncaster region and the Humber, there is little evidence to support Cox's view that pre-canal Goole 'served as an important distributing centre' for coal.[5] Although land tax assessments record the existence of a customs officer at Goole at the turn of the century, he was gone by 1810. His presence cannot adequately be accounted for, though it may have been for the prevention of smuggling. It is plain that before the arrival of the AC Goole's role as a riverport was a very minor one indeed; from the late eighteenth century Keadby at the Trent terminus of the Stainforth and Keadby Canal (SK) had become a more convenient connexion with Hull for the Don valley towns, while traffic on the Aire had also been reduced. The potentialities of Goole's position at the junction of two Yorkshire navigations were not to be realized before the coming of artificial waterways.

Thus the hamlet of Goole in the early nineteenth century was a relatively static agrarian community, largely living its own life behind its half-tamed rivers and partly-reclaimed moors. Even in 1822 there was little indication that an entirely new way of life was about to be imposed. To one writer the pre-canal settlement was no more than a collection of 'miserable huts',[6] while Parsons in 1837 noted that: 'Fifteen years ago Goole was an obscure and insignificant village, and for anything which then appeared it was likely to remain so'[7]. Here, as in Runcorn, Lower Mitton and Whitby, the stage was set for the irruption of the canal into an area where a placid agrarian existence had persisted for uninterrupted centuries.

The Decision-making Context

The transport history of the West and East Ridings of Yorkshire in the eighteenth century is largely a history of canal and river navigations. From time immemorial poor roads had stimulated navigation on the river Ouse, the history of which is told elsewhere.[8] Although by the early eighteenth century the river was in poor physical shape, it was heavily used. Various attempts were made in the seventeenth and eighteenth centuries to improve the waterway, but the opening of Naburn Lock in 1757 was the only major improvement. Below the junction of Ouse and Trent the Humber was the goal of most of the navigations which in the latter century were projected to connect those rivers with Yorkshire's western and southern industrial zones.

The Ouse, however, opened up very little mining or manufacturing country. It was its right bank tributaries, the Aire and Don, which gave access to the coal, cloth and iron of the West Riding. The Don, terminating as the Dutch River, carried a considerable traffic even though there were major problems associated with its navigation. Though the natural outlet for much of south Yorkshire, the Don valley line suffered the same piecemeal improvement as a waterway as it was to experience in the Railway Age. After initial improvements, Sheffield ware with its return cargo of Swedish iron began to use the Don, despite the unimproved nature of the Dutch River, neglected since the hasty departure of Vermuyden[9]. Traffic increased as navigations such as the Dearne and Dove, and Barnsley canals were connected to the Don, which was finally linked to Sheffield by canal in 1819. By this time, however, the

Dutch River outlet had become less used because of a revival of the Don-Trent route in the shape of the SK line.

Unlike the Don the Aire was little used in medieval times, yet was to become in the nineteenth century the busiest of Yorkshire navigations. In the seventeenth century goods had moved by land between the West Riding and small ports, such as Rawcliffe and Airmyn, on the lower Aire. In the following century there was some rivalry between the Don Navigation and the AC, and the Don company was also thwarted, by the opposition of local landowners, in its attempt in 1731 to get powers to improve the Dutch River and to remove two of its bridges, one being that at Goole. A century later the AC was to provide Goole with a far more important raison d'etre than a mere bridge-point.

Space does not allow the presentation of a detailed history of the AC, one of the most powerful companies in eighteenth century England. In fine, the economic situation which in 1699 led to the formation of the AC, of which the Knottingley–Goole Canal was but the final outlet, was much the same as that which promoted the Bridgewater Canal some sixty years later. Textiles and coal demanded outlets; the AC was at first able to provide these by improving an existing waterway which already had 'coals at the heels' of it. The AC was designed chiefly 'for advancing ye Trade of ye Northern woollen Manufacture', a trade which accounted for much of the 2000 tons of goods which moved annually between the West Riding and Hull.[10] It was promoted largely by Leeds merchants, but the gradual support of landowners interested in coal sales enabled the company to effect river improvements as far downstream as Weeland.

A steady improvement of the upper reaches of the two rivers as far as Leeds and Wakefield was marked throughout the eighteenth century by cuts to avoid meanders, the construction of locks, and deepening. Later in the century, however, the lower Aire had become so inadequate to support the growing trade that the pressure of complaints from traders precipitated a crisis. Accordingly, the navigation began to construct a canal from Haddlesey on the Aire to Selby on the Ouse, the original port at Airmyn being allowed to run down. In 1778 the Selby Canal was opened and by 1781 most of the installations and employees had been transferred from Airmyn to the new canal port.[11]

Served by land carriage, Selby had long been the West Riding's main riverport, but with the completion of the canal a boom was initiated. The lowest Ouse bridgepoint, with an already-established shipping interest, Selby thrived as a break-point between canal barges, the largest of 60 tons burden, and the 200 ton vessels on the Ouse. By 1825 the port's river trade was at its height; a branch customs house facilitated clear access to the sea, inland connexions by steam packet, coach, and waggon were frequent, and local industries were thriving. In the 1820s over 800 vessels per year cleared coastwise.[12] But Selby's was a brief glory. Within forty years of the completion of its canal, schemes were set on foot to abandon the AC's second port in favour of a third.

AC records indicate that despite the opening of the Selby Canal some vessels, when empty, still used the lower Aire to avoid paying tolls. Yet the Selby Canal was itself proving inadequate. With a mean draught of only 3ft 6in this small canal had to take most of the goods passing along an expanding system of Pennine waterways. By 1816 three trans-Pennine through canals had been completed to link the industrial hinterlands of Mersey and Humber. These lines from Manchester and Liverpool ended at either Leeds or Wakefield, the interior termini of the AC. Immense profits accrued to the latter, and further improvements were made in the upper reaches of the system. The situation downstream, however, was becoming serious. In the second decade of the nineteenth century a number of schemes were advanced by independent groups for avoiding the AC, by now regarded as a dangerous monopoly. The eventual result of this agitation was the creation of the canal port of Goole.

At least two canals were projected as early as 1817 to give better access to the Humber while avoiding the lower AC system. One, supported by West Riding merchants, planned to join the Aire and Don from Knottingley to Doncaster, with a branch to the Dutch River just above Wentbridge. The other was planned to connect the mining area of south Yorkshire with the same neglected outlet. The schemes roused the AC to a second paroxysm of activity and, bringing its influence to bear, it had the Went Bill thrown out of Parliament. In the face of attempts to revive it, the AC was compelled to search for yet a third tideway terminal for its system.

The undertakers were faced with three possibilities: to continue to use an improved Selby Canal; to revert to the lower Aire if powers could be obtained for its improvement; or to construct a second canal avoiding the lower Aire *in toto*. It had been clear to them for some years that the Selby Canal was rapidly losing its ability to carry all the vessels demanding access to the Ouse. By 1785 it was growing increasingly shallow owing to the inwash of sand, and a company engineer, fresh from dredging, stated that: 'The Selby Canal is the only deficient Part of the Navigation it was originally made too shallow'.[13] In 1817 trade to and from Selby had 'greatly declined' despite the overall growth of traffic between Leeds and Hull.[14]

By this time the lower Aire was in a parlous state. As early as 1790 the AC was benevolently bestowing small pensions on Aireside employees who, like the river, were 'rendered incapable of doing anything'.[15] When it was reported in 1818 that the Selby Canal was so choked that vessels could hardly navigate singly, let alone pass one another, the undertakers took the third course by resolving to cut a canal from Haddlesey to the Dutch River at New Bridge. They doubtless felt that not only would this line be cheap because short, but would also be effective in quelling the clamour of West Riding traders for rival canals. Hardly had this decision been made when Lord Downe of Cowick Hall 'expressed himself in general terms decidedly hostile to the measure' and George Leather, the Bradford engineer, was ordered to move the line further away from the Hall.[16] In the same year John Rennie was called in to give a second opinion on the best means of securing a new communication between Aire and Ouse. By November he had convinced the undertakers of the folly of the Dutch River link, and soon produced an alternative. His death in 1821 left the execution of the plan to Leather, who had made a definitive survey of the route in 1819.

The concept was clearly Rennie's; his report of 30 December 1818 provides the first detailed study of the feasibility of a canal from Knottingley to Goole. This report, based not only on a painstakingly detailed survey but also on Rennie's excellent engineering ability and sound historical sense, is one of the most explicit documents in the history of canal decision-making.[17] The engineer quickly disposed of the lower Aire which below Haddlesey was 'exceedingly crooked and full of shoals'. Indeed, he showed the Aire even above Haddlesey to be in places 18 in. too shallow for contemporary barges and intimated that the new canal should leave the river at Knottingley. Turning his attention to the Selby Canal, he confirmed the earlier opinion that dredging could not cope with infilling. However, improvement was almost impossible on account of a clause in the Act of 1774 which restricted the water level in the canal.

The difficulties presented by the Ouse had been largely ignored before Rennie's time. Not at all complacent, he examined the river at high tide when it was 'considered to be in a tolerably good state'. Finding eleven large shoals and numerous other obstacles he pronounced the Ouse above the Dutch River 'very indifferent and by no means suitable to the immense Trade, especially in Neap Tides during which the Small Coasting Sloops are frequently detained several Tides in getting to

Selby'. Regarding the Ouse below Selby as being overburdened with shipping and recognizing that shallows persisted below the Dutch River mouth, Rennie was nonetheless convinced that the Don outlet was the highest point on the Ouse to which ships of a moderate size might navigate at suitable states of the tide, which there rose a critical 4ft higher than at Selby.

The question, therefore, was how to reach from Knottingley a point near the Dutch River mouth. In September 1818 Rennie had surveyed the Haddlesey–Newbridge line suggested by the AC directors. He was perhaps not unaware of previous complaints of the Dutch River's inadequacy for navigation, and was given ample opportunity to appreciate local difficulties when his boat, drawing a mere 3ft of water, lay aground for seven hours above Goole Bridge. The engineer found: the banks, jetties and bridges unsafe and sources of dangerous eddies and currents; the bottom uneven; the water shallow; and the quantity of suspended warp such that the pattern of shoals was constantly changing. 'On the whole' he stated, a canal leading into the Don 'would be wholly inadequate'.

He therefore 'took an extensive view of the country between Ferrybridge and Goole', and produced an alternative proposal which was largely carried out when excavations eventually began. Geology and relief were of negligible influence, only two locks being necessary. In fact the main features conditioning Rennie's specific route were drainage systems, while their accompanying marshes together with large estates were the causes of minor deviations. Once the Selby Canal, the Aire, the Ouse as far down as the Don outfall, and the Dutch River itself had been eliminated as inadequate for navigation, Rennie's canal route was severely restricted in scope. Since crossing large rivers was costly in time, money, and disputes, the canal had to terminate on the Ouse between the mouths of Aire and Don. From Ferrybridge, west of Knottingley, the canal followed the Fleet Drain; on reaching Newbridge it followed the Dutch River to meet the Ouse on the northern outskirts of Goole. The very point of entry into the Ouse was determined by the Participants of the Hatfield Chase Improvement who demanded that unless the AC should keep the Don banks in repair, the canal should not approach within 50 yd of the drain.[18] This was agreed to, and the canal was cut so close to the drain that only a narrow strip, a few yards wide, separates the two.

However, before cutting began Lord Downe and Ralph Creyke of Rawcliffe Hall requested the AC to abandon the scheme and, by carrying the canal across the Don and Thorne Waste, to provide a passage to Hull via Trentmouth. Though Leather was ordered to survey this route, difficulties were great, and the two landowners were finally reconciled to the Goole line on condition that the canal should be moved even further south to avoid their estates. Not satisfied with this, Lord Downe caused the undertakers to abandon their proposed branch into the Dutch River at Newbridge, thus cutting them off from direct water connexion with the Don valley towns.[19]

The Bill suffered much opposition. Broadsheets denounced the company's proposal to restrict the types of vessel using the navigation, this being regarded as a move towards a carrying monopoly on the part of the AC fleet. A 'Leeds Committee' of landowners and merchants, opposing the undertakers' desire to increase tolls, bewailed the fate of the Went Canal and condemned the power of a navigation whose revenue had doubled in the last twenty-five years.[20] The untiring Lord Downe was able to insert a clause to regulate boat halers, whom he believed to be itching to despoil his demesnes. In its altered state the Bill received the Royal Assent on 30 June 1820.

As early as 1823 Leather was reporting that excavation was behind schedule, and during the next two years he frequently postponed the canal's opening date.[21] Delays were occasioned by the difficulty of moving materials, by the obstruction of local landowners, and by the scarcity and increased cost of both materials and workmen in the national boom of 1825. Warping and drainage were dislocated, while Lord Downe continued to harry the company. After a fortnight's delay because of 'unprecedented drought' the canal was opened with due ceremony on 20 July 1826. Toasts ranged from 'Jolly Tars and chearful Swains' to 'Success to the Port of Goole'. Partly publicity stunt, partly traditional, the colourful festivities fired imaginations; it was 'an event which must constitute a prominent . . . feature in the history of the port to which it relates—now just emerging from obscurity'.[22]

The Initial Terminal

In the early nineteenth century the AC undertakers had a commercial and social importance equivalent to that of the Duke of Bridgewater half a century before. Indeed, the company was facetiously referred to as the fourth estate of the realm. It is not surprising, therefore, that the founding of Goole was reported not only by the Yorkshire press but also in London newspapers.[23] *The Hull Advertiser* best illustrates the impact of Goole on the locality; in the years immediately following 1826 scarcely a month passed without some reference to the new port. Within three years, a large proportion of the advertisements relating to the Marshland and Howdenshire districts was mentioning the canal port.[24] 'Hook, near Howden' became 'Hook, near Goole' as local people began to recognize the beginnings of a local re-orientation of activity. 'For sale . . . at Reedness, four miles from New Goole' was a typical entry, and one farmer was sufficiently impressed to advertise his farm as 'being about fifteen miles from Goole'. From about 1834, few major directories failed to mention the port, and by the time of Lewis' *Topographical Dictionary* (1842) Goole had become an established fact. In pursuance of its first national survey the Ordnance Survey was quickly on the scene and by 1853 the town had appeared even on 6in sheets.

The Knottingley-Goole Canal entered the township of Goole alongside the Don, 'parallel interests, as well as parallel considerations, having suggested parallel lines'.[25] A fair number of houses stood in the way of the canal. Almost the whole of this community, with smithy, inns, and mill, was razed in the name of progress. The undertakers, realizing that if the goodwill of the chief landowner could be obtained the smaller would probably follow suit, set out to woo one Admiral Sotheron as early as 1819, the year before their Act was passed. In 1820 Leather was made land valuer for the company, and negotiations began in earnest. Within four months the admiral had tentatively agreed to sell 'the whole of his land on the North side of the Dutch River'[26] Smaller proprietors then proved equally willing to sell, and deeds signed in 1823–24 cover almost the whole of the area required for the terminal port.

The company added many small plots to Sotheron's basic block of seventy-five acres, purchased in 1823, and by 1834 the whole area of Hook and Goole townships lying between Murham Lane and the Dutch River belonged to the navigation. Unlike the small acreages taken up by the other canals, the Goole estate contained almost 200 acres. Nevertheless, there was no surfeit of space on the margin of the Ouse, and the estate was later to prove as restrictive as those of Ellesmere Port and Stourport.

Goole was planned on an altogether more extensive scale than previous canal terminals. An engineering sub-committee was set up in 1820 to consider Rennie's plans. Since Selby's 'want of Docks suitable to the reception of Brigs [had] been much complained of', Rennie considered 'the best means of forming a communication between the Canal and the

River Ouse at Goole [was] by means of an intermediate Bason and Locks, insead of locking directly from the Canal into the River'.[27] A rectangular basin, little more than a widening of the canal, was Rennie's first plan. Of sufficient size to hold fifty to sixty sail of barges, the dock was to be laid out in 1821. Rennie's death supervening, responsibility for the dock works devolved upon Leather, whose report of 1822 outlines the evolution of the initial dock system.[28] Rennie had soon added a second dock to his first; both were planned to open separately into the Ouse. Though eminently suitable for a cramped site, the scheme was elaborated in anticipation of the enlargement of the Goole estate. The final plan involved both ship and barge docks, connected by inner locks via an intermediate basin to separate river locks. Leather drew out the dying engineer's third plan, and thought sufficiently highly of it to put it into operation without major modification.

Superimposing the plan on Rennie's chart of Ouse soundings, Leather verified the old engineer's claim that a deepwater channel, caused by the constriction of the Ouse, existed off Goole. Moreover, to the advantages of deep water was added that of relatively still water. The eddy caused by tidal flow along the Dutch River maintained still water just above the drain's outfall, an aid to the manoeuvring of vessels into and out of the locks. Congestion in the Ouse was to be avoided by allowing vessels to wait in the harbour basin. Though the water level of the docks was maintained by canal water, the whole system could be used as a vast lock, vessels riding in with the tide (Fig. 12).

Built as planned, the system was remarkable for its unified conception: the harbour basin, 250ft × 200ft, draught 17–19ft; the ship dock, 600ft × 200ft, draught 18ft; and the barge dock, 900ft × 150ft, draught 10ft, were fully interconnected. While the ship dock was planned to take up to sixty river vessels, its partner was 'calculated to accommodate about two hundred sail' of small coasting and inland craft.[29] Over a small branch of the barge dock, designed as a fly-boat terminal, a four-storey warehouse rose, allowing transhipment to proceed under cover. 'An immense fireproof Bonding Warehouse' was erected on the east side of the ship dock, while sheds sprang up in response to an early demand for more warehouse room. Offices were built near the Dutch River, while 'a number of handsome houses for the agents and officers of the establishment' flanked the river locks.[30] Occupying a singularly commanding position on the island between harbour and docks, a custom house was erected after 1828, and a patent slip was provided to facilitate the repair of 300–400 ton vessels.

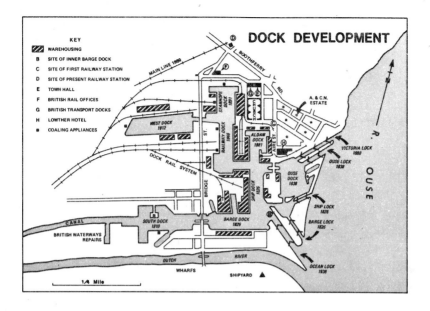

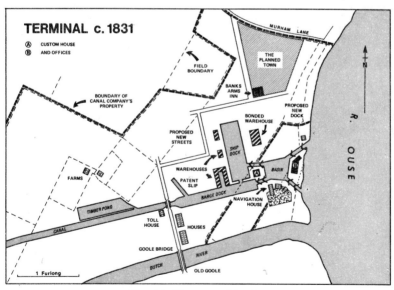

Fig. 12. The port of Goole.

After 1826 excavations were begun to provide material for raising wharves, while a timber pond and boundary wall round the bonding warehouse were also constructed. As early as 1826 Leather anticipated modern dockland mobility by recommending that 'an Iron Railway . . . be laid along the sides of the Docks . . with branches at proper intervals'.[31] Most spectacular of all, the construction of an even more elaborate dock system, requiring at least an additional five docks, was mooted by Leather as early as 1825, though the scheme was passed over as too expensive and complex (Fig. 13).

Although bricks, stone, and ironware arrived by water, the scarcity of building materials was so great that in 1823 spoil from dock excavation was piled up and used for brick-making. Many of the 20,000 bricks used for facing the early buildings must have come from this source. New Goole was built entirely of red brick, the clays of the estate furnishing adequate supplies of material for a surge of brick-making; large brickponds persisted for a number of years. The town arose bodily from the ground on which it stood, a growth capped entirely with imported slate. Planned and created as a unit by a wealthy company, Goole had the potential for success. Springing suddenly on the scene, the town was accepted equally quickly; the first print of Goole appeared within four years (Fig. 14). Behind the manually operated river-lock gates rise substantial warehouses, while a forest of masts locates the docks. In the river sailing vessels are accompanied by the steam packet *Ebor*, symbol of both a new technology and a new port.

The Establishment of a Seaport

The Knottingley–Goole Canal soon proved its worth. Providing less than 17 per cent of the AC's income from old and new navigations in 1831, the line was responsible for 40 per cent of all income by 1850. Grain and wool were upstream staples, while coal vied with textiles in the downstream trade. Other commodities, however, were carried in relatively increasing proportion, for though total receipts increased with the volume of coal carried, the proportion contributed by coal fell from nearly 30 per cent in 1820 to less than 23 per cent in 1838.

In order to attract this traffic to the new line, canal, dock, and estuarial facilities had to be provided and the use of alternative routes shown to be disadvantageous. The application of selective tolls reduced the attractiveness of the shorter Selby Canal, and though the drawbacks on

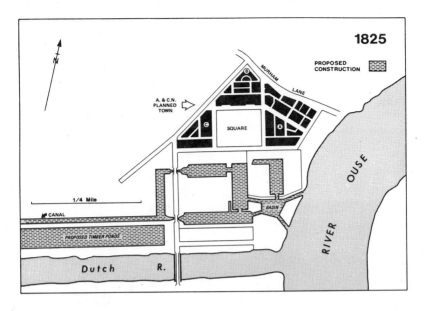

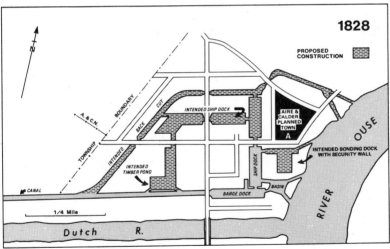

Fig. 13. Grandiose port development schemes at Goole, 1825–8.

F

Fig. 14. The new canal port of Goole, 1831, from the Ouse, on which steam is already challenging sail.

coal were equalized in 1831 this did not apply to coal shipped coastwise at Selby.[32] Moreover, although improvements to the Selby cut were made during the period 1828–36, traffic was reduced by the prolongation of obstructive repairs and the prohibition of nocturnal navigation.

Promotion of Goole at the expense of its erstwhile establishment at Selby was undoubtedly the AC's aim. In 1826 the company's trading establishment was transferred bodily from Selby to Goole, and two years later the latter had, with twenty-two workers, the largest complement of company employees at any one place, including Selby (4) and Leeds (19).[33] In the first weeks, however, traffic was slow to appear on the canal. Leather attributed this to: the general trade depression; the desire of crews to visit their families at Selby; the lack of tradesmen and competent officials at Goole which, in true frontier town fashion, provided poor quality provisions at high prices; difficulties in obtaining hauling horses; and a natural resistance to the new venture, the longer line being regarded by many as a means of extracting extra tolls. The solution to these problems was obvious; Leather advised the company to build up a substantial town at Goole so that 'Selby never can stand in competition with Goole'.[34]

Goole was established during a period of stagnation in Hull, whose indecision over dock construction was the opportunity of several upriver ports.[35] The AC had petitioned for Goole to be commissioned a port for foreign trade almost a year before the completion of the canal. While the Board of Customs found this application to be premature and contrary to its avowed policy of concentrating revenue collection, by 1827 the completed works at Goole had so favourably impressed the comptroller that he was willing to minimize earlier objections regarding the expense of a new customs post, the risk of smuggling, and the difficulties of Ouse navigation. Angry complaints from Hull were brushed aside. All, and Hull not least, could see that the strategic breakpoint position of Goole was likely to attract shipping. Goole was declared a foreign trade port in 1828; with port limits extending from the Trent outfall to include all the Ouse tributaries, this was a severe blow to both Selby and Hull.

The latter's opposition rose to a fever pitch on 6 April 1828 when the first seagoing vessels, the steamer *Lowther* and the brig *Stapler*, left Goole for Hamburg. After 1826 the *Hull Advertiser* made frequent reference to the new port in which its presumption in taking over the Ouse tributaries was criticized and the grounding of vessels in the Ouse hailed with delight. To overcome the latter difficulty the AC in 1828 arranged for a special pilotage system, which remained in existence until the organization of the Humber Conservancy Board in 1907.

In the early years, however, the flourishing foreign trade in no way compared with the importance of coasting. In the first seven years of its life, Goole's average annual number of ships received inward was 158, with 127 clearing outwards. Comparable figures for coasters were 1240 and 1619. The registration of non-canal vessels averaged 27 per year, reaching 77 in 1836. Customs revenue trebled in the three years 1828–30.[36] By 1828 Hull's shippers were worried men. In its first seven years Goole annually imported over 5 million pounds of wool and exported 11 million pounds of cotton twist; Hull's share in the latter trade immediately declined. The number of coasters using Hull fell by half between 1827 and 1828, and the coastwise trade never recovered. Selby's coasting trade fell more heavily; it was only one quarter that of Goole by 1832.[37]

Despite the obstacles placed in its way by both Hull and Selby, Goole in the early thirties had seemingly triumphed. Sailings between Goole and Hamburg were frequent, and vessels traded as far afield as Archangel and North America. Regular processions of carriers' flyboats on the canal were matched by a daily service of speedier steam packets between Goole and the West Riding coaches. A number of packets also ran daily to Hull, and there were regular services to Selby, Thorne, Newcastle, Yarmouth and London. Though less a resort than a lively embarkation point, Goole was nevertheless accorded a major place in Parsons' *Tourist's Companion*, while Holland believed the colourful spectacle of Ouse shipping and the 'long liquid turnpikes' leading thereto to be 'well worth a day's journey to Goole'.[38] Head likened the Knottingley–Goole horse packet to 'a triumphal barge, so gaudily . . . was she decorated'.[39] Arriving by the complementary river approach, a tidewaiter burst into verse:

'The machinery and docks are extremely complete;
And the offices also remarkably neat;
With the elegant stores of that size
That the craft of the rivers may load or discharge
In the dock of the warehouse, unusually large:
Which excites a degree of surprise.'[40]

The New Town

To the first inhabitants such a description might well have contained more than a grain of truth, for the town planned by the AC on the advice

of Leather was commodious for its time. In 1822 Leather had reported:
'The establishment of trade and the consequent rise of a town will enable
[the AC] to sell off or let building ground, so as to add greatly to the profit
of the concern'.[41] In the following year applications for building leases
reached such proportions that he reported that speculators would be
likely to commence construction on adjacent non-company land. He
therefore recommended the AC to ratify his uniform plan to which all
builders would be required to conform.

Leather's plan was extremely elaborate (Fig. 13). In form it resembled
a common Mediterranean plan; an elevation on the original depicts a
classical arrangement consisting of imposing arcaded facades enclosing
on three sides a square opening forwards to the waterfront. In view of the
company's expected expenditure on contemporary dock proposals, the
capital required to establish such an ambitious settlement was not
forthcoming. When the eastern third only of the plan was approved, a
Building Committee was set up. Acting like a modern planning
authority, the committee considered plans and, jealously retaining
freehold, granted leases of ninety-nine years for building land.

The first task was to lay out the major streets, the first of which was
completed by 1823. Because of the low-lying nature of the area and its
consequent liability to flooding, the streets were built up several feet
above the general surface, material for this operation being taken from
concurrent dock excavations and from surrounding land. The latter was
subsequently relevelled by warping in the traditional Humberland
fashion, the whole process being an admirable, though unusual, example
of the technique of 'cut and fill'.

By 20 July 1826, when the canal was opened, several dwellings had
been completed, and the AC took a private census of the new town (Table
II). The majority of the population was clearly concentrated in
temporary navvies' huts, and the frontier town atmosphere was
emphasized by an ill-balanced population structure, only 38 per cent
female. The contrast between the agrarian hamlet south of the Dutch
River and the new town to the north must have been immense. With an
almost perfect sex balance and a density of six persons per dwelling, the
hamlet faced a thriving boom town, drastically overcrowded with eleven
persons per dwelling. Such overcrowding was doubtless detrimental to
both health and morals, considerations second only to profit in the eyes of
the paternalistic directors of the AC. The need to accommodate a flood of
immigrants was thus met by a surge of building; the total number of
houses in the planned town rose from 21 in 1826 to 178 by 1829, when the

Table II

Aire and Calder Navigation Census of Goole, 1826

Housing type	Number of Dwellings	Males	Females	Total
In huts built for the workmen	97	328	216	544
In old dwellings	6	26	15	41
In houses in the new town	18	128	70	198
In lock-keepers' houses	3	8	4	12
Total: north side of the Dutch River	124	490	305	795
In houses on the south side of the Dutch River	74	213	215	428
Grand Total	198	703	520	1223

level of crowding had been reduced to six persons per dwelling.[42]

The result of this activity was the creation of 'New Goole', a triangular settlement which by the 1840s contained over 250 building structures. From the start each street was planned to perform some specific function, building-unit shape and size varying accordingly. Aire Street became the major commercial street, containing stores, inns, saloons, and other provision for the wants of seamen. Ouse Street, built unusually wide to accommodate an open market, had a mixture of shops and dwellings. In both streets, dwelling space was located behind, above, or below the commercial premises. East Parade's imposing structures were intended for the professional classes. Behind these facades the poor clustered in the small terraced cottages of the centre and north, but penetrating towards the south-eastern corner of the town by means of cross streets. This corner, with the 'Banks Arms' (built by Sir Edward Banks, the chief contractor), the 'Public Rooms', 'Commercial Buildings', and the chapel, was the hub of the town, as befitted the nearest point to the docks.

Leather's plan of 1828 contains a riverside view of an opulent and well-built town. The picture, however, with its long facades of white, many-windowed buildings crowned by a forest of masts, was an idealized image of the early nineteenth century port. The architecture of Goole, however, did display considerable and impressive uniformity, product of the company's rigorous control. The spirit of this control is apparent in Leather's report of 1826, which stressed the virtues desirable in the AC's

Goole agent: '. . . as the town is all your own, much will depend upon his forming the habits and manners of the people'.[43] The building plan translated this paternalism into substantial reality. Formal terraced uniformity and an outward display of quiet opulence were the keynotes.

The architects, Woodhead and Hurst of Doncaster, produced a building style in no way original, but rare on this scale (Fig. 15). The outward appearance of the town was apparently designed from the point of view of persons arriving by water conveyance. Facing the harbour, the solid three-storey respectability of East Parade was calculated to impress the new arrival. In Aire Street appearances were maintained by a uniform Georgian facade, still the most impressive street in Goole. In Ouse Street long two-storey vistas were relieved at block corners by taller structures designed as inns or retail premises. Workers' housing, as in George Street, consisted of an unrelieved monotony of grim, squat, two-storey cottages, the smallest, yet the most crowded, dwellings in the town.[44] The northern frontage, North Street, remote from the docks and facing bare fields, was constructed somewhat later when restrictions had been relaxed.

Tending to reinforce the uniformity of style and brickwork was the insistence on bevelled block corners. Rounded corners are common in port areas, probably to assist the cornering of loaded drays, but rarely have they been used on such a scale as to provide the leitmotiv of a whole planned town. At strategic positions the chamfered corner would accommodate a shop front or door, and in the northern section the association of corner shops and working-class housing anticipated the characteristics of later bylaw housing.

Perhaps a rear view of the low-class housing best illustrates the AC's concern with outward show. Here blank brick walls were broken only by the smallest of windows. Moreover, only the major streets were raised, the unmade back alleys remaining at the original ground level. Housing was constructed on this original level; thus the ground floors, though exposed to daylight at the rear, took on the character of cellars at the front. In Ouse Street some buildings had six rooms; while the street-level front room served as a grocery or beershop the rear and upper rooms housed the family, for a second family frequently occupied the ground floor. In George Street was manifested the strange form best described as 'one up, one down, and one quasi-cellar'. Courts and back-to-backs, however, were few. The most impressive structure was the 'Banks Arms', renamed the 'Lowther' seven years after being purchased by the AC in 1828. Tall, sharp-edged and powerful, standing out against a uniform background, it

FIG. 15. George Street, Aire and Calder Navigation estate, Goole. Behind the taller edifices of East Parade (background) is typical terraced workers' housing (2 rooms plus cellar) with shop on chamfered corner.

effectively reflected the opulence of the company (Fig. 16). Although much of the planned town was demolished in the late 1960s, the 'Lowther' remains the most imposing building in Goole, and a peeling mural of the harbour, in the former directors' boardroom, reflects the lost glories of the port.

Although all builders within the estate had to conform to AC regulations, whereby all buildings were to be of brick or stone, with blue slate roofs, no such restrictions hampered the speculators who began to build outside the estate as early as 1829.[45] But the overall impression was one of company control. Holland informed the tourist that 'this suprising town' would gladden his eyes with 'ships with their streamers flying, new streets . . . mansions and shops of almost metropolitan appearance, [and] immense warehouses'.[46] White's description, however, best illustrates the success of Woodhead and Hurst: 'The New Town of Goole stands . . . north of the docks, and from the magnitude and opulence of its buildings, presents an air of considerable importance, especially when viewed from the river in connection with the docks and shipping'.[47]

Amenities were quickly established to cater for a population which as early as 1837 contained 12 shipping agents, 13 shoemakers, 3 shipbuilders, 2 surgeons, 6 schools, 16 inns and beerhouses, 3 banks, and 5 insurance agents.[48] Pursuing its self-imposed task of civilizing the frontier town, the AC extended certain of its facilities even to those areas outside its estate. Sewered drainage, a gasworks, and a waterworks were provided, and a cholera hospital set up during the epidemic of the early thirties. Assistance was given for the founding of a weekly market, an annual fair, National schools, a Literary and Scientific Society, an annual regatta, a fire engine, and a soup kitchen for the poor. Just north of Leather's original central square, the AC provided stone and land for a parish church, completed in 1848. The spire is still one of the dominant features of the Goole dockland. By placing together the edifices of commerce and religion the company symbolized its commitment to the supervision of almost all aspects of life in its planned town. Moreover, the lack of municipal buildings reflects the assumption by the AC of the position of paternalistic dictator.

Port Expansion and Trade Recession after 1835

Almost at once the dock system proved inadequate for the trade. As early as 1827 it was decided to excavate a third dock especially for steamships.

Fig. 16. Aire Street, Goole; sheds and railway lines face cafés and public houses, normal dockside equipment. In the foreground the Lowther Hotel (formerly the Banks Arms) was the first building erected in canal Goole.

Although an Act was obtained in 1828, difficulties of land purchase prevented work being set on foot until 1835, the dock being finished three years later. A berthing jetty was provided near the new entrance lock, which at 210ft × 58ft was then the largest in England. By 1841 a graving dock for the repair of steamships had been added (Fig. 12).

But the hopes which led to these improvements, based on Goole's first flourish, were not to be fulfilled. After its first decade of unremitting growth, Goole's foreign trade stagnated until after mid-century. Attempts by private individuals to establish regular sailings to foreign ports, although often supported by the AC, achieved little. 'The opposition, made by the Merchants of Hull, in the Establishment of Steam Vessels to Hamburgh and Rotterdam . . . by a reduction of freight has crushed (for the present) the growing Trade of Goole'.[49] Traffic on the Goole canal, however, increased rapidly. Between 1834 and 1845 the traffic in corn, stone and lime more than doubled, and coal tonnage rose from 200,802 to 313,449 tons. The proportion of total AC receipts provided by the Goole canal rose steadily until it reached almost 42 per cent in 1850. Thus the Goole canal, and the coal carried upon it, began to assert themselves as the AC's financial backbone in the period of foreign trade stagnation which soon followed the creation of the canal port. The original boom and its apparent levelling-off are reflected in population trends for Goole (Table III).

Table III
Goole: Per Cent Population Increase 1821–51

Period	Goole	Goole and Hook
1822–31	273·6	170·9
1832–41	70·5	62·0
1842–51	3·5	29·3

Building was, however, spilling over into Hook township. The trends for Goole and Hook together indicate a respectable continuation of the boom, the joint population rising nearly sixfold, to 4619, in the period.

Goole's trading problems after the later 1830s were in great part due to the impact of rail carriage. Having failed to crush the new port by attempting to impose its dock dues on Goole ships and to hinder steam towing to the port,[50] Hull played a major part in the promotion of a Hull–Leeds railway.[51] In the late twenties the AC had found difficult the discouragement of private attempts to produce canal bypasses on the

Leeds–Castleford and Wakefield–Ferrybridge sections of its navigation. After being coerced into improving these upper portions, it was then faced with a project which planned to render its new canal completely obsolete. By 1830 the AC was fighting for the very existence of its new port, a mere four years after its birth.

While the AC denounced the railway as a 'direct attack', Hull interests promoted Selby as a rail-water breakpoint and hoped for the downfall of what they regarded as a monopolistic enterprise.[52] With the opening of the Leeds and Selby Railway in 1834 the revival of Selby's coasting trade and coal shipments was followed by a decline in AC revenue due to a lowering of tolls necessitated by the comparatively low rates of the railway. In view of the difficulties of Ouse navigation below Selby, however, the railway was extended to Hull in 1840.

By its astute wooing of the railways, Hull attained some measure of success in its attempts to crush Goole. Coal traffic declined, and during the period 1843–7 railway control of the Calder and Hebble Navigation (CH) caused the virtual cessation of the traffic in cotton bales down the AC line. Selby, eclipsed in 1826 and revived in 1834, was left high and dry again in 1840, and declined to the status of a minor port. After fourteen years of uncertainty, Goole's anti-Selby jingle had at last proved valid:

'Selby was a sea-port town
When Goole was but a marsh;
Now Goole it is the sea-port town
And Selby fares the worse.'

Free of Selby's competition, Goole still had to contend with Hull. Yet the new port not only retained a fair trade but also began to broaden its economic base by attracting canalside industry. Where a lone windmill had stood in 1805, shipyards were established and 356 vessels totalling 25,840 tons were launched in the period 1828–32.[53] The patent slip was able to effect repairs to the largest vessels using Goole, then rarely exceeding 300 tons burden, while a fourth shipyard was added in 1839. A brewery had appeared in 1830, a foundry by 1834, and a 'sugar house' by 1849. These developments, while not compensating fully for the stagnation in trade, provided alternative employment and a basis for future expansion.

7. Notes

1. W. Dugdale, *The History of Imbanking and Drayning*, Bowyer and Nichols, London (1772), p. 120.
2. W. G. East, 'A Note on Historical Geography', *Geography*, 18 (1933), 282–92.
3. G. Dunston, *The Rivers of Axholme*, Browne, London (1909), p. 33.
4   Day book of William Smith of Potter Grange (1818–62), Garside Historical Collection, Goole Public Library.
5. R. M. Cox, *The Development of the Coal Industry in South Yorkshire before 1830*, unpublished M. A. thesis, University of Sheffield (1960), p. 203.
6. *Hull Advertiser* (21 July 1826).
7. E. Parsons, *The Tourist's Companion*, Whittaker, London (1835), p. 169.
8. B. F. Duckham, *The Yorkshire Ouse*, David and Charles, Newton Abbot (1967).
9. A. W. Goodfellow, 'Sheffield's Waterway to the Sea', *Transactions, Hunter Archaeological Society*, 5 (1941), 246–53;
    T. S. Willan, *The Early History of the Don Navigation*, Kelley, New York (1965).
10. R. W. Unwin, 'The Aire & Calder Navigation: I—The Beginnings', *Bradford Antiquary* New Series 42 (1964), 53.
11. ACN 1/4 (20 September 1781).
12. E. Baines, *History, Directory, and Gazetteer of the County of York*, Vol. 1, (1822), pp. 93, 273.
13. ACN 1/7 (25 July, 17 August 1796).
14. ACN 1/8 (5 July 1817).
15. ACN 1/7 (19 August 1790).
16. ACN 1/8 (25 September 1818).
17. Rennie's report, ACN 1/28 (30 December 1818).
18. ACN 1/28 (3 March 1820).
19. ACN 1/8 (22 July–9 September 1819, 19 January 1820).
20. Collection of posters, ACN 4/187 (12 February 1820).
21. Leather's reports, ACN 1/29 (1822–6).
22. *Leeds Mercury* (1 July 1826); *Hull Advertiser* (21 July 1826).
23. *Morning Chronicle* (26 July 1826).
24. e.g. *Hull Advertiser* (9 January, 12 March, 21 May, 27 November 1829).
25. J. Holland, *The Tour of the Don*, Sheffield Mercury, Sheffield (1837), p. 491.
26. ACN 1/8 (5 August 1819); 1/9 (27 July 1829, 14 November 1821).
27. ACN 1/9 (21 July 1821); Leather's report, ACN 1/28 (23 July 1822).
28. Rennie's reports, ACN 1/28 (30 December 1818, 18 December 1820).
29. E. Parsons, op. cit., p. 71.
30. *Hull Advertiser* (21 July 1826); ACN 1/9 (3 August 1829).
31. Leather's report, ACN 1/28 (5 August 1826).
32. ACN 1/9 (5 December 1831).
33. ACN 1/29 (20 October 1828).
34. Leather's report, ACN 1/28 (5 August 1826).

35. W. G. East, 'The Port of Kingston-upon-Hull during the Industrial Revolution', *Economica* 11 (1931), 190–212.

36. HM Customs Records (London) 32: 145 (1831), p. 197; 32: 145 (1835), p. 290.

37. HM Customs Records (London) 32: 147 (1832), p. 181.

38. J. Holland, op. cit., p. 495.

39. G. Head, *A Home Tour through the Manufacturing Districts of England in the Summer of 1835*, London (1836), p. 231.

40. J. Phillips, *A Trip to Goole, on Board the Sythe-a poem*, Peck and Smith, Hull (1834).

41. Leather's report, ACN 1/28 (23 January 1822).

42. Leather's report, ACN 1/28 (5 August 1826).

43 Leather's report, ACN 1/28 (5 August 1826); see also Lease Book, ACN 3/3.

44. J. D. Porteous, *The Company Town of Goole: An Essay in Urban Genesis*, Occasional Papers in Geography No. 12, University of Hull (1969)

45. *Hull Advertiser* (6 November 1829).

46. J. Holland, op. cit., p. 492.

47. W. White, *History, Gazetteer and Directory of the West Riding of Yorkshire*, Sheffield (1837), p. 290.

48. Ibid., pp. 304–6.

49. HM Customs Records (London) 32: 145 (1835), p. 154.

50. ACN 1/9 (1827–34).

51. W. W. Tomlinson, *The North Eastern Railway*, Kelley, New York (1967), p. 202; *Hull Advertiser* (28 August 1828).

52. *Hull Advertiser* (12 March, 14 May 1829).

53. J. Holland, op. cit., p. 494.

Canal Ports and
Technological Change

The Fate of Towns and Cities is every jot as unstable as the
State and Happiness of Men.

Camden, Sixteenth Century

8

The Challenge of the Railways, 1830–1918

> Upon the whole the railroad is a pestilential, topsey-turvey, harum-scarum whirligig. Give me the old, solemn, straight-forward canal—three miles per hour for expresses, and two for jog and trot journeys—none of your hop-skip-and-jump whimsies for me . . .
>
> New York canal shareholder, 1830

Although cheap waterborne traffic enabled Britain to enter an age of unprecedented industrial expansion, both coastal and inland navigation suffered when railway goods carriage came into its own in the 1840s. Bypassing old riverports, the railways condemned them to decay. Many canals which did not merge with railway companies went into decline, small shipping places stagnated, and the process of port replacement was accelerated. Some canals fought back by expanding facilities, by at last becoming carriers under the Act of 1845, by river improvement, and finally by support of ship canal schemes. Railway glamour, however, caught the public's imagination and rendered most inland steam navigation schemes stillborn; the attitude of the New York canal shareholder was soon to become an anachronism. Just as canals had superseded river and road carriage, so their eclipse by the new medium was encouraged by the Board of Trade's belief that only increased speed and cheapness of transport could maintain the prosperity of manufacturing communities.[1] These being the criteria, the triumph of the railways was inevitable, given the general application of the following rates of carriage between Sheffield and Manchester in the 1830s:

actual, by canal: 8 days at 28s per ton
actual, by road: 2 days at 34s per ton
expected, by rail: 4 hours at 20s per ton[2]

Towns influenced by canals were readily able to adjust to the new situation; for them the problem was largely a matter of adaptation to and accommodation of the more efficient medium. Canal-created ports, however, had a vested interest in a transport system now rapidly becoming outmoded. Theirs was a more difficult problem, the dilemma of whether to continue in the old way or convert wholeheartedly to the new.

Runcorn

The demise of Bradshaw, the purchase of the MIN, and the agreement with the LNWR gave the Bridgewater trustees a strong bargaining position vis-a-vis the railway. The sudden railway-induced drop in receipts of the early 1830s was reversed, so that by 1849 the duke's waterways were carrying 1,500,000 tons per annum, more than twice as much as had been conveyed in 1830.[3] New passenger services for a short time succeeded in reducing the passenger receipts of the LNWR. With the opening of the Liverpool and Bury Railway in 1849, however, an intense rate-cutting campaign began 'and though it entailed serious losses each strove to maintain and extend their operations'.[4]

Unable to ruin the private canal carriers because of the support given them by the trustees, the railways began a concerted attack on the highly-prized cotton trade. Of 130,000 tons of raw cotton carried locally by water in 1849, 26,000 were for Manchester and 104,000 for places beyond. Hoping to secure not only half the former but also the whole of the latter, the railways attempted to force cotton off the Bridgewater system. But while negotiations dragged on the course of competition clearly favoured the canal and until the 1870s the trustees maintained their powerful position through an increasing number of agreements with almost all the local railways

These relationships between the trustees and the railways are described in detail in Mather's *After the Canal Duke*.[5] At Runcorn the effect of railway competition was selective. A steady fall in the volume of foreign shipping was clearly related to the reorientation of overseas trade towards ports with railway connexions, such as Birkenhead and Garston. Fleetwood began to abstract Runcorn's Scottish pig-iron trade when developed by the Lancashire and Yorkshire Railway after 1847. But coastwise trade and the number of vessels registered at the port increased, while the value of exports rose from £6,888 in 1860 to £51,789 in 1868.

With about 300,000 tons passing through the docks in the early fifties, and a pressure of trade so great in 1852 that the canal fleet was unable to handle it, dock extensions were imperative.[6] Without new facilities, the trustees knew that their plans to capture more of the salt, grain, and iron trades would be stillborn. After much vacillation, Alfred Dock was begun in 1854, and the Runcorn and Weston Canal some three years later. Equipped with hydraulic cranes, the new basin, completed in 1860 together with the canal connexion to the Weaver system, bespoke the trustees' intention of abstracting a greater share of the latter's salt and pottery trades. The Weaver trustees were thus stimulated to pursue a policy of improvement which included locks to take 300 ton steamers upriver, the Anderton lift to facilitate interchange with the TM, and new docks at Weston Point.

The railway which entered Runcorn was on the whole welcomed by the town, for it aimed less to capture the canal trade than to reduce the distance by rail between Liverpool and the Midlands. Sporadic efforts to bridge Runcorn Gap had been made throughout the coaching era. Runcorn being regarded as a 'spot picked out by nature . . . for a bridge'.[7] Renewal of interest came with long distance railway projections (Fig. 17). As early as 1829 a scheme for a Liverpool–Runcorn line had been denounced by Bradshaw.[8] Fifteen years later the GJR promoted its corollary, a Preston Brook–Runcorn line 'having for its ultimate object extension into Liverpool'.[9] Board of Trade objections to this piecemeal measure led to its withdrawal. In the late 1850s the LNWR, as the GJR's successor, fearing the construction of a rival line through Runcorn, promoted a Runcorn Gap link line between its Cheshire and Lancashire trackage.

Almost immediately the railway purchased Runcorn ferry, and while its bridge was under construction between 1863 and 1868 managed the crossing in such a way as to make passengers eager to travel by other means.[10] A station was opened in 1868, and a branch to the Bridgewater docks made to preserve the rights of the trustees 'who show themselves everywhere'.[11] The fulfilment of a century of bridging plans, the railway dominated Runcorn's townscape with its deep cutting through Runcorn Hill, its high level crossing of Top Locks, and its castellated stone viaduct. Incidental benefits conferred upon Runcorn were great; no longer 'five miles from anywhere', the town lost its cul-de-sac position at once.

Though newly invaded by the railway, Runcorn in the early 1870s was still primarily a canal port. Between 1873 and 1884 about 500,000 tons of goods passed annually through the docks (Table IV).

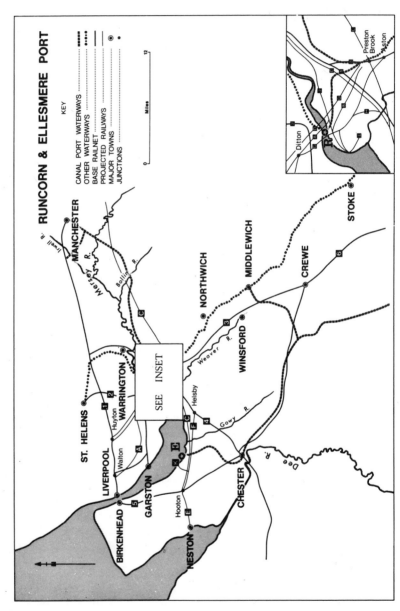

Fig. 17. Runcorn and Ellesmere Port in the Railway Age.

KEY

Base railnet:
1. Liverpool and Manchester Railway (constructed 1826–30).
2. St Helens Railway and Canal (1846–53).
3. Grand Junction Railway (1833–7).
4. Birkenhead, Cheshire and Lancashire Junction Railway (1846–50).
5. Chester and Birkenhead Railway (1837–40).
6. Chester and Crewe Railway (1837–40).

Railways projects to Runcorn (R) 1826–1920 and Ellesmere Port (E) 1845–1918:
A. Liverpool and Runcorn (projected in 1826).
B. Runcorn and Preston Brook (1844, 45).
C. Birkenhead, Lancashire and Cheshire Junction (1845).
D. Huyton to Preston Brook (1845).
E. Hooton and Neston (1851).
F. Hooton and Helsby (1858).
G. Aston to Ditton (LNWR, 1860).
H. Runcorn and Frodsham (LNWR, 1873).
J. Warrington and Runcorn Light Railway (1900).
K. Hooton Light Railway (1918).
L. Weston Point Light Railway (1920).

Table IV
Trade of the Bridgewater Docks, Runcorn, 1873–84 (tons)

	Imports		Exports		
Year	Coastwise	foreign	Coastwise	foreign	Total
1873	256,251	59,481	199,394	27,843	542,969
1884	215,541	22,246	196,200	12,411	446,398

Coastwise and import trades were most important. Two-thirds of the
coastwise imports consisted of clay, while half the coastwise exports was
salt, much of the remainder being coal. Salt also made up a considerable
proportion of foreign exports. Urban expansion followed that of trade. A
contemporary local guide expressed amazement at the changes wrought
in the landscape following a 'great influx of working men'.[12] House
building continued steadily around Top Locks and along the canal.
Industrial expansion also followed the canal, expanding so much into
Halton township east of Runcorn that the proportion of the latter's
rateable value represented by industry fell after 1851 to about 30 per cent.
Quarrying proceeded apace, several tramways being constructed
between the quarries and Weston Point docks.

Most notable, however, were the major extensions of the soap and
alkali works, and of shipbuilding specifically for the chemical trade.[13]
Founded on East Lancashire's demand for textile reagents, after mid-
century the 'chemical revolution' exploited Runcorn Gap's position as a
waterway node equidistant between Lancashire coal and Cheshire salt.
With the establishment of plant in 'Widnes near Runcorn' in 1847 a
considerable interchange of capital and experienced personnel grew up
between the two settlements.[14] After initial discouragement on the part of
the Bridgewater trustees, large-scale chemical works arrived in Runcorn
after 1860 in the shape of Wigg's copper and alkali works, built alongside
the Old Quay Canal east of Runcorn.

Weston also developed after mid-century, largely through the
expansion of works established on the Weston Canal by Runcorn
chemical manufacturers. One of these works demanded 500 workers, and
was largely responsible for the 80 per cent population growth of Weston
in the period 1852–81. Both Weston village and Weston Point expanded,
and to the paternalism of the Weaver trustees was added that of the
chemical manufacturers. The excavation in 1883 of Tollemache Dock
was followed three years later by the erection of a salt works served by a
brine pipeline. By 1890, however, Runcorn and Weston had been

outstripped by Widnes as chemical producers; on the Cheshire side of Runcorn Gap landscape devastation never reached the extent experienced in the Lancashire town, soon rechristened 'Little Hell'.[15]

Paralleling urban and industrial growth, the passing of the Runcorn Improvement Act in 1852 promoted a spate of public building, encouraged by the Bridgewater trustees who, as second largest landowners in Runcorn, provided two commissioners. Market hall (1856), public library (1858), court house (1859), and public hall (1860) were erected within easy reach of the town hall. Though its fairs had become obsolete and its parishes reduced in size after 1850, Runcorn retained its local influence by founding three newspapers before 1870, two of them shared with Widnes. An indicator of urban expansion, the gas company increased its consumers thirteenfold between 1838 and 1885.

But the period of expansion came to an end in the 1870s. Between 1852 and 1881 Runcorn's population had increased by 70·5 per cent, its buildings by 76·3 per cent. The thirty years 1882–1911, however, saw rates of only 17·1 and 22·4 per cent respectively. Several new factors were at work after 1870. Though the Bridgewater system was more than holding its own against railway competition, from 1856 persistent attempts were made to dispose of it. The need of the duke's beneficiaries for a less fluctuating source of income culminated in 1872 in the sale of the canals to the railway-controlled Bridgewater Navigation Company. The new administration was selective in its prosecution of the trade of Runcorn. By 1876 Fenton and Arnold docks, names redolent of the Potteries, had been excavated, and a series of warehouses for pottery storage added in order to compete effectively with newer railway ports (Fig. 5). Runcorn's foreign trade stagnated, and declined after 1885, but coastwise traffic, still the bulk of the trade, grew at a faster rate after the railway takeover, as did the registration of vessels.

The attainment by Runcorn of Urban District (UD) status in 1894 was of minor importance compared with the advent of the most radical change in the waterway system since the duke's first canals more than a century before. Improvement of both Mersey and Irwell was long overdue. By the 1880s neglect of the rivers had reduced the size of vessels able to reach Manchester to 50 tons, and nothing had been done in the estuary where the lowest neap tides often failed to reach Runcorn. The story of the Manchester Ship Canal (MSC) is told elsewhere.[16] The plans of 1883–4 for a canal terminating above Runcorn, with a midstream trained channel from thence to the Mersey Bar were violently opposed by both Liverpool and Runcorn. Erstwhile enemy of Runcorn, the Liverpool Dock Board even considered purchasing the Bridgewater canals and working goods to Manchester as a way of preventing the realization of the ship canal.[17] However, by finally compelling the MSC to hug the Cheshire shore, Liverpool effectively secured the future of Runcorn as a port.

In 1885 the Bridgewater Navigation Company's canals were sold to the MSC at a handsome profit. Before it was obliterated by its successor, the MIN line carried much of the materials for the works, and during 1892–3 Runcorn docks were closed during the construction of the outer embankment. The strong feelings aroused in Runcorn by this measure were only allayed by the construction of a 1,500 ft layby below the docks. Two locks, the larger 600 ft × 45 ft, gave access from Weston Point docks to both Mersey and Weaver, while the Bridgewater Lock, 400 ft × 45 ft, provided Runcorn with direct access to the Mersey.

Ship canal promoters prophesied the flocking of industry to the banks of the canal, which they regarded as a 35 mile length of dock. Runcorn UD, however, despite its nodal position along an arcuate strip of the MSC, did not feel an immediate benefit. After sharing somewhat in the phenomenal rise of Widnes throughout the period 1852–81, it shared also in the depression of the chemical industry which set in in the 1890s. Coal strikes and the growing preference for cheaper electrolytic products caused a wholesale decline in salt decomposition in the Runcorn Gap area where the less efficient Leblanc process was dominant. In 1895 'the suphuric acid plant of the three works in Runcorn stood quite idle all year, and the salt cake and bleaching powder plants . . . were kept going only for a few weeks'.[18]

Nevertheless, 1886 saw the arrival of the district's first really large scale industry. The promoters of the Castner–Kellner electrolytic plant chose the Runcorn Gap area for its admirable position, but sited the works at Weston Point because of the large area of cheap flat land available for expansion along the waterfront. Expansion indeed took place several times before the Great War. The ship canal also effectively relocated the Wigg and Salt Union works on deep water; both expanded in the Leblanc revival after 1905. Moreover, the hopes of competitors that the Castner works would fail through lack of soft water, railway access, and cheap power, were dashed when the Salt Union built a large electricity generating station in 1910–11. Sufficient power was produced from waste steam to provide supplies to towns as far afield as Ellesmere Port and Crewe. Abstraction of water from Liverpool's Vyrnwy pipeline and railway sidings acquired in 1922 solved the other problems. Through the impact of these activities Runcorn, of which it was said in 1879 that 'with the exception of the railway and canal works, there is nothing much to be seen',[19] could be described in 1913 as 'a seaport, a great emporium of inland navigation, an industrial centre, and the local capital of an historic district'.[20]

Despite these activities in the Runcorn Gap area, the town of Runcorn grew only slowly in the late nineteenth century. A short-lived boom in exports, beginning in 1892, was over by 1896. Moreover, the volume of coastwise shipping began to decline with the opening up of Manchester to seagoing vessels. Having seen the Old Quay Canal obliterated by the MSC, and having lost control of both Bridgewater Canal and its docks to the ship canal, Runcorn also lost its identity as part of the Port of Manchester. Nevertheless, foreign imports, having fallen by 75 per cent after the advent of railway control, exhibited a rapid rise after 1892. Moreover, after the slump of 1896 both export and coastwise trades began a slow upswing.

With the spectacular rise of large-scale chemical manufacture Weston village fared far better. While Runcorn's population grew by 17 per cent in the period 1882–1911, that of Weston, one-eighth the size, grew by 27 per cent. Widnes also outstripped Runcorn. The vagaries of the ferry service after 1894 led the twin towns to complete a transporter bridge in 1905, although before the development of motor traffic it made no profit. Moreover, the industrial revival in the early twentieth century did not wholly alleviate the problems of unemployment in Runcorn. Town health reports for the period immediately before the Great War are full of pleas for the establishment of further industry, and in 1911 'a low birthrate and a grave outlook' were noted. The depressed position of canal-based Runcorn in this period of regional growth in shipping and chemical manufacture can be seen in its character as a major canal boat centre, the only local authority in Britain to issue over 1,000 canal boat dwelling certificates,[21] and in its ignominious failure in 1903 to gain political control of ancient Halton and thriving Weston.[22]

Stourport

Railways running between the Midlands and the lower Severn were soon to render Stourport obsolete as a transhipping port. In the early days of rail, in view of 'the distressed state of the trade' and the failure of its

proposed 'Coalition of the Canals in this district', the STW made large
financial contributions towards opposition to railway projects.[23] The year
1844, however, found the company supporting both the Birmingham and
Gloucester, and the Oxford, Worcester and Wolverhampton (OWWR)
railway against the Liverpool and Birmingham's (LBR) audacious plan
for a Worcester–Wolverhampton line to 'run along the bank of the now
improved Navigation from Worcester to Stourport, and thence along the
side of our Canal . . . and thus necessarily carry off, not only the long, but
also the short traffic'.[24] As if stunned by 'projects threatening the interests
of this Company in every direction', and recognizing the value of
OWWR guarantees to the Severn Commission, the STW concluded in
1847 that it was 'highly desirable that this Company should amalgamate
with some railway company on the basis of guaranteeing to the Company
their present dividend'.[25]

The OWWR, completed in 1852, added Worcester to the growing list
of Severn ports having rail connexion with Stourport's hinterland. At the
same time a projected Birmingham–Wolverhampton railway proposed a
Stour valley branch, the only line projected directly to Stourport before
the 1890s. On the basis of these two lines, a number of other railways were
projected, with reference less to Stourport itself than to its fortuitous
position near the axis of two persistent directional influences. First, three
lines were promoted between 1845 and 1859 to connect the Welsh
Marches with the Midlands. The exigencies of terrain, however, were
responsible for directing these lines across the Severn at Bewdley; only
one envisaged a branch to meet the proposed Stour valley line. Secondly,
and crossing these lines at a high angle, Severn valley railway projects
attempted to link Shrewsbury and Worcester.

In 1845–6 such a line was proposed by the SURC with reference to the
Stour valley scheme, to which the STW had been persuaded to drop its
opposition.[26] The abortive line would have passed through Lower Mitton
below the canal bend; a more reasonable scheme, passing between the
two Mittons, was not proposed until 1852. Having quickly obtained
sanction for this line from Shrewsbury to the OWWR, the Severn Valley
Railway (SVR) delayed its completion until running rights were jointly
taken up by the Midland and Great Western (GWR) companies.
Opened early in 1852, the line was of no great advantage to Stourport.
Running only between market towns, single tracked for most of its length,
and closely following the Severn's meanders, it had little future as a
conveyance for heavy goods. Contemporaries regarded it as useful for 'the
seeker after both health and pleasure', but believed the Severn to afford

'better accommodation for the conveyance of heavy articles'.[27] Cutting transversely across the STW's canal and with its great embankment across the Stour meadows, the line was the symbol rather than the source of the STW's failing grasp upon the goods traffic moving between the West Midlands and the lower Severn.

A local poet aptly described the despair of boatman and coachman:

'Since steam, grim conqueror, spoils their trade
And causes all their hopes to fade'.[28]

Specific trades, such as fruit carriage, were early lost to the speedier medium. Dividends began to fall rapidly after 1862, and by 1913 the company could declare a dividend only one fifth as great as that declared fifty years before. As canal traffic declined the STW made little attempt to improve its line, devoting most attention to improving facilities on the Severn. In particular the company desired a lock below Diglis to enable 'small steamers and seaborne craft' to penetrate to Stourport. The Severn Commission decided upon a lock at Tewkesbury, but was unable to proceed until the STW, already heavily committed financially to the improvement venture, provided £40,000 in 1856. Anticipating extensive amelioration of the navigation, the STW purchased two steam coasters, each capable of carrying over 100 tons of cargo, in 1860. But they were given up four years later, though continuing to work between Worcester and French and Irish ports for several years.[29]

Although seven steamers were reported working between Gloucester and Stourport in 1860, Severn traffic declined because of the deterioration of the lower river. Despite further river improvement, traffic fell from 349,393 tons in 1863 to 292,326 tons in 1898. The eventual realization of 7 ft of water up to Stourport in 1890 came too late to revive the canal port and arrest the failing fortunes of the STW. Indeed, the port had been in physical decline since the 1860s, when the loss of general trade, coupled with coal and iron strikes, had drastically reduced receipts and permitted the infilling of the redundant Cheapside Basin. As coal increasingly became the major waterborne commodity, attempts to close the TS Canal filled the STW with alarm. In the face of the liabilities of the Severn towpath companies and the attempts of Gloucester to impose port dues on upriver vessels, the STW tried every means of maintaining traffic. A GWR plan of the seventies for a dock near Stourport came to nothing. The rapid demise of ambitious late nineteenth century schemes for a Birmingham–Bristol ship canal, though inevitable, was hastened by the refusal of the STW to give support to a line which would reduce both its traffic and its identity. Any implementation of a Royal Commission proposal of 1909 for an improvement of the Severn sufficient to allow 600 ton craft up to Stourport was stifled during the Great War.

An attempt in 1890 to lend STW support to the Severn and Canal Carrying Company (SCCC), by then one of the largest remaining carriers using both waterways, had no result. Indeed, the SCCC removed its fleet repairs from Stourport in 1909 when the Sharpness Company, owners of the WB Canal, took control of it, though 1912 found the STW helping the SCCC to purchase new tugs. By this time, however, the middle and upper Severn trades were failing; the last barges traded to Bridgnorth in 1895. Stourport traders were no doubt of the opinion that their haven must be the next to be eclipsed in the process of downstream port replacement, for Worcester and Tewkesbury were increasing their transhipping functions with the aid of dock extensions, the Sharpness Company, and good rail connexions. The condition of the long neglected STW Canal did nothing to prevent this redirection of traffic. In reply to boatmen's pleas for dredging, the company in 1893 could recommend only that smaller loads be carried.[30] As early as the eighties the decay in STW control over the Midlands–Severn traffic was reflected in Stourport's dockland, which appeared:

'A sad contrast to its former self. Railways have robbed the Severn and the canal of the traffic, which now passes by instead of into its commodious basin. We found the Company's great hotel . . . with rooms sufficient to make up a hundred beds . . . diminished to the proportion of one of the smallest inns in the town, its extensive rooms being let off to form dwelling houses. One solitary barge, loaded with sand . . . was all that the *Athlete*, capable of tugging a hundred such, could muster on the Monday morning.[31]

Urban expansion during the whole of this period was conspicuous only by its absence. An extremely low rate of growth in both population and building characterized the particular economic malaise of a canal port town left high and dry by railway competition. In the 1880s, as at mid-century, the whole of Stourport's built-up area could have easily been fitted into the grounds of nearby Moor Hall, the former residence of a canal carrier. Significantly, the hall was to become the home of a carpet manufacturer. So noticeable was the combination of declining water traffic with the simultaneous expansion of the industrial sector that the working population of Stourport appeared as early as 1868 to be 'principally engaged in trades and manufactures'.[32] Even the town's industrial base began to shake off its former dependence on water transport; as early as 1847 the STW was forced to contemplate the construction of its own craft, 'boatbuilders and carriers being afraid to incur the expense . . . in consequence of the competition by railway'.[33] Though the construction of small vessels continued, the last Severn trow built in Stourport was launched in 1861. Improved access, however, was instrumental in promoting the most significant trend of the period, the expansion of the textile and metal trades.

Though a tin works took over part of Stourport's earliest carpet factory, three further carpet mills were erected during the sixties and seventies. Seeking cheap Stourside sites free from the congestion of Kidderminster, these works brought some employees with them. Having risen by a mere 0·6 per cent between 1862 and 1871, the combined population of the Mittons rose by a decennial mean of 18·2 per cent during the two subsequent decades, although much of the employment was for females only. Stourport and Lower Mitton had little share in the expansion of bricks and mortar. Vested rights over land on the Bewdley and Harlebury sides of the town added their weight to the pull of Kidderminster and the railway in focussing building activity in Upper Mitton. Here Newtown, in the form of terraced artisans' dwellings, arose between 1875 and 1886, though the forces of reinvigoration were soon spent. The Mittons reached their prewar population peak of 5,596 in 1891, net emigration accounting for a loss of 7·3 per cent of the joint population in the period 1892–1901, a loss not made up in the following decade. Stourport greeted the new century with a trade depression, low marriage and birth rates, and untenanted houses and retail property.[34]

Signs of the STW's diminishing influence had been apparent as early as mid-century. Thereafter, although the dockland estate remained a unit, many company houses and some land parcels were sold off. In particular, the infilled Cheapside Basin was sold after 1865 for extensions of the vinegar works and as a site for the Stourport Gas Company, significantly the enterprise of a canal carrier, but at least until the seventies, when industrialists became a major force in the town, the canal company retained its seigneurial character.

In the 1870s the growth of Newtown coincided with the expansion of amenities in the provision of which the STW took no part. A new Severn bridge, a newspaper, and a yearly regatta found support from manufacturers, but a new parish church begun in 1881 mirrored Stourport's subsequent stagnation in its unfinished appearance throughout the period. Inaugurated in 1894, and annexing Upper

Mitton in 1897, Stourport Urban District Council (UDC) finally absolved the STW of further responsibility for the town. Influence from further afield emerged in the nineties when two railway schemes were specifically projected to the town from the east. The successful Kidderminster and Stourport Electric Tramway, completed in 1898 along High Street, was designed not only to take an increasing number of female workers to Kidderminster textile mills, but also to provide easy access to riverine Stourport for Midlands holidaymakers. While the tramway produced a guidebook and ran an extensive Sunday service, the STW played some part in developing its port area as a tourist centre. Stourport UDC negotiated with the company for land for a river promenade and bandstand, and by the outbreak of the Great War a large space surrounding the Engine Basin had been given over to a permanent fairground.

Ellesmere Port

While the Birkenhead and Chester Railway (BCR) of 1840 dealt the death blow to the canal passenger trade, iron ore traffic through Ellesmere Port was unable to expand because of rate cutting by the LNWR in favour of Garston railway docks, while early attempts to obtain a rail link for Ellesmere Port were overridden. The decline of population in the decade 1852–61 was attributed by the census to 'the facilities of railway conveyance having caused a partial cessation of canal traffic'.

Improved relations with the LNWR helped bring about a revival in the early 1860s. As the LNWR soon realized that the SU could be used to rival the North Staffordshire Railway which was working the TM, the SURC was able to capture a great share of iron ore imports. In 1857, rather than extend facilities at Preston Brook, the Bridgewater trustees began to reroute their ore traffic via Ellesmere Port; at the same time Birkenhead and Liverpool were hindering each other's development of the trade. With these aids Ellesmere Port was able to take advantage of a measure of independence from Liverpool gained in 1847 when the port became a creek within the port limits of Runcorn.

Increasing industrialization in the Midlands not only demanded an expansion of Cambrian iron ore, Irish grain, and Welsh slate imports, but also the increased movement of pottery goods. Crate and clay warehouses were erected at Ellesmere Port in 1864, and coasters were able to depart with loads of finished metals and pottery ware, though most of these goods were still transhipped into estuarial vessels for export via Liverpool.

At this time Ellesmere Port secured a railway (Fig. 17). Birkenhead's bid to rival Liverpool included a plan for direct rail links with South Lancashire, avoiding the delays incurred in the journey via Chester. Accordingly, a short rail link between the BCR line at Hooton and the Chester–Warrington line at Helsby was promoted. Having no desire to stimulate any port but their own, the promoters created Whitby Locks station outside Ellesmere Port only when compelled to do so by the Marquis of Westminster. Even before its completion in 1863 the line was taken over jointly by the LNWR and GWR. It had little effect on Ellesmere Port. Liverpool workers with sufficient means to commute daily from the Wirral via the Mersey tunnel of 1886 were not attracted to Whitby Locks. The canal port's share in the rising Merseyside population was due wholly to commerce; in 1860 the LNWR and GWR complained that railborne general merchandise traffic between Chester and Liverpool had remained static for some years, 'the Shropshire Union Canal affording the means of successful competition'.[35] Further, the SURC in 1870 completed a horse tramway from Whitby Locks station to the docks, where facilities were expanded in response to increasing traffic. Earl Grosvenor's wharf was purchased and a new grain warehouse erected in 1870–1. The Mersey fleet, in continuous expansion since mid-century, by 1869 consisted of 2 tugs, 12 floats and 81 flats.

Industry was slow to appear in Ellesmere Port, but the solitary shipyard of the 1840s found companions after mid-century. About the same time a soap works was erected on the canal side, an apparently unsuccessful offshoot of the general expansion of the Merseyside chemical industry. In 1863 the SURC took possession of the works and sold it; production had ceased by 1890 (Fig. 18). Two developments after 1870, however, were not only different in type from the above but were also harbingers of the future. By 1889 the Diamond Oil Company's canal-side distribution depot had been joined by a second plant.[36] A pointer to the more immediate future was the decision of N. S. Burnell, owner of a small Liverpool galvanizing works, to open a similar plant at Ellesmere Port.

Congestion of Liverpool's dockland and heavy dock charges

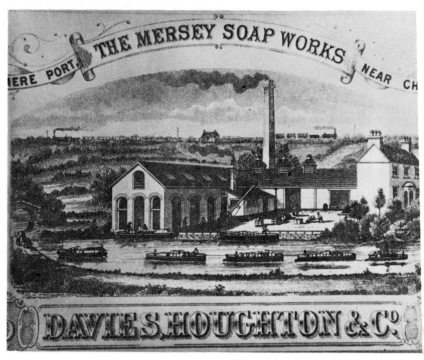

Fig. 18. The Mersey Soap Works alongside the Wirral Line at Ellesmere Port, late nineteenth century. In the background trains pass by Whitby Locks Station.

required Burnell to look elsewhere. A site was needed which would minimize the haul of imported alloy, unloaded overside into barges at Liverpool without paying dock dues, and of Wolverhampton metal, much of which also moved by water. Ellesmere Port, located at the major waterway breakpoint between the two cities, was ideal. With great freedom of choice in such a non-industrial settlement, the plant was located at the point which allowed the maximum efficiency of operation. Built in 1883 at the junction of railway and canal, the plant was able to assemble materials from any direction at minimum cost. Ease of dispatch of the finished product on flats mooring at the plant's own wharf proved a major advantage.

The development of the port and its associated industry created a population boom. Fluctuating markedly until 1861, the population of he township more than doubled in the period 1862–81. Although aided by the railway, this expansion was more accurately ascribed by the 1871 census to 'the briskness of business . . . in transferring cargoes from boats on the canal to vessels on the Mersey'. At first the influx was housed in the vacant dwellings of the 1850s though the quickening of activity led to the construction of about seventy new dwellings in the decade 1872–81, of which the SURC provided ten. Amenities were gradually extended. In 1863 the SURC built a gas works, although only company houses were supplied despite the complaints of the remainder of the populace. The supply was, however, extended to the new church completed in 1869.

Ellesmere Port's return to prosperity was marred by estuarial troubles. The shifting Mersey channel occasioned delays and groundings, and the tidal basin was badly silted by 1863. Various remedial schemes were aired, including the diversion of the Rivacre Brook, the complete removal of Pool Hall Rocks, and a revival of the proposed canal extension to Netherpool. So desperate was the situation the SURC in 1870 bought a strip of land along the Mersey shore for the canal extension. The opposition of R. C. Naylor of Hooton Hall, however, quashed this venture. A new entry into deep water was therefore cut, and was immediately successful. By 1873 the depth of water at the tidal basin was 3 ft greater than in 1871.[37]

How far the canal port would have been able to sustain its boom if the MSC had stopped short at Runcorn Gap is debatable. The SURC ably petitioned against this early scheme after the 1883 plan, which had revived an earlier scheme for a Dee–Mersey ship canal through Ellesmere Port, had been abandoned.[38] The arrival of the MSC provoked a revolution in the form and function of Ellesmere Port of far greater magnitude than that stimulated by the BLJ sixty years before.

Before ocean-going vessels first gained improved access to the canal port in 1911 the SU had begun to pursue a publicity campaign, emphasizing the advantageous situation of the port in relation to major industrial and commercial areas. Good relations with the MSC ensured the provision of wharfs and a layby, while vessels of up to 400 tons were allowed to use the ship canal up to Ellesmere Port free of charge.[39] Between 1892 and 1912 about £170,000 was invested in the port. During 1882–4 almost all the warehouses east of the tidal basin had been erected, their functional nomenclature (Fig. 9) emphasizing the heavy traffic in iron, pottery goods, and grain. The

G

greatest change, however, was the substitution of the MSC for the Mersey as the dock frontage. West of the North Pier a quay wall 1800 ft long was built to enable vessels of up to 4,000 tons to lie alongside in 24 ft of water. The rail tracks left by the ship canal contractors were bought, paving the way for the abolition of the horse tramway. Much land was also bought between 1891 and 1914 in anticipation of a building boom, and in 1895 the SURC land available 'for future extensions' was far larger than the whole dockland of 1885.[40]

Ellesmere Port received its full share of the migration of industry to the MSC's banks. East of the town a 350 ft × 70 ft dry dock was created by a private company, while a timber yard and creosoting plant were laid out to the west. In 1898 a copper smelting works was built on land adjoining both canals, the site being taken over by a cement works in 1912. Grain milling interests soon recognized the possibilities of a ship canal site. The three mills which arrived in Ellesmere Port in 1903–6 had all previously operated in interior areas served by the SURC, and retained their inland markets by using the canal. Waterfront sites at the canal port proved cheaper than at other points because of the SURC's special lease agreements, and grain storage facilities were provided in the form of a six-storey warehouse opened on the North Pier in 1899. All three mills were placed together west of the main dock; the SU then ran a narrow barge dock along their Mersey frontage and railway sidings along the other. Such direct handling facilities could not be ignored.

The above-mentioned industries were influenced in their seaport location by the development of transoceanic sources of raw materials. The arrival of the Wolverhampton Corrugated Iron Company (WCI) in 1905, however, was determined by changes in both sources and markets. Raw steel, increasingly obtained from South Wales or price-cutting Belgian cartels, arrived cheap at Britain's western coastline, especially where seaport dues could be avoided. Further, as much of the galvanized sheet production was exported via Liverpool, Ellesmere Port's cheap canal-side sites proved ideal. Railways were reluctant to transport the characteristically small loads of finished sheets, while a coastal site also saved the long haul and back haul of raw steel and finished goods between the coast and the Midlands. The siting of the new plant near Burnell's mill reemphasized the advantages of a position alongside both rail and canal lines. Somewhat different was the establishment of an indigo factory on marshland east of the port. The firm chose the MSC site in view of its bulky raw material imports, proximity to an already established chemical area, and ease of product transfer to the Pennine textile zone by both water and rail.

By 1910 the two metal firms were employing about 2,000 workers. Between 1902 and 1911 the town's population rose by over 153 per cent, largely because of immigration from the Wolverhampton area. Although 802 houses rose in the short period 1901–14 to accommodate this immigrant contingent, overcrowding became an established feature of the town.[41] Housing was taken in hand by the industrialists themselves and the availability of land conditioned its development. The MSC having purchased much of the area to the east of the town and a large parcel to the west, the only means of expansion north of the railway was to infill the interstices between SURC and MSC property.

Compared with this uncontrolled piecemeal growth, development south of the line was a planned entity. One of the largest and most modern mills in Britain at the time, the WCI was faced with an acute housing demand from the 60 per cent of its workers who migrated with it. Congestion to the north being apparent, the WCI, the sole industrial concern located south of the railway, decided to provide housing nearby. A series of streets, gridded to run parallel with and transversely to the railway, were laid out in the years immediately before the Great War, though this conflict prevented the estate's complete realization. Despite such improvements, however, the lack of overall urban planning was apparent, and Ellesmere Port soon gained a reputation as the Wirral's 'most objectionable and untidy symbol of the industrial era'.[42]

Shops and public houses multiplied to meet the needs of the expanding populace. In the eight years before 1910 three new schools were built north of the railway, though new churches, perhaps more sensitive to demographic trends, were built to the south. The old canal port town, however, was the recipient of most of the new facilities: banks; the local cooperative (1899) and building (1906) societies; music hall (c.1908); and library (1910) were all located along Station Road, connecting Whitby Locks Station with Dock Street. Only with the removal of the horse tramway in 1896 was the east frontage of this street developed, and for some years a curious contrast of development and building style was apparent between its two sides.

Though the proportion of the town's population supported by the SURC quickly fell below the 95 per cent of 1855, the company vied with the Marquis of Westminster and the LNWR in providing donations for parsonages, local societies, school extensions, and other schemes until long after this date.[43] During the seventies and eighties the company was active in many spheres. In 1893–7 streets near the docks were finally made up and after years of pleas gas provided to areas outside the SU estate. In 1902, however, Ellesmere Port and Whitby UD was created, and the parishes of Overpool, Netherpool, Stanlow and Great Stanney added in 1910. The SURC had little influence on urban development and organization in the new century, except in its estate in what was becoming known as the 'old town'. Though in this area canal company paternalism remained a vital force until the Great War, overall influence had been lost through the influx of new industries and a large body of immigrants with little knowledge of either local or SU traditions.

Goole

Unlike the earlier canal port towns, Goole was given little opportunity to develop fully as a canal-river transhipment point before the intervention of railways. Goole had been in existence merely three years when railways first began clamouring for entry; fourteen years after its foundation the port's role had apparently been usurped by railway links between Leeds and Hull.

With its excellent position, Goole was a natural goal for early railroads, which recognized the value of ports at the effective limit of inland navigation for coasters. The confused relationship between the AC and the railways has been explored elsewhere.[44] Briefly, a large number of railway projects appeared during two distinct bursts of activity coinciding with the national manias, and pursued routes towards the Ouse so similar as to suggest 'a repetitive pattern guided by persistent geographical influences'.[45] Almost all were planned as branches from the basic West Riding railnet whose major lineaments were apparent by the later 1830s.

The battle for railway access to Goole can be seen in terms of a three-way convergence (Fig. 19). From 1829 a series of lines repeatedly failed to extend down the Don valley, despite the obvious commercial and topographical advantages of such a route. Schemes for lines from the lower Trent valley after 1845 also failed to materialize for a considerable period. The third line of convergence saw the most intense competition. From 1829 demands for direct west–east links between Goole and the industrial West Riding, and thence with Lancashire, had the support of powerful interests, not least certain AC directors.

As early as 1836 the AC directorate, with the recent revival of Selby in mind, concluded that to oppose railways blindly would be to invite ruin, whereas the selective encouragement of the five railway projects then aiming to terminate at the Ship Dock might easily help establish Goole's position as a port. In every case the AC reserved the right to construct the terminal portions of any lines reaching the edge of its Goole estate. Its determination to remain uninvolved outside the estate is seen in its refusal to consider the Doncaster and Goole Railway's proposal for an AC-owned Goole–Newbridge line 'common to all such Railways as shall come from the South, West or North, in order to avoid a collision between the rival railways'.[46] When, however, companies such as the Manchester Leeds and Goole attempted to acquire powers to take up land on the AC estate 'contrary to previous understandings', the AC's powerful parliamentary lobby proved an insuperable opposition.

While sporadic schemes along the Aire and Don valleys continued to seek sanction, the AC, shaken by the costs of opposition, began the first of a series of prolonged negotiations with connecting Pennine navigations in an effort to present a united front against the mounting railway attack. Little came of this move, or of the AC's revival of the plan to connect its canal with the Dutch River for access to South Yorkshire. By 1844 the railway had gathered strength for a fresh attack, in the face of which the AC determined to accept the 'most advantageous' of the 'numerous plans which have been projected for connecting the port of Goole with some of the neighbouring railways'.[47]

In 1845 four major companies contested the right to open up Goole to railborne Pennine traffic. All had strong Manchester connexions. The AC records make the mechanics of this crucial time of decision-making fairly clear, three alternative policies being open to the directors. Total opposition was ruled out as 'hopeless of success' and likely to damage Goole in view of recent rail connexions to the rival ports of Grimsby, Gainsborough, and the Hartlepools. Support for the least objectionable line was rejected on the grounds that there was no way of knowing which Bill would gain parliamentary support. The third course, 'to allow them fair and equal chances, restricting opposition to a defence of rights on the Goole estate' was therefore pursued by default.

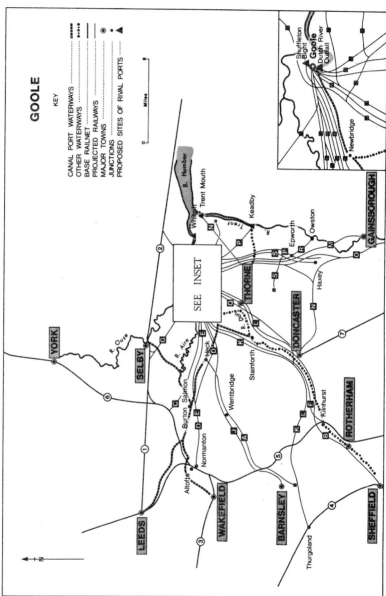

FIG. 19. Goole in the Railway Age

KEY

Base railnet:

1. Leeds and Selby Railway (constructed 1830–4).
2. Hull and Selby Railway (1836–40).
3. Manchester and Leeds Railway (1836–41).
4. Sheffield, Ashton and Manchester Railway (1837–45).
5. North Midland Railway (1837–40).
6. York and North Midland Railway (1836–40).
7. Great Northern Railway (1896–9).

Railways projected to Goole 1830–1910:

A. Heck and Wentbridge (1826, 28).
B. Sheffield and Goole (1830).
C. Burton Salmon to Goole (1836).
D. Manchester, Leeds and Goole (1836, 37).
E. Wakefield, Pontefract and Goole (1844; constructed 1845–8).
F. Doncaster, North Midland and Goole (1836, 37, 39).
G. Selby to Goole (York and N. Midland, 1844; constructed 1903–10).
H. Goole to Newbridge (1836, 44).
J. Manchester, Barnsley and Goole (1844).
K. Goole, Doncaster and Sheffield and Manchester Junction (1844).
L. As K, with line change and branch (1845).
M. Axholme, Gainsborough and Goole (1846).
N. South Yorkshire Railway's Axholme Extension (1851).
O. Great Northern Railway's Axholme Extension (1847).
P. Goole, Haxey and Keadby (1865).
Q. A series of Doncaster to Goole projects from railway mania to the North Eastern Railway's Thorne–Staddlethorpe Branch (constructed 1863–9).
R. Goole, Epworth and Owston (1883).
S. Goole and Marshland Light Railway (constructed 1898–1909).

Despite the efforts of both rival railways and threatened canals, the Wakefield, Pontefract and Goole Railway (WGPR), with Manchester and Leeds backing, obtained an Act in 1845.[48] That the successful line should be the one which most nearly duplicated the route of the AC waterways is not surprising in view of the powerful interests supporting it.[49] Moreover, the line, following the path of the heaviest west–east traffic, was more likely to aid the development of Goole than the trans-Pennine canals, created too late and on too small a scale, and by this time partially under railway control.

As if confident of its forthcoming twenty-year rail monopoly of Goole, the WPGR began to assert itself. Early in 1846 the company demanded a branch line to the tideway at Shuffleton Bight, outside the AC estate. Besides this threat, the AC became apprehensive lest the railway should avoid its docks altogether by terminating on the canal side outside the estate and, by arrangement with a local landowner, use the latter's right to erect wharfs and ply boats into the Ouse free of charge. Only after an intense struggle did the AC obtain restrictive clauses, while it also purchased land at Shuffleton 'so as to effectively secure it from the hands of a Rival'.[50] The price paid for the preservation of the AC's transhipping monopoly was the construction of a fourth dock for railway use (Fig. 12). The rival port bogey was raised by other companies in 1845, 1851 and 1883, and as late as 1913 the WPGR's successor, the Lancashire and Yorkshire Railway (LYR) was considering the excavation of docks at Old Goole.[51] Only the onset of the Great War prevented the establishment of this rival railway port south of the Dutch River.

Both the LYR line, its Aire Street station and the Railway Dock were opened in 1848. Fears of violent competition between rail and canal were dispelled by an intercompany agreement which gave the railway effective control of the textile traffic through Goole. Agreements, however, broke down in the fifties on account of what the AC regarded as the railway's 'gross irregularity, not to call it by a harsher name'.[52] The subsequent rate war was wholly detrimental to the navigation. By 1855 the AC was begging the South Yorkshire Railway to make Goole its coal port, and in the following year the company reached its nadir by considering a proposal to lease or sell the navigation jointly to the LYR and the North Eastern Railway (NER).[53] Only spirited action on the part of a hard core of proprietors and intercompany dissension among the railways enabled the AC to retain its independence.

Thoroughly chastened by this experience, the company could offer only feeble opposition to the construction of a link line to shorten the rail distance between Doncaster and Hull (Fig. 19). Forced upon the NER by powerful competitors, this line was completed in 1869, providing Goole with its long delayed Don valley connexion, its second and principal station outside the AC estate, and a major engineering achievement in the swing bridge over the Ouse at Hook.[54] A Trent valley line was not provided until the construction of the Goole and Marshland Light Railway system at the turn of the century. A short line from Selby, built largely to avoid congestion on the main West Riding lines to Hull, was completed in 1910–12, seventy-seven years after its first proposal. Thus at least two of the four railways which finally emerged from the welter of proposals were lines which simply passed through Goole on their way to Hull.

The LYR, initially kept out of Hull by the manoeuvres of the NER, was thus led to develop Goole as its major east coast outlet. Under this competitive stimulus the AC was able to emerge from the doldrums of the fifties into a period of continuous improvement, including leasing the Barnsley (1854) and CH (1865) canals. The losses incurred in running these were more than made up by the channelling of traffic, particularly Barnsley coal, on to the AC system. As textiles became a railway staple and grain imports fell off after the 1850s, coal increased in importance as a staple canal commodity. Between 1850 and 1870, while Selby's coal export declined slightly, and that of Hull increased only by a third, Goole's coal traffic rose threefold to a volume over 75 per cent that of Hull. With its new NER link, however, which also speeded the demise of passenger services on the Ouse, Hull was able to increase its coal exports from 193,000 tons in 1870 to 463,000 tons in 1879.[55]

Goole's eventual revitalization was largely due to the reorganization of AC management on an aggressive professional basis, after the shareholders' loss of confidence in the inept amateur directorate of the early fifties.[56] On the canal steam haulage was encouraged; between 1852 and 1858 the mileage covered and tonnage carried by steam-hauled boats more than doubled while the cost per mile fell by two thirds. Foreland connexions were revived, for in 1854 it was realized that 'it is indispensible to the future success of the Navigation that a communication by steam be established between Goole and the Continent'.[57] However, only with the foundation of the Goole Steam Shipping Company (GSS) in 1864, backed by both AC and LYR, did continental liner services, after three decades of false starts, finally get under way.

The most important single improvement of this period can be ascribed

to W. H. Bartholemew, the engineer-manager who was largely
responsible for the AC's progressive policies in the late nineteenth
century.[58] As early as 1842 the mode of transhipping waterborne coal at
Goole was being reconsidered, and became a major issue with the
establishment of a waggon tip system by the LYR. In the early sixties,
amid a mass of improvements to docks, timber ponds, and towing and
hauling operations, Bartholemew developed the compartment train
system. Based on railway principles, and reminiscent of the tub-boat
trains of the Shropshire and Shrewsbury canals, the system originally
consisted of groups of six steel compartments which were pushed from the
rear. As later developed, and still in operation, the compartment boat
train involves the organisation of up to nineteen rectangular steel barges
or 'tom puddings' into an amphibious goods train. By this means a crew of
four was able to carry up to 1,200 tons of coal. At Goole hydraulic lifts,
hoisting each compartment from the water, tipped its contents into the
hold of a waiting collier. This cheap and efficient means of bulk mineral
transport enabled the AC to hold its own as a coal carrier, against intense
railway competition, until the Great War. Within fifteen years the
medium was carrying over one fifth of the coal passing through Goole,
and though in 1900 railborne coal accounted for 60 per cent of Goole's
coal export, compartment boats had reduced the rail:water ratio to
equality by 1913.

   Although coal carriage rarely accounted for more than one third of the
AC's revenue, in terms of tonnage and therefore of shipping, coal ranged
between 61 and 69 per cent of the whole traffic throughout the period. It
was a prospective increase in this enormous volume of coal traffic, never
less than a million tons annually after 1862, and contingent upon the
extension of railways linking Hull, Grimsby and Goole with the booming
concealed coalfield east of Doncaster, which led to a renewed burst of
improvement of the AC dock system from the 1870s (Fig. 12). The
construction of Aldam Dock (1882), Victoria River Lock (1888),
Stanhope Dock (1891), Victoria Pier extension (1908), and finally South
and West docks (1910–12), more than doubled Goole's dock space, static
for a generation, in thirty years of construction. Further, the threat of a
revived plan to make Keadby a major South Yorkshire coal port forced
the AC's hand on the issue of a link between its canal and the Don system.
Proposed since 1828, the New Junction Canal of 1905 gave the prolific
coalfield a ready outlet by compartment boat to the expanding Goole
docks.

   In conjunction with hinterland and foreland developments,

improvements to the Ouse at Goole had been made in the sixties. However, the progressive extension of the GSS fleet and the increasing coal and textile exports with their corresponding imports, demanded a radical reappraisal of the Ouse as a seaway. To cope with this unprecedented traffic, and partially in response to what might be called a minor ship canal mania on the part of Leeds and Sheffield, Bartholemew engineered the Lower Ouse Improvement scheme, on a scale wholly new to that river. The Act of 1884 made the AC conservator of the Ouse between Hook and Trent Falls, and the provision of a trained channel towards the latter point continued well into the twentieth century.[59]

The first decade of river improvement alone cost the AC £274,495, but whereas before the improvement a 500-tonner was considered large, in the 1890s vessels of 2,000 tons could reach the port along a channel some 3 ft deeper at low tide. The gradual upswing of foreign trade became a boom at the turn of the century; in the period 1865–1904 the number of foreign vessels entered rose from about 400, of 70,000 tons, to 1,360, of 555,000 tons. In a similar period the tonnage both entered and cleared coastwise rose nearly fivefold. While the registration of sailing vessels fell dramatically, the tonnage of registered steam craft of over 50 tons burden increased fiftyfold between 1845 and 1904. A similar expansion occurred in the registration of canal boats at Goole, which rose from 400 in 1878 to 814 in 1899. In 1913, its peak year, the port of Goole handled 3,895,514 tons of traffic and 1,448,555 nrt of shipping.

With such a trade expansion after the crisis of the 1850s, Goole became a major immigration centre. Only once did the decennial rate of population increase, averaging about 30 per cent between 1852 and 1911, fall below the national urban rate. It was noted in 1901 that the rural district surrounding Goole had lost many of its young adults to the thriving port, the population of which rose rapidly from 4,618 (Goole and Hook) in 1851 to 20,916 in 1911.[60]

The corresponding extension of the built-up area came in the 1860s. A second 'New Town' was laid out north of the AC estate, while other subdivisions arose in Old Goole, towards Hook, and on the western side of the NER line. In these fields a uniform terraced pattern of red brick artisans' housing sprang up, accompanied by a market hall (1876), and a fire brigade and waterworks (1881–3). Between 1853 and 1894 eight journals and six places of worship were founded. Between 1900 and 1913 a further three churches followed the wave of buildings over the railway line to the west. At the core of the town five theatres, opened between 1887 and 1914, were founded on the same wave of prosperity which led the AC to pursue its extensive improvements and thus attract the necessary patrons.

Much of the urban expansion can be attributed to the AC's lack of foresight in the planning of new dock space. In its unsuccessful application for the position of sanitary authority for Goole under the Public Health Act of 1872, the company had stated that much land was available for dock extensions. The implementation of these extensions, however, involved the stopping up of streets, the cutting of railway lines, rendering useless the LYR station, and where the older docks were widened, the wholesale demolition of housing near the Dutch River bridge. A rough and ready species of slum clearance, this led to a housing shortage in the early twentieth century, relieved only by the hasty erection of terraces on the northern fringes of the town. Moreover, it was partially responsible for the characteristically misplanned nature of Goole, 'that grotesque combination of bricks and docks, railway crossings and green fields'.[61]

Only the industrial sector failed to expand after the 1870s, when the port had shipbuilding, ropemaking, flour milling, iron founding, and chemical and fertiliser interests, all dependent upon and located near the dock system. Though the AC had provided lavishly for Goole by establishing almost all of its early amenities from slaughterhouse to gas and water supplies, its failure to encourage industrial development was bitterly castigated by the local press. As late as 1888 the *Goole Times* was inveighing against the suppression of public opinion in the town, occasioned by the AC's position as chief employer.[62] But the UDC, its area constituted piecemeal from neighbouring townships in 1894, also made little progress in attracting manufacturers. In 1900, under the headline 'Goole's Greatest Need—Manufactories', the *Goole Times* poured scorn on its efforts and, debating how long the coal boom could last, prophesied the loss of youthful population to 'inland' centres should industry fail to appear.[63]

By 1913, though Goole was experiencing a prosperity never before known, with several busy near-Continental shipping lines and nine vice-consular agents, a growing uneasiness was apparent. Future expansion, though regarded as inevitable by most, was recognized by a perceptive few to be conditional upon the town's ability to free itself from AC control and expand its industrial sector: 'if Goole was not so much in the grip of a monopoly, and facilities were extended to fresh enterprises, the town would [continue to] grow with amazing rapidity'.[64] The general feeling, however, was still one of unbounded optimism, and the town's merchants and civic leaders were all too unfortunately sure that 'Goole and the Aire and Calder Navigation ought always to be found rowing in the same boat'.[65]

Port Development to 1913

Superseded by railways in the Age of Pioneers (1830–43), each canal port received its own railway in the Age of Interlopers (1848–69). Though dock branches were built, except for Goole direct railway projections to canal ports were few and unsuccessful. The four ports varied greatly accordingly to their potential for survival as canal-based ports in the new economic environment (Table V).

Table V
Canal Port Characteristics, 1851–1913

Characteristic	Runcorn	Stourport	Ellesmere Port	Goole
Little canal competition	X			X
Canal mainly 'wide'	X			X
Industrial canal	X	X		X
Major modern improvements	X			X
Active railway interest	X		X	X
Steam haulage on canal	X		X	X
No defecit (1909)	X	X	X	X
'Good condition' (1909)	X		X	X
Maximum draft (feet)	4	4	4	6
Max. load on canal (tons)	c.80	c.35	c.30	250
Max. load on river (tons)	15,000	140	15,000	2,000
Traffic on canal (1905, tons)	3,208,000	722,640	605,161	2,810,988
Net revenue (1905, £)	n.a.	5,165	6,765	111,511
Lock ratio (miles per lock)	2·93	1·04	1·48	2·33
Circuity index (canal)	1·39	1·27	1·68	1·11
Circuity index (superseding railway)	1·03	1·13	1·32	1·04

Sources: Royal Commission (1909), Saner (1906).

Clearly, the vitality of Runcorn and Goole, given efficient management, contrasted strongly with the likelihood of Stourport's becoming moribund.

Attempts were made with varying success to stem the rerouting of traffic onto rails by means as various as canal improvement, steam towing, carrying, river improvement, ship canal plans, and attempts to overcome inter-canal jealousies in the pursuit of through rates. Each port experienced periods of estranged relations with rail-served ports downriver. While Goole survived a series of projected rivals, Stourport slowly succumbed to lower Severn competition. On the Mersey the general principle of downstream port succession was reversed by the MSC, which carried off a great part of the former low class traffic between Runcorn and Manchester, and gave an edge to Weston Point's competition in the Runcorn Gap area. Nearly all the traffic between the Potteries and Liverpool remained waterborne, however, up to 100,000 tons per annum passing through Runcorn. Despite the GWR's assertion of 'a fair traffic' at Runcorn in 1905, on the Bridgewater Canal coal movement had almost ceased, and it was said that neither the Bridgewater fleet nor the byetraders were able to make ends meet. Coal had become the principal commodity passing through Stourport 225,000 tons being handled in 1905. By 1913, however, at Stourport, pleasure boats were once again beginning to outnumber trading craft. A similar amount of coal reached Ellesmere Port which, as a free port, had built up a small trade by 150–300 tonners with the Mediterranean and Southern Ireland.[66]

The AC fared best largely by using characteristically railway techniques, as compartment boats were thought to be, an idea no doubt uppermost in Fay's mind when he declared: 'the Aire and Calder is like one of the ordinary railway companies'.[67] Certainly the trade figures for the port, as for Runcorn on a far smaller scale, showed an overall upswing through the period. While Goole's coasting was restricted mainly to the south and east coasts, two thirds of Runcorn's coastwise trade was divided equally between Ireland and the South West. In foreign traffic, Goole's overwhelming concentration on the North Sea trade was an extreme case of the overall emphasis on short-sea Continental trading, especially after the loss of Runcorn's American trade to Manchester after 1894 (Table VI)

Table VI
Orientation of Foreign Trade, 1913 (per cent)

Foreland	Runcorn (1894)	Runcorn	Ellesmere Port	Goole
Near Continent	30·04	50·00	95·07	63·64
Scandinavia	18·18	30·77	2·11	27·28
Iberia	3·04	11·54	1·41	4·54
North America	48·48	7·69	1·41	4·54

Source: Sampling of daily Bills of Entry

Unlike Runcorn, Goole feared no usurpation of its function by inland centres, even though the first seagoing steamer reached Leeds through enlarged AC locks in 1901. While the LYR-owned GSS line operated almost 67 per cent of all ships using Goole, the AC relied increasingly on the home and foreign demand for coal. The intimate link between total canal tonnage, the volume of coal carried, and compartment boat traffic found direct expression in the population growth rate of Goole, which tended to fluctuate in phase. Like Runcorn, but unlike Stourport and Ellesmere Port, Goole became one of Britain's major canal boat registration points. Of the four canal ports, Stourport alone failed to extend its dock system after mid-century. At the other extreme, Goole provided the clearest indication that traditional canal-based ports might possibly survive well into the Motor Age.

8. Notes

1. Report of Board of Trade Railway Department, *PP*,XXXIX (1845) p. 359.
2. R. E. Leader, *History of the Company of Cutlers in Hallamshire*, Cutlers' Company, Sheffield (1905), p. 177.
3. F. C. Mather, 'The Duke of Bridgewater's Trustees and the Coming of the Railways', *Transactions, Royal Historical Society* Fifth Series 14 (1964), 131–54.
4. G. O. Holt, *A Short History of the Liverpool and Manchester Railway*, Railway and Canal Historical Society, Caterham (1965), pp. 15, 17.
5. F. C. Mather, *After the Canal Duke*, Oxford University Press, Oxford (1970).
6. 'Runcorn Group' report, BTHR (London) Gen. 4/210 (1860).
7. J. Dumbell, *A Letter Relative to a Bridge at Runcorn*, (1813), pp. 5, 16.
8. F. C. Mather, 'The Duke of Bridgewater's Trustees', . . . op. cit., p. 141; Cheshire CRO: deposited plan QDP 86.
9. Report of Board of Trade Railway Department, loc. cit.
10. BTHR (London) Gen. 4/210 (1864–7).
11. H. Booth's letter to the LNWR, BTHR (London) Gen. 4/210 (21 March 1859).
12. W. Marsh, *Excursionist's Second Guide to Runcorn*, (1871), p. 6; Cheshire CRO: deposited plan DDX 172/1.
13. *Chester Courant* (10 June 1863).
14. D. W. F. Hardie, *A History of the Chemical Industry in Widnes*, I.C.I., London (1950), p.64.
15. Reports of the Alkali Inspectorate, *PP*,XXIII (1860) to XX (1890).
16. B. Leech, *History of the Manchester Ship Canal*, Sherratt and Hughes, Manchester (1907);
    D. Fairhall, 'The Manchester Ship Canal', *Geographical Magazine* 35 (1962), 32–46;
    N. Y. Oldham, 'The Manchester Ship Canal', *Geographical Journal* 3 (1894), 486–91.

17. S. Mountfield, *Western Gateway: The History of the Mersey Docks and Harbour Board*, Liverpool University Press, Liverpool (1965) p. 58.
18. Reports of the Alkali Inspectorate, *PP*,XIX (1891) onwards.
19. J. Murray, (publisher), *Murray's Handbook for Shropshire and Cheshire*, London (1879), p. 159.
20. J. Rochard, *Runcorn, Frodsham and Helsby Illustrated*, Gravesend (1913?). p. 3.
21. Poor Law Report, *PP*,XXXVIII (1898–9), 214.
22. *Runcorn Guardian* (2 May 1903).
23. STW 1/6 (12 December 1844).
24. STW 1/6 (24 December 1844).
25. STW 1/6 (16 September 1845).
26. STW 1/6 (2 March 1846).
27. *Berrow's Worcester Journal* (1 February 1862).
28. Griffiths (1862), quoted in I. L. Wedley, *Old Stourport*, Kidderminster (1912), p. 8.
29. STW 1/7 (1 September 1853, 11 August 1856, 4 February 1864).
30. STW 1/8 (7 April 1893).
31. J. Randall, *The Severn Valley*, Randall, Madeley (1882), p. 428.
32. J. Noake, (publisher) *Guide to Worcestershire*, London (1868), p. 428.
33. STW 1/6 (4 February 1847).
34. MOH report, Stourport (1901).
35. GWR and LNWR joint minutes (30 March 1860), quoted in T. W. Roberts, *The History and Development of Ellesmere Port from 1785*, unpublished M.S., Ellesmere Port Public Library (1960), p. 66.
36. P. Sulley, *The Hundred of Wirral*, Haram, Birkenhead (1889), p. 158.
37. T. W. Roberts, op. cit. Ch. 5, *passim*.
38. SURC 1/37 (14 May 1844).
39. B. Leech, op. cit., Vol. 2, p. 112.
40. SURC 1/37 (14 August 1891–27 February 1914).
41. MOH reports, Ellesmere Port, (1910–14).
42. E. H. Rideout, *The Growth of the Wirral*, Bryant, Liverpool (1927), p. 30.
43. SURC 1/7 (9 September 1873).
44. J. D. Porteous, 'A New Canal Port in the Railway Age: Railway Projection to Goole 1830–1914', *Transport History*, 2 (1969), 25–47.
45. J. H. Appleton, 'The Railway Network of Southern Yorkshire', *Transactions, Institute of British Geographers*, 22 (1956), 159–69.
46. ACN 1/9 (26 October 1836).
47. Auditor's report, ACN 1/28 (5 August 1844).
48. *Railway Times* (1 January 1848), p. 19, (29 January), p. 112.
49. G. G. Hopkinson, 'Railway Projection and Construction in South Yorkshire and North Derbyshire 1830–50', *Transactions, Hunter Archaeological Society*, 9 (1964), 8–26.
50. Auditor's report, ACN 1/28 (3 August 1846).
51. *Goole Times* (11 April 1913).
52. Auditor's report, ACN 1/28 (6 August 1855).
53. ACN 1/10 (15 September 1856).
54. G. G. MacTurk, *A History of the Hull Railways*, Hull Packet Office (1880), p. 148; BTHR (London) LIB 4/55.
55. W. W. Tomlinson, *The North Eastern Railway*, Kelley, New York (1967), p. 705; *Railway Times* (29 January 1848), p. 112.

56. *Goole and Marshland Gazette* (13 September 1856).
57. ACN 1/10 (28 August 1854).
58. *Yorkshire Post* (20 November 1919).
59. B. F. Duckham, *The Yorkshire Ouse*, David and Charles, Newton Abbot (1967), Chapter 7.
60. MOH report, West Riding of Yorkshire (1901).
61. *London Daily Dispatch* (6 August 1900).
62. *Goole Times* (27 July 1888).
63. *Goole Times* (6 April, 14 September 1900).
64. *Goole Times Almanack*, Goole (1912), p. 88.
65. *Yorkshire Post* (9 January 1903).
66. *Royal Commission on the Canals and Inland Navigations of the United Kingdom* (1907–9) III, p. 14 question 21876, p. 15 qu. 11888, p. 101–3 qu. 20300–9, p. 176 qu. 23160, p. 504 qu. 23917–8: V, p. 23 qu. 33437, p. 24 qu. 33454.
67. Ibid., III, p. 123 qu. 21045–50.

9

Canal Ports in the Motor Age, 1918–73

> The remarkable development of the internal combustion engine during the present century has not only revolutionized road transport but has completely altered the whole economic situation.
>
> Royal Commission on Transport, 1930

The phenomenal growth of road transport after World War I was responsible for a second downgrading of the role of the canal in Britain's internal transport system. Road transportation rivalled rail as Britain's major carrying medium by 1939, and the railways responded with drastic reorganization and rationalization. In contrast, the canal system remained substantially unchanged after 1918, for the continued decline of canal traffic meant less even to the canal ports than had the rise of the railways a century before. In the Motor Age the canal ports' possession of four modes of internal transport, estuarial, canal, rail, and road, gave them potential advantages in terms of future growth possibilities.

Runcorn

During World War I the chemical and tanning industries of Runcorn expanded, though foreign dock traffic was severely reduced. In the general postwar boom, however, foreign trading through Runcorn revived rapidly. Imports exceeded the value of £1 million for the first time in 1918; thereafter port traffic in general followed the national trend, and exports failed to reach £160,000 in any one year until 1945.

In tonnage terms Runcorn docks did not follow the regular upward trend of the parent ship canal. A small traffic in both directions in the

1930s, 73 per cent of all exports being coal, was reduced by two-thirds in World War II, and had failed to recover to even half the prewar level by the early 1950s (Table VII).

Table VII
Runcorn: Total Imports and Exports 1932–62 (tons)

Movement	1932	1942	1952	1962
Import by vessel	64,703	20,931	16,512	117,953
Import by barge	10,886	4,877	18,872	2,021
Export by vessel	19,364	6,062	8,726	53,126
Total	94,953	31,870	44,110	173,100

Source: MSC Company, Bridgewater Department

Moreover, the partial recovery in imports was almost wholly due to barge traffic; coastwise pottery materials, almost 74 per cent of all imports in 1932, had fallen to less than 50 per cent in 1952, by which time the eight import categories of 1932 had been reduced to a mere three. Indeed, after World War II the basis of Runcorn's traffic was radically altered. Conscious both of the increasing road haulage of pottery goods and of growing congestion in Liverpool, the MSC successfully redeveloped the seemingly redundant Runcorn by encouraging general cargo continental shipping. Exports, wholly chemicals in 1952, rose sixfold in the following decade with the resumption of salt exports as the major item (57 per cent). In the same period imports became more diversified in their sevenfold rise covering fourteen major categories. Wholly new imports, notably synthetic rubber and plastics, accounted in 1962 for about 57 per cent of the traffic handled, while pottery goods, 20 per cent of all imports, persisted at about one fifth of their 1900 volume.

Though the port remained viable, the original canal did not. The impact of road haulage, the failure of bye-traders, and the non-replacement of an aging barge fleet led to a general reduction in canal traffic. Revived usage in World War II, however, encouraged the parent company to replace the wooden fleet, 200 strong, with 25 larger steel craft. In the late 1960s these still carried about 150,000 tons annually, mainly bulk cargoes within the Manchester area. Of 33,400 tons of feldspar and clay, making up 60 per cent of Runcorn's imports in 1956, only 10 per cent was forwarded up the lock flight to the Potteries by narrow boat. A decade later this trade had deserted Runcorn.

The figures of the canal inspectorate, recording an increase in canal boats registered at Runcorn from 1,116 to 1,162 between 1914 and 1939 cannot be taken at face value; half the registered boats were permanently out of commission.[1] Though the 473 inspections of 1937 revealed a transient canal population at Runcorn of 1292 adults and 946 children, the numbers fell rapidly after 1945 as boats were laid up. Up to 1939 traffic on the canal remained over one million tons annually, but had fallen to half this volume in the 1950s. Coal comprised 80 per cent of the traffic, and though the consumption of canal-borne coal by Runcorn industries doubled in the period 1947–54 to reach 34,000 tons, this was a temporary phenomenon.[2] Only the persistence of a very few boats kept inspection alive into the sixties: 'The number of Canal Boats passing through the Urban District during the year 1961 was probably the lowest recorded since the Bridgewater Canal was built'.[3] By 1962 canal traffic had practically ceased; company policy ended canal access to Runcorn docks. The 1960s saw the total eclipse of both traffic originating east of the port and of direct transhipping between estuary and canal; the closure of the second lock flight brought to an end Runcorn's era as a canal port:

Table VIII
Bridgewater Canal: Commercial Traffic at Runcorn 1961–6 (tons)

Traffic	1961	1962	1963	1964	1965	1966
Total Bridgewater Canal traffic	404,272	365,213	328,821	316,976	256,111	273,516
Coal to Runcorn Docks by canal	18,614	6,554	—	—	—	—
Canal traffic from Runcorn Docks	2,827	863	546	1,437	543	—
Total canal traffic through Runcorn Docks	7,540	5,637	17,286	26,173	26,949	14,398
Runcorn canal traffic as percentage of all Bridgewater traffic	7·2	3·6	5·4	8·7	10·7	5·3
Transit trade	26,981	13,054	17,832	27,600	27,492	14,398

Source: MSC Company, Bridgewater Department

After the passing of an Act in 1966 the MSC, despite strenuous opposition from canal interest groups, began to fill in all docks except Fenton, Alfred and Tidal Dock (now Francis), together with the Runcorn and Weston Canal and the second lock flight. This work was completed in 1971 except for Old Dock. The Preston Brook–Runcorn section of the Bridgewater Canal, its uses in the 1970s largely confined to the provision of industrial water and pleasure boating, now terminates abruptly at Top Locks. In 1973, 200 years after its inauguration, Runcorn remained a port, with a 70-acre dockland, but it was no longer a canal port. Inland conveyance, in the absence of canal connexion, is now undertaken by the Bridgewater Department's lorry fleet, a service begun in 1923. Numerous improvements have rapidly expanded Runcorn's trade, port traffic rising from 90,126 tons in 1960 to over half a million in the early 1970s.

Weston Point docks have remained more closely tied to their originating canal, though a traffic of over one million tons annually before 1913, falling to little over 30,000 tons in 1950, has today become the regular handling of about 500,000 tons. The port, now operated by the British Waterways Board (BWB), also resembles its former rival in its 7:3 ratio of imports to exports, the former again largely consisting of fertilizers, pottery materials, and general goods. Though capable of taking vessels of up to 1600 tons, the port is bypassed by smaller vessels, 400 tonners being able to penetrate up the Weaver as far as Winsford. The port's recent revival, however, partly due to redevelopment, closely resembles that of Runcorn and follows the national trend towards the increased use of small ports for general cargoes. In both ports heavy investment which revitalized traffic after the lean years of the early fifties may be directly related to the letting of the first contract for a trans-Mersey road bridge at Runcorn in 1956. Completed in the sixties, the high level viaduct has been placed in close juxtaposition to its railway predecessor, and now visually dominates the town (Fig. 20). The demolition of the singularly inadequate transporter bridge was permitted rather than necessitated by the new bridge.

The transport function of Runcorn, however, played only a minor role after 1918 as chemicals and tanning became the economic mainstays of the community. Their rise to prominence was emphasized by the decline of older trades such as quarrying, metal processing, boat building, and other port-related activities. With a combination of advantages which included efficient port facilities, cheap water carriage, adequate water supplies for processing and effluent disposal, and a trained labour force, tanning expanded in the inter-war period. Wholly located on the Bridgewater Canal, the industry took in hides and skins by water as late as the 1940s. Road transport became dominant after 1945 in view of the shortage of flats, their heavy soiling by this 'dirty cargo', and the need for

speedy delivery of the very small consignments produced. By the early 1950s only coal intake justified the canalside location. Moreover, the decline in demand for sole leather, together with the rise of synthetics, reduced the industry from three works with over 1000 workers in 1951 to a single plant with 270 workers in the later 1960s.

The sudden collapse of this staple industry enormously enhanced the already overwhelming importance of chemical manufacture. The conjunction of positional advantages, the MSC, brine piping, and the Castner process confirmed chlorine and caustic soda production as the basis of the array of chemical products emerging from Runcorn today, and in this sense the town retains the stamp of this particular stage in the development of the British chemical industry.

The increasing output of chlorine-based products, constant reorganization, and the proliferation of new processes and products demanded the constant construction of new works and extensions. In 1937 every major works in Runcorn and Weston was merged into the expanding Imperial Chemical Industries (ICI) complex. By 1945, with the final demise of the larger works along the Bridgewater Canal, this single company was operating six separate and highly complex factories in the Runcorn area, all orientated towards the MSC. The final confirmation of Runcorn's position as a major heavy chemical producer came with the creation of the ICI's Mond Division in 1964, accompanied by the construction of a large administrative and research complex on Runcorn Hill. Combining activities previously carried on at Liverpool, Widnes and Northwich, the hill top structure not only reaffirms Runcorn's nodal position in chemical manufacture but also symbolizes the economic and social domination of the town by a single firm. In 1966 35 per cent of the working population in the Runcorn Employment Exchange area was employed by ICI alone.

Despite this enormous interwar industrial expansion, Runcorn UDC produced biennially after 1917 a promotional handbook lauding the town's ability to provide cheap sites adjacent to railways, canals, and docks, with ready supplies of hard and soft water, Cheshire brine, local gas, electricity and industrial gases, an abundance of labour, especially female, and the availability of fine landscaped areas for residential

FIG. 20. An aerial view of Runcorn. The Bridgewater Canal, lined by industrial establishments, has been exposed by demolition for the Runcorn–Widnes roadbridge, which separates the railway bridge from the transporter bridge, now demolished. Remains of the duke's canal estate, now dwarfed by the Manchester Ship Canal operations, can be seen as waste land, far left.

development, notably around the natural park of Runcorn Hill. Most of the chemical developments had taken place east of Runcorn or in Weston, and the tendency for Runcorn's inhabitants to seek work outside the UD became an alarming trend before the town was able, in 1936, to annex an area far larger than itself, including Weston, 3000 people, and the major chemical works.

Until the late forties, local authority housebuilding languished and a rising population was partly accommodated by company housing erected by both tanning and chemical proprietors. ICI, for example, was compelled to extend a 500-dwelling housing estate at Weston Point. After World War II, however, both private and public house construction revived, and company housing began to be sold off. With a population a little under 30,000 in the late 1960s, Runcorn had become a major chemical centre and had shed most of its former role as canal port. Even greater changes were initiated in 1964, however, when the area was chosen for the site of Runcorn New Town. Work began in the late sixties on the first phase of a public transport based town in the shape of a figure eight. Designed to absorb Merseyside overspill population, the new city is expected to reach a population ceiling of about 100,000 in the 1990s.[4]

Stourport

During the Great War lack of labour and strong rail competition prevented the STW from working its waterway even to its much reduced capacity.[5] The retention of control by the Canal Control Commission until 1920, dissension among connecting canals, and a desire to raise tolls without resorting to a special Act, were among factors which influenced the STW's decision to seek the aid of the Ministry of Transport under the Transport Act of 1919. Accordingly, the company increased all charges by at least 100 per cent and made attempts to recover loans made since 1842 to both SCCC and Severn Commission. In 1921 the latter owed the STW £101,690, 57 per cent of its total debt.[6] But as Severn traffic improved with the growing distribution of oil, chocolate crumb, and other specialized commodities, the commission was able to pay off its arrears during World War II.

In terms of traffic the canal languished. Electrically-propelled barges and the inland carriage of oil products never became economic propositions. Coal continued to reach Wilden ironworks by water until the Hatherton Branch was closed in 1949 after nationalization. The carriage of coal to local electricity generating stations had almost ceased by 1944 in the face of both rail and road competition. Annual boat inspections at Stourport graphically illustrate the demise of canal traffic. From 69 in 1916–21, the number had fallen to a regular 13 between 1939 and 1948. In 1952 it was reported that 'the canal basins in Stourport are no longer used for commercial traffic'.[7]

Severn traffic to Stourport docks vanished with World War II. In 1937 the SCCC gave notice to quit warehouses at Stourport as its river craft could no longer ascend the river locks, while the warehouses themselves were unfit for modern use. Anxious to retain both docks and canal in use, the STW vainly proposed the construction of two new warehouses and a new barge lock, in return for the SCCC's taking up a long lease. In response to the SCCC's lack of enthusiasm the STW replied: 'Our hopes of the locks being used to continue traffic from the River to Wolverhampton were somewhat dashed by the insistence of your Company on a bridge which will carry twenty tons—by road!'[8] Equally vain attempts to interest oil companies in the docks were continued until World War II, when new wharfs at Diglis and the symbolic dropping of the word 'canal' from the title of the SCCC confirmed the demise of Stourport as a canal port. Dredging and lock renovation came to an end with the dissolution of the Ministry of War Transport. By 1944 so much material had been thrown into the canal by the crews of grounded boats that the maximum loading of coal boats was fixed at 2ft 11in. The STW was relieved to submit to nationalization in 1948.

Below Stourport, however, river wharfs flourished after 1928 when the petroleum industry's preference for the cheap coastwise shipping of products was extended up the Severn by the creation of depots at the effective head of navigation for estuarial craft. With the construction of water-fed wartime storage tanks a small oil wharfage zone emerged between Stourport and Lincomb, and further companies arrived after 1945 to take advantage of Stourport's unique situation for the cheap Midlands distribution of products brought from Avonmouth by 150 ton barges. This traffic increased in the 1950s, and was augmented by an extensive transhipping business operated by British Transport Waterways at nearby Nelson Wharf. Despite the competition of oil pipelines, a 50 per cent increase in Severn traffic occurred in the decade 1950–9, though this level of traffic was not long sustained.

Despite this retention of the transhipping function, however, Stourport as early as 1913 was clearly a manufacturing town, concentrating upon tanning, carpets, vinegar and metal processing. With the arrival of three large scale industries in the 1920s this manufacturing bias was further emphasized. In the early twenties the Shropshire, Worcestershire and Staffordshire Electric Power Company was seeking a site for a new generating station more centrally located within its extensive supply area than the original Smethwick plant. A site was chosen below the Severn–Stour confluence for ease of access to waterborne coal and water for condensing.[9] Opened in 1927, the plant was flanked by a second station in 1950, although further expansion was limited by site congestion and the capacity of the Severn to supply water.

Electricity supply was an ideal location leader, especially in view of the post-1918 trend for the dispersal of firms from congested urban areas to smaller towns. Soon after the completion of the first power station a large steatite firm moved to Stourport from London, the reasons for the move being cited as the availability of barge traffic, railway access, clean air, vacant flat land, a local labour pool, and the proximity of clay and coal supplies. The pull of Midland and northern markets for the gas fittings then produced was also important. The works now concentrates on insulators and refractories for the electrical industry. Removing from London in the early thirties, a wire and chain manufacturer became Stourport's third major employer. The establishment of these three large growth industries by the early 1930s, together with the consolidation of the carpet industry, was sufficient to unleash a mild boom at a time when much of the country languished in economic depression.

Since World War II Stourport has been invaded by numerous small firms whose major markets are in the Black Country. Flexible road transport, cheap power, and readily available vacant industrial sites have attracted these highly specialized linkage industries from the West Midlands conurbation. Perhaps the best summary of the factors influencing individual decisions to remove to Stourport is that of the manager of a small plant which left Kidderminster in 1956: 'pleasant location, availability of suitable labour, lower rates, ready access, and less general congestion than the neighbouring Black Country'. The latter area also supports Stourport via a regular seasonal inflow of holidaymakers, reflected in the concentration of gift shops and cafés in Severnside streets. A funfair, promenade, and pleasure cruisers cater for those who lack the cabin cruisers now occupying the former STW docks. After two centuries as a canal port, the Stourport dockland has totally reverted to its originally minor function as a resort.

The urban expansion which accompanied the industrial changes of the interwar period further emphasized Stourport's loss of its original canal port function. Despite local authority building, the steatite company was obliged to construct 142 houses which in 1929–30 accounted for nearly 85 per cent of all dwelling completions. Weekend cottages began to develop alongside the Severn, and from the 1950s holiday caravan sites were laid out. After 1945 Stourport expanded across the Severn with the development of a large council estate, which has been further developed to take Black Country overspill population.

In recent years the growth of light industry and tourism has tended to alter the character of Stourport. The 1960s saw increased emphasis on manufacture as water traffic became ever less important. Early in the decade the BWB leased off Nelson Wharf, for the most viable river trades, in timber and aluminium, were being carried privately. This traffic has now come to a halt. The transhipment of oil products also declined and finally ceased in the sixties as barge traffic gave way to pipeline and bulk rail movement. All three oil terminals below Stourport were eccentrically located with respect to the Midland terminals of the Thames–Mersey pipeline. At the former canal port's dockyard, the New Basin has been infilled to serve as a timber yard, and both the Tontine and the remaining warehouses are being converted into flats. With renovated locks, however, the remaining docks allow the passage of about 1300 pleasure craft per year, and provide moorings for 200 (Fig. 21). But more local employment is provided by the local prefabrication of materials for use in the motorway system.

Ellesmere Port

Between 1910 and 1950 the tonnage carried along the MSC increased over threefold, doubling in the 1940–50 period alone. In 1922 the ship canal company assumed sole control of the canal port, the original canal company having fallen upon evil times. Before World War I, almost all the half million tons carried annually on the SURC canal system was in the hands of the company, though methods remained traditional, horse haulage being everywhere the norm except upon the Wirral line. With higher costs and a marked fall in iron and pottery cargoes, the LNWR in 1921 felt no longer able to finance canal losses.[10] Amalgamating with the LNWR, the SU disposed of its effects at Ellesmere Port and disappeared from view. Forty years earlier this might have wholly destroyed Ellesmere Port; in the 1920s the loss was hardly noticed.

Private trading continued on the canal. Flour and steel firms retained

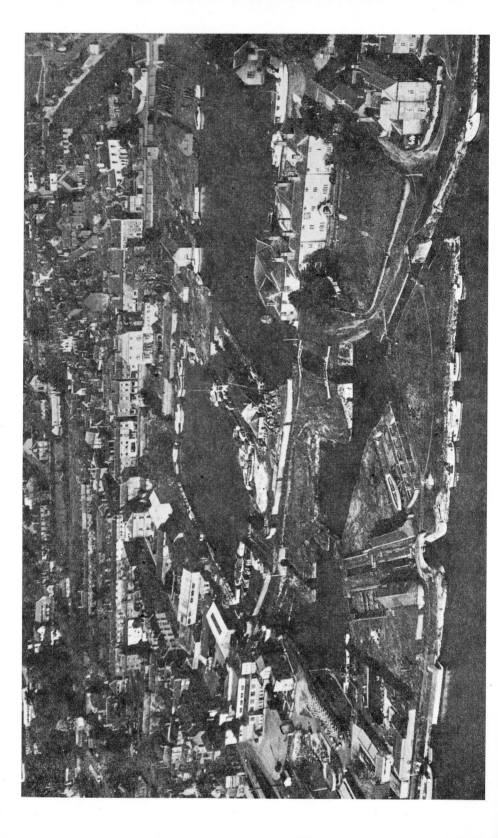

large fleets, but that of the latter was greatly reduced when barge traffic between Ellesmere Port and Shotton steelworks ended in the 1930s. By 1940 the volume of traffic had fallen by two thirds in a single decade. By 1949 neglect had resulted in silt accumulation to within 12in of the water surface of the main dock and the number of canal boats inspected had fallen from 103 in 1944 to 35. Two years later this tally had been reduced to 8.[11] The last regular traffic to the Midlands, in waste tar, came to an end in the late 1950s. Although grain continued to arrive by barge for a time, direct off-loading soon became the rule; the 10–15,000 ton grain trade of the 1960s ignored the derelict SURC docks. From the 1950s a few pleasure boats took up moorings in the silted inner docks, but only half sunken barges remain today. Telford's china clay and grain warehouses were demolished during the period 1971–2, at which time the infilling of New Dock Arm was begun. Of the original docks, only the Tidal Basin remains in use.

Like Stourport, Ellesmere Port by 1918 had become an industrial town, its growth owing a great deal to the perspicuity of the MSC in foreseeing national economic trends and its success in attracting a portion of Britain's newer industrial development to the ship canal. Oil traffic quickly rose to second place, after raw cotton, in the value of Port of Manchester imports. Clearly anticipating such an expansion, the MSC began to construct an oil dock as early as 1916. Oil importation demanded deepwater sites close to major markets but, in the interests of safety, at some distance from residential areas. The fortuitous conjunction of a solid sandstone outcrop at Stanlow, just above Ellesmere Port, with a large expanse of flat, vacant land provided the ideal site for oil dock construction (Fig. 9). Opened in 1922, the first dock was followed by a larger one in 1933, and the ship canal, deepened to 28ft throughout before World War I, in 1927 was excavated to 30ft from its Mersey outfall to Stanlow.

Such elaborate provision proved an overwhelming attraction for oil companies. Six companies established storage, blending, and distribution depots at Stanlow in the period 1922–33; in the latter year Lobitos built the first Stanlow refinery. But the MSC was in no way content to reorient Ellesmere Port's economy solely towards oil. The deepening of the ship canal allowed oceangoing ships of up to 15,000 tons to reach the

FIG. 21. An aerial view of Stourport. The canal (top right) terminates in an intricate dock system now occupied by fairground and pleasure boats. In the foreground is the Tontine Inn; at the further side of the docks the large houses of eighteenth century canal carriers face the fossil canal port.

refurbished port. In this connexion the MSC's policy of reserving canalside land for industrial use bore fruit in quantity. Soon after the second deepening of the canal the Bowater group, attracted by a 1000ft wharf below Ellesmere Port, established a large newsprint mill to serve the northern dailies. The arrival of oil and paper works more than offset the decline in cement, flour, and metal production which began in the depression. But the WCI and another steel firm, in part turning over to the production of containers for the oil industry, were still the dominant employers before 1939, providing 2400 jobs in comparison with 1306 in oil and 890 in paper.

Policies initiated before 1945, however, secured for oil refining the role of Ellesmere Port's staple industry. Strategic factors accounted for wartime expansion, and throughout the war years the Lobitos refinery processed the whole of England's domestic output. Moreover, the Petroleum Board laid pipelines between Stanlow and the Thames; these were later extended to form PLUTO by means of which, according to Lord Curzon, 'the Allies floated to victory on a wave of oil'. After the war the need for cheap redistribution of oil products by water and the national policy of developing Merseyside to balance Thames installations confirmed Ellesmere Port as an oil centre. Shell established a refinery at Stanlow in 1949. In the early 1970s its integrated oil and chemical complex covered over 2000 acres, and the company was using not only the two oil docks and Stanlow laybye, but also three large private wharfs, the whole capable of handling the annual cargo of 500 small tankers. By the early 1960s Stanlow refinery, with a capacity of over 10 million tons per annum, accounted for half Shell's British capacity and about one sixth of the total capacity of Britain. Ancillary industries, such as carbon black and detergents, together with electricity generation and a variety of other servicing occupations, created an industrial complex which became ever more intricate as the paper mill began to produce oil product containers and bitumenized pipes.

As the MSC was soon quite unable to take the larger oil tankers, the 19 acre Queen Elizabeth II dock, capable of taking four 30,000 ton vessels, was constructed at the ship canal entrance in 1954. Despite the growing size of tankers, foreign companies established oil depots at Stanlow in the early 1960s; Stanlow had become a going concern and it was sufficient for these companies that the area was 'oil-oriented'. Threatened by the advent of the super-tanker, Stanlow was later connected by pipeline with Tranmere, eleven miles below and capable of taking 65,000 ton vessels. Modern tankers of up to 200,000 tons will require a pipeline some 100 miles long from a deepwater 'single buoy mooring' terminal now under construction off Anglesey. Future expansion of refining at Ellesmere Port, however, may be limited. With national oil pipelines it has now become feasible to locate a super-refinery, with site and water requirements no greater than those of the Trent valley power stations, in the heart of the Midlands market.

The oil industry, despite future limitations, was chiefly responsible for the burgeoning growth of Ellesmere Port from a population of 18,911 in 1931 to over 60,000 in 1971. With 5,000 inward commuters in 1947 and 7,000 two years later, a desperate need for housing dominated the town.[12] Public housing was in some instances built specifically for a single firm, such as the Pooltown estate for the paper mill, but most new firms had at first to provide company housing. Indeed, the WCI began a model village at Wolverham, which was left half completed in 1926 with the onset of economic depression. In the late 1950s Ellesmere Port was designated a reception area for Liverpool overspill population, approval being given for the transfer of some 20,000 persons. This scheme has radically altered the economic and social life of what was previously regarded as an 'independent isolated industrial town'.[13] By 1959, when the first families were transferred, 8079 persons were entering Ellesmere Port daily to work, while 500 acres, largely owned by the MSC, remained available for industrial development.[14]

Some of this land was developed in 1961 when a further new industry was directed to Merseyside by government demands that new motor vehicle plant be located in areas of economic difficulty.[15] This in turn was to stimulate the growth of Ellesmere Port's port which, although owned jointly by the BWB and the MSC, is managed by the latter. Among other recent developments, a major car shipping terminal has been built. The continued attraction of the traditional centre of production, the West Midlands, confirmed Ellesmere Port as one of the three major Merseyside sites, with ample water supplies and a 393-acre site at Hooton Park. In its provision of direct employment for about 10,000 workers, the new works may further exacerbate the intense commuting inflow and urgent housing problems of the former canal port.

Goole

At the outbreak of the Great War Goole remained essentially a transport-based town. The enemy occupation of its foreland, together with the transfer of many of its vessels to government use, dealt the port a savage blow. A postwar boom in shipping, shared with most British ports, soon collapsed. The value of imports thereafter remained stable at about £12 million, while exports fluctuated between £11 and £20 million in the 1921–30 decade. Though annual imports between 1932 and 1939 were reduced to about half the value of those of the previous decade, exports continued at a fairly high level. Cotton piece exports slumped by almost two thirds in the period 1918–36, but coal shipments remained high. Yorkshire coal production was not as badly affected by the depression as that of other areas, and though foreign demands, accounting for half the shipments in the 1920s, declined in the following decade, the coastwise trade remained.

Though Goole did reasonably well in the interwar period largely because of this coal trade, the position of the AC Canal was not as favourable. With the diversion of rolling stock to other uses in the Great War, shipment of coal by compartment boat had accelerated to 50 per cent of Goole's intake. After 1926, however, a relative decline set in and throughout the thirties the railways carried about two thirds of the supply.

Despite improvements to its waterway system, the AC focussed its interest on its port at Goole. Although the amalgamation of near-Continental shipping lines plying also from Hull and Grimsby operated to the detriment of Goole in the 1930s,[16] the continuation of a fairly high level of export trade, the decline of sail and steam, and the increased size of colliers to 2000 tons, gave impetus to AC plans for dockland improvement. Its most ambitious scheme, for a central wet dock to be excavated to the east of the existing docks and north of the canal, was repeatedly urged in the 1920s as a means of revitalizing the port. The trading situation, however, was not deemed sufficient to warrant it, despite the assurance of a further coal source when a Thorne colliery company was persuaded in 1927 to ship its coal through Goole rather than via a light railway to a proposed Ouseside wharf.[17] Thus the dockland of 1913, with 39 acres of water in eight commercial docks surrounded by three miles of quays, remained almost unchanged in the modern period (Fig. 12).

The most substantial change was the opening in 1938 of an entrance lock planned by Bartholemew before World War I. Ocean Lock's dimensions, 375ft × 80ft, were sufficient to accommodate any vessel likely to use the lower Ouse, even if substantial improvements were made (Fig 22). After 1918 such improvements mainly consisted of the continuation of channel training schemes interrupted by the conflict. By 1926 the Trent Falls Improvement Act had become necessary; this measure empowered the AC and the Humber Conservancy to train the channels at the confluence of Ouse and Trent. Large scale improvement ended with World War II, for no further amelioration was possible without turning to the Humber itself. The sheer cost of improving the navigation of the latter has discouraged any such attempt, and Goole shipping thus remains subject to the difficulties involved in navigating tortuous channels.

The opening of Ocean Lock confirmed the AC's faith in Goole, which believed as late as 1938 that 'the road to real prosperity for the port was being finally trod'.[18] Hopes were rudely dashed with the blackout of lights on the Ouse during World War II. Nocturnal navigation being impossible, Goole suffered far more severely than in the previous conflict. A quick postwar recovery was made, however, and Goole was the first of the Humber ports to surpass its prewar volume of trade in the major commodities.[19] The export of manufactured goods was responsible for this, accounting for two thirds of the total value of the trade.

In terms of volume, however, Goole remained a coal port, a situation which was little changed by nationalization in 1948. Coal traffic peaked in 1953 when 2,448,238 tons were shipped, accounting for 93·9 per cent of Goole's exports and 83 per cent of all trade. Recent coal shipments have averaged about 1·5 million tons per annum, and the growth of imports has as yet reduced only slightly the position held by coal in the traffic statistics (Table IX).

Table IX
Trade of Goole by Volume, 1949–65 (Per cent)

Trade	1949	1965	Mean over period
Exports as percentage of all traffic	81·00	75·00	80·76
Coal as percentage of exports	82·60	90·50	89·79
Coal as percentage of all traffic	62·10	73·40	72·40

Source: British Transport Docks Board

The modern trend towards the use of small ports in the face of growing congestion and labour disputes in the larger has benefited Goole, always well known for its quick turn-round. Total traffic has exceeded 2 million tons annually since 1952, and imports, notably of timber which doubled in volume in the year 1965–6 alone, have played an increasingly

important role. This trend may be vital for the port's survival. As yet, however, the traditional trading pattern remains. Although vessels of over 2000 tons may use the port, in practice motor vessels of a few hundred tons dominate the traffic. Coastwise shipping, more than ever concerned with coal carriage, retains its established routes to east and south coast ports. Thirteen cargo liner services cover the near-Continental seaboard from Boulogne to Wismar, although two thirds of all sailings concentrate on Rotterdam and Amsterdam. Symbolically linking two major Common Market conurbations, a few small craft of less than 200 tons make the journey between Goole and the Ruhr.

Industrially, Goole has fared less well. The general malaise which overcame shipping during two wars, coal strikes, the loss of foreign markets, and the port quota system of coal shipment which adversely affected Goole in the 1930s, effectively arrested industrial development. Between 1918 and 1938 no new manufacturing plant of any size was located in the town, whose few industrial workers were wholly employed in pre-1913 works mainly linked with shipping. As these could not cater fully to the demand for non-port employment, workers began commuting between residences in Goole and industrial sites further afield.

The bridging of the Ouse at Boothferry in 1929 did not improve Goole's position, for the town was bypassed by road traffic running between Hull and industrial areas to south and west. In the 1930s 'the chief occupation of the inhabitants [remained] directly or indirectly connected with shipping'.[20] Highly sensitive to national economic trends, this overdependence plunged Goole into unemployment during the thirties, a situation only slightly ameliorated by the postwar establishment of several small firms and by a clothing factory directed to the town in 1947 in an attempt to diversify the employment structure. This factory has been especially valuable in providing female employment in a town where heavy manual labour had been at a premium for 120 years. The few light industries established since 1950 have had little impact on the overall port orientation of the town, and on the growing trend towards a daily efflux and reflux of labour. Locked into a paleotechnic economy, Goole's position in the early 1970s is one of unenviable stagnation.

This malaise is mirrored in the decline of Goole's population from over

---

Fig. 22. An aerial view of Goole. The dock system and canal lie immediately north of the Dutch River and shipyard. The Aire and Calder planned town fronting Ouse Dock, in which a compartment boat fleet is assembled, is now largely demolished.

20,000 in the period 1911–31 to 18,470 in 1966. Even with the inclusion of Hook, now physically contiguous with the larger settlement, the decline in the 1931–61 period was from 20,885 to 20,010. At no time since World War I has port traffic exceeded its peak of 3,895,514 tons (1913), and despite renewed efforts there has been a general failure to attract substantial industries unrelated to port activities or local agriculture. In part this springs from a basic antipathy between the aims of urban and port authorities. The latter, controlling the large vacant area formerly reserved for the abortive central wet dock, has not encouraged industrial development thereon. Situated at the heart of the dockland, this idle land is a symbol of Goole's present economic malaise. In contrast, Selby has expanded rapidly; its annual port traffic had reached well over half a million tons by the early 1970s.

Goole's future depends largely upon circumstances beyond its control. Despite the obvious viability of the AC system, which carried 3·4 million tons in 1965, the national docks board, in part because of the poor river approaches, has shown 'a lack of great confidence in the future expansion of Goole Docks'.[21] Recent developments include container berths and the infilling of the original basin of 1826 to serve as a car shipping terminal. Moreover, the port's major roles of coastwise coal exporter and distributor of manufactured goods to and from the near-Continent are threatened by modern Humberside developments. The Lancashire–Yorkshire motorway, now completed, will further enhance the position of Hull and Immingham at the expense of the Ouse port. Immingham in particular has arisen in the very period of Goole's decline and, handling more efficiently many of Goole's staple cargoes, enjoyed twice the commercial traffic of the older port as early as 1964. Plans to transfer coal exports by liner train to Immingham, and for a Humber bridge, implicitly involve robbing Goole of its remaining raison d'etre as a coal shipper and an inland import-distribution centre at the lowest bridgepoint on the Ouse.[22]

Port Development After 1918

Even before World War I, canal traffic was becoming a less potent force in the economic life of canal-created ports. Since 1918 the canal ports have been caught up in national trends based upon flexible motor transport, the rise of extreme industrial specialization, the governmental direction of industrial location, and the development of footloose light

Table X
Canal Port Characteristics, 1914–73

Facility	Runcorn	Weston Point	Stourport Docks	Stourport Riverside	Ellesmere Port Docks	Ellesmere Port Ship Canal	Goole
Docks commercially used 1973	3	2	0	0	0	2	8
Water acreage of docks, 1973	10	8	—	—	—	?	39
Substantial quayage	X	X			X	X	X
Maximum size of vessel (tons) taken by docks	2,000	1,600	—	—	—	15,000	2,400
.. by wharfs	12,500	12,500	—	150	15,000	15,000	2,400
Functioning dock railway						X	X
Maximum draft of vessels in docks (ft)	$17\frac{1}{2}$	15	—	—	—	$28\frac{1}{2}$	$17\frac{1}{2}$
Near-continental liner services							X
Canal still used commercially, 1973	X	X	X			X	X
Substantial use by pleasure craft	X	X		X			
Dock and wharf extensions, 1914–73	X			X	X		X
.. closures 1914–73	X	X	X		X		X
Downriver navigational improvements, 1914–73	X				X	X	X

X represents the existence of the characteristic.

industry. In view of these developments, each town has had at least some opportunity to shed its canal–river transhipping function, almost obsolete after 1918, in favour of a new economic orientation.

The capacity of the canal ports to retain their traditional port function changed significantly after 1914, as Table X indicates. Two trends are readily apparent. Stourport and Ellesmere Port, abandoning their original canal and dock space to pleasure craft, have sought to develop wharfage for specialized commodities along the banks of the major river or ship canal. Goole and Runcorn, in geographically analogous positions, have, on the other hand, modernized their old dock systems for general cargoes and retained in part the commercial function of the canal. If traffic to private wharfs is excluded, however, only Goole remains a fully-fledged independent port. Nevertheless, there has been a continuation of water traffic of some sort to each of the four ports into the early 1970s. Despite the apparent confirmation by inter-urban motorways of the canal ports' initial loss of raison d'etre in the Railway Age, the flexibility of the road vehicle has been a factor enabling each town to remain a port, though not necessarily a canal port.

Table XI
Location of Industry by Transport Site, 1966

Location	Runcorn	Stourport	Ellesmere Port	Goole
Percentage of works located by				
road	26	50	26	60
rail	0	10	9	5
water	74	40	65	35
Percentage of water-located works sited along major river or				
ship canal	43	60	87	60
tributary river	29	20	0	20
barge canal	28	20	13	20

Indeed, all but Goole are now primarily manufacturing towns. In this connexion it is interesting to investigate industrial location in terms of transportation facilities, bearing in mind that in all canal ports industry originally located itself exclusively alongside the canal. Individual transport lines depend for their attractiveness not only upon the alternative media available but also on their relation to relief and on the type of industry served. An industrial survey carried out by the author in 1966 suggests that while railways tend to be unattractive to canal port industry, water sites are prized. In terms of employment, almost 100 per cent of industrial workers in both Mersey ports were employed in works located on waterside sites, though in Stourport and Goole this figure fell to 35 and 47 per cent respectively, road sites accounting for almost the whole of the remainder. While these figures can be regarded only as indicators, a breakdown of all plant sites confirms the Merseyside water site emphasis and the trend away from water in the towns less well endowed in terms of river approaches (Table XI).

Moreover, the canal which brought each town into being in no case accounted for even 30 per cent of water-located plant. Emphasizing still further the unimportance of the barge canal, the latter was able to substantially outweigh the tributary river as an industrial site only in the case of Ellesmere Port, where the Gowy has been culverted.

The survey was also concerned with the usage of the available transport media by canal port industry (Table XII).

Table XII

Transport Usage by Industry, 1966 (Per cent)

	Runcorn	Stourport	Ellesmere Port	Goole
Inward				
Road	67	74	51	50
Rail	31	11	6	7
Water	2	5	38	43
Other	0	10	5	0
Outward				
Road	78	85	71	83
Rail	13	3	11	0
Water	9	6	11	17
Other	0	6	7	0
Overall				
Road	73	79	61	66
Rail	22	7	9	4
Water	5	6	24	30
Other	0	8	6	0

In all cases road haulage, conforming to national trends in accounting for over 60 per cent of all transport usage, was somewhat more important for the removal of products than for the assembly of raw materials, indicating the general weight loss during processing associated with the tendency to use bulky raw materials more readily moved by rail or vessel. On the other hand, shipbuilding products, as in Goole, naturally move away by water. Despite the tendency of both Stourport and Ellesmere Port to use pipelines, and Runcorn's exceptional use of railways, a dichotomy is readily observable. Whereas road, rail, and other media in Stourport and Runcorn accounted for over 94 per cent of all goods moved, they were responsible for only 70 and 76 per cent in Goole and Ellesmere Port respectively, where water transport averaged 27 per cent of all movement in 1966.

Although continued water traffic to the privately-owned Mersey ports seems assured in view of the cooperation of the MSC with monolithic oil and chemical concerns, the situation of Stourport and Goole is less fortunate in the context of recent national policies on coal and oil handling. However, whereas the run down of Severn traffic at Stourport has hardly been noticed in the light of a thriving economic structure, in the case of Goole a similar process would prove socially and economically disastrous.

9 Notes

1. MOH reports, Runcorn (1914–64).
2. Calculated from figures given in A. J. Williams, *The Impact of the Construction of the Bridgewater Canal on Land Use in Adjacent Areas*, unpublished MA thesis, University of Manchester (1957), pp. 78–85.
3. MOH reports, Runcorn (1961–2).
4. A. Ling, *Runcorn New Town*, Development Corporation, Runcorn (1967).
5. STW 1/9 (11 January 1917).
6. STW 1/9 (10 November 1921).
7. MOH reports, Stourport (1916–52).
8. STW 1/10 (14 April 1938).
9. STW 1/9 (9 November 1922).
10. C. Hadfield, *The Canals of the West Midlands*, David and Charles, Newton Abbot (1966) p. 249.
11. MOH reports, Ellesmere Port (1944–64).
12. *Liverpool Echo* (7 September 1949).
13. W. Smith, *The Distribution of Population and Location of Industry on Merseyside*, Liverpool University Press, Liverpool (1942), p.23.
14. *Liverpool Daily Post*, (21 January 1959); *Liverpool Echo* (14 May 1959).
15. R. C. Estall and R. O. Buchanan, *Industrial Activity and Economic Geography*, Hutchinson, London (1966), pp. 172–186;

R. C. Estall, 'New Locations in Vehicle Manufacture', *Town and Country Planning* 32 (1964), pp. 154–8.

16. B. F. Duckham, *The Yorkshire Ouse*, David and Charles, Newton Abbot (1967), pp. 173–6.
17. *Goole Times Almanack*, Goole (1928).
18. *Goole Times Almanack*, Goole (1939).
19. J. M. Bellamy, 'Trends in the Foreign Trade of United Kingdom Ports', *Port of Hull Journal*, 45 (1957), pp. 7–11.
20. MOH report, Goole (1933).
21. L. N. Fraser, *A Growth Policy for the North*, H.M.S.O., London (1966), p. 57.
22. *Goole Times* (3 February 1968).

Retrospect

The inland navigation of this country has been a main ingredient of its prosperity. Canals have made towns, opened secluded regions, peopled solitudes, and communicated to numerous inland provinces of the country the vast advantages that result from our insular position . . . canals have joined the factory and the port, the country and the town . . . Enthusiasts . . . saw in canals the pledge of millenial regeneration and happiness.

The Times, 9 May 1846

10
Conclusion: A Canal Port Model

Observe the Genius of the Place in all.

Alexander Pope

In attempting to demonstrate the existence of the canal port as a recognizable specialized urban type, this investigation seeks to avoid the closed nature of a merely descriptive study. In model-building or the construction of a typology, the concern is less with congruence than with the teasing out of fundamental features of structure and process which, common to all individuals, form a basic entity stripped of superficial differences. A model may be a generalization, an ideal or a basis for prediction. The composite model put forward in this chapter partakes of all three attributes. It is initially concerned with a consideration of the genesis of the British canal port, followed by its economic, social, and physical development in the Canal, Rail and Motor ages. Grangemouth, a Scottish canal town, is then tested against the model canal town as derived from the four English examples. Finally, the typical port development of the canal town is outlined and compared with James Bird's model, 'Anyport'.

Canal Port Genesis

The pre-canal settlement stood on the lower reaches of a river which connected a large coastal seaport with an interior agricultural, mining, and manufacturing hinterland. Though no more than a day's journey from the nearest market town, the township lay off the main roads and was approached by unimproved cart-tracks differing little from its own field paths. Although it stood near the confluence of two rivers, lack of demand and the size of the major river precluded bridge-building, though ferries were available. They remained little frequented, however, for travellers usually avoided such remote spots, preferring to cross by the bridges of nearby towns.

Though the township had an intimate connexion with both rivers for power, fishing and shipping, the latter pales into insignificance when compared with the volume of traffic passing along the major river in early industrial times. As a confluence settlement, the pre-canal township lay at a potentially important position between the rapidly industrializing hinterland and the outer seaport which dealt with both coasting and foreign trades. Most working vessels, however, sailed past the settlement, the economy of which remained essentially agrarian. Occupations other than farming were only of minor importance, and little produce left the hamlet. The latter consisted of a number of cottages clustered around a church, an inn, and a few larger houses inhabited by the local gentry.

Communications were poor. The industrializing hinterland remained separated from the thriving seaport by inadequate transportation by river vessel and packhorse, and despite attempts to improve these media economic growth and social progress were hampered in both hinterland and port. The ready movement of bulky commodities, notably coal, was hampered, and take-off into sustained growth was prevented. The solution to this problem was the construction of a canal.

The canal was planned to be as short and cheap as possible, consonant with economic viability and the need to reach a terminus below which a free river gave unimpeded access to the major seaport. Because of the efficiency and availability of estuarial craft, it was not thought necessary to project the canal directly to the seaport; an optimal point of intervening opportunity was instead chosen. The choice of this position was not haphazard. The canal terminus lay on a major river carved into a belt of New Red Sandstone and backed by Coal Measures, a superb position in the context of the Industrial Revolution. It lay, moreover, at the lower end of a valley which had long functioned as a line of communications in the region. The general situation of the canal terminus was thus determined by a combination of topographical configuration and economic opportunity.

The actual site was chosen according to its merits from a variety of proposed termini considered by or offered to the promoters. Specifically, Runcorn could have been supplanted by Hollins Ferry, Barton, Hempstones, or indeed, many points on the Weaver; Stourport by the

Severn ports of Shrewsbury or Bewdley; Ellesmere Port by outlets on Severn or Dee; and Goole by the resuscitation of Airmyn, the continued use of Selby and the Dutch River, or by Lord Downe's plan for a Trent outfall. The terminus chosen was the compromise most satisfactory to promoters, engineers and the public. In the specific cases mentioned, the points chosen have such analogous positions in the regional context that a diagrammatic situational model may be constructed (Fig. 23).

The final outcome was no great triumph for the canal in terms of shortening the distance between hinterland and port. Specifically, taking Manchester, Ellesmere, Wolverhampton and Leeds as the interior towns demanding access respectively to Liverpool, Bristol and Hull, it is possible to compare the effective interurban distance before and after the advent of the canal. Taking the 'desire line' or airline distance as unity (1·00), circuity indices for interurban movement by river or land in pre-canal times ranged from 1·35 to 1·85, averaging 1·56. The canals reduced this figure to 1·36, with a range of 1·11 to 1·68. Thus the mean reduction was merely 0·2, equivalent to a saving of one mile in eight. It is impossible to obtain valid figures over a sufficiently lengthy period to afford an adequate comparison of the time taken between seaport and interior centre by the rival media. However, more efficiently organized and unimpeded by shoals, floods, and other river obstacles, the artificial waterway effectively reduced the time taken to transport goods between the two points, in itself a major inducement for merchants to transfer their goods to the new medium. The canal, however, came into its own in terms of the cost of carriage; between Liverpool and Stourport, for example, the rate per ton fell from £5 by land to £1 10s by canal. No other contemporary form of transport could offer such cheap rates.

Confident in its ability to attract traffic, the canal company began to equip its terminus as a transhipping point. Unlike many canal companies, whose waterways terminated in simple river outfalls surrounded by bare fields and graced only by a lock keeper's cottage, the company was not slow to heed Pope's exhortation to 'Bid harbours open'. The terminus rapidly became a terminal with the immediate construction of docks. Specific examples exhibit some variation in the dock system produced. The Mersey ports, with basins at both summit and river levels joined by locks, contrast with Stourport's basins at an intermediate position in the lock series, and Goole's docks at canal level, locking directly into the river. As each port had basins above river level, however, all originally partook of a characteristic which is usually

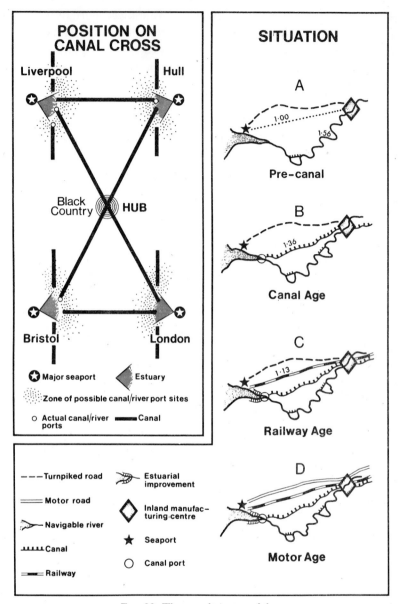

Fig. 23. The canal port model.

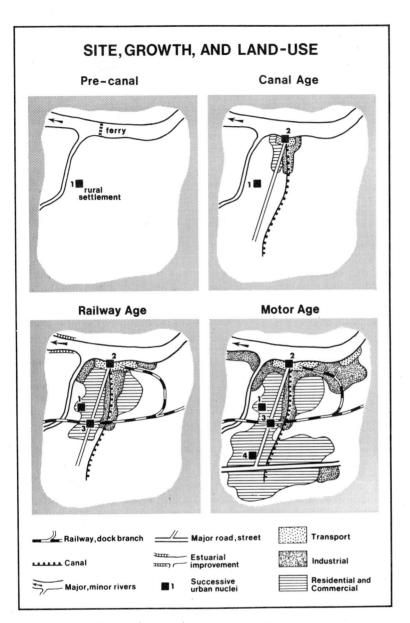

SITE, GROWTH, AND LAND-USE

Pre-canal

Canal Age

Railway Age

Motor Age

⟋ Railway, dock branch	⟋ Major road, street	⠿ Transport
Canal	Estuarial improvement	Industrial
Major, minor rivers	■1 Successive urban nuclei	Residential and Commercial

Canal port model, *continued.*

regarded as unique to Goole, the maintenance of water level in the docks by fresh water from the canal.

In detail, the canal terminal occupied a fairly cramped company estate, the canal reaching river level by means of multiple locks between which side basins were intercalated to facilitate the movement of vessels. Broad locks were provided to enable river craft and seagoing vessels to enter the docks, where transhipment between estuary and canal was effected. Substantial warehouses and cranes lined the docksides, and quays and stables were provided, together with facilities for vessel repair. Essential structures included office, toll house, and a number of cottages and larger dwellings to accommodate permanent employees, who included an agent or harbourmaster, and one or more lock keepers, wharfingers, and tonnage clerks. Pride of place, however, was taken by the impressive hotel within which a large room was set aside for a boardroom. Situated on the waterfront, the hotel was calculated to dominate both waterway and settlement. A vital, compact entity, the embryo port town contrasted strongly in both form and function with the surrounding rural landscape.

New towns demand a supply of people. One of the strongest influences of the new canal port was its role in stimulating streams of immigration from the surrounding region. By careful analysis of the 1851 census Enumerators' Returns, it is possible to trace the pioneering population *ab origine*. This is made possible at the individual family level by noting the successive birthplaces of household heads and their children. Typical individual migrant paths suggest the importance of the outer seaport, interior industrial centres, and ports superseded by the canal port as collecting points for migrants from a wide area, prior to their final move to the canal port. Intricate but logical paths, such as the following, were common:

Brighouse–Horbury–Wakefield–Thorne–Goole;
London–Liverpool–Manchester–Goole;
Dublin–Liverpool–Chester–Ellesmere Port.

The three indicated are typical paths followed by persons connected respectively with canal, rail, and sea transport.

In terms of absolute numbers, the largest sources of canal port population were the very inland manufacturing centre and seaport that the canal port was created to connect. Emphasizing the port's orientation towards shipping rather than manufacture, the seaport's contribution substantially exceeded that of the major inland centre. Amongst other towns, river ports superseded by the canal terminal made the largest contributions. These contingents from established ports were of great importance in the pioneering phase, for they provided an initial reservoir of experience in shipping and cargo-handling.

When the contributions of settlements relative to their size is assessed, however, most suppliers of numerically large contingents could well afford to lose these emigrants. For example, Leeds, Howden and Airmyn each had supplied 77 persons to Goole by 1851, but the proportions of their respective populations represented by this figure are 0·05, 3·45, and 13·73 per cent. Settlements contributing the largest proportion of their populations were universally situated in a compact zone around the canal port; in the extreme case of Ellesmere Port, Whitby and Overpool contributed as much as 22 and 24 per cent of their respective populations to the new town. Such major emigrations were frequently to the lasting detriment of villages and even towns in the canal port's vicinity. After the establishment of the new terminal, population curves for nearby villages show a check in the rate of growth, with stagnation or decline in some cases. Superseded ports suffered greatly from the impact of the canal port. In the case of Stourport and Bewdley, for example, the older river port was clearly unequal to the competition. According to the 1851 census: 'changes in internal navigation . . . having deprived . . . Bewdley of much of the commercial importance formerly resulting from its situation on the Severn, the decline of the carrying trade is assigned as the cause of the decrease of population'.

Canal Port Development

In this section it is convenient to consider changes in the canal port's population and occupational structures, physical urban form, and relationship with the canal company at three significant dates: the termination of the Canal Age towards the middle of the nineteenth century; the eve of the Great War, the turning point between Railway Age and Motor Age; and the present day. Initially, the canal port was concerned largely with 'frontier town' problems, notably the purchase of land, the organization of installations, the importation of labour, the establishment of urban amenities, the task of attracting regular traffic, and the problem of survival in the face of rival canals and the control of the estuary by the major seaport. Before 1850 few foreign vessels arrived, and the new settlement functioned primarily as a goods and passenger breakpoint between seaport and interior.

The Canal Port in the 1840s

A collage of comments from mid-century directories and travellers' accounts indicates the canal port in the 1840s to be a populous, neatly-built, bustling mercantile town, its basins commodious and flourishing, and the whole a direct product of an immense traffic on both canal and river. Lewis' *Directory* subsumes all other observations.[1] In it the canal port is considered as a port, entirely the creation of a canal company, and as a town, wholly different in form and function from the pre-canal hamlet. Respectively the work-place and home of the inhabitants, port and town were symbolized by the two poles of docks and church. The town had been called into existence to serve the port, and both were dominated by vast company warehouses.

The port had survived surprisingly well in the face of estuarial difficulties and concerted opposition from its usurped rival, the outer seaport, and proposed or realized canal and rail by-pass schemes. Prosperity still rested mainly on the original transhipping and storage function, and bulky cargoes prevailed, for the canal had 'coals at the heels of it', the Duke of Bridgewater's criterion for success. Industrial intrusions were not as yet of great importance, and plant was almost wholly located alongside waterways. These attributes were reflected in the occupational structure; service or tertiary occupations employed almost two thirds of all workers, and over one third of tertiary workers were in transport. Moreover, an overwhelming 90 per cent of all transport workers were employed in water transport occupations, and these comprised about 20 per cent of all employment in the canal port.

Largely working class, the town had experienced an approximately fivefold population increase in the period 1802–51. Like most expanding immigrant towns, including the new towns of modern Britain, the population consisted mainly of young families, two-thirds of the inhabitants being below the age of thirty. As befits a port dealing with heavy cargo-handling work and construction, males made up over 51 per cent of the population, the national mean being 49 per cent.

Heavy immigration led to urban expansion. Almost wholly oriented around the canal company's dock estate, the town core had effectively captured the township's focus of activity from the pre-urban nucleus. Within the estate and on its periphery a characteristic layout of docks, warehouses, residences, and public buildings had developed as the formal expression of the primary urban function. Largely the work of speculative builders, expansion outside the company estate took the form of outward-extending sectors of estate land uses, residentially and commercially along the main street, industrially along the canal and related waterways. In contrast with the planned arrangement of the company-built urban core, the speculators built in a piecemeal fashion, so that a complete contrast of architecture and urban form existed between core and periphery.

Situated at a major transport breakpoint in England's interior urban frontier, its functions largely connected with movement, and greatly dependent upon both hinterland and foreland for its livelihood, the canal port at mid-century had certain affinities with settlements then being established in the American West. The high proportion of immigrants, with its concomitants of rapid growth, demographic imbalance, and 'melting-pot' characteristics, enhanced the port's pioneering character. Lack of amenities and regular complaints concerning drunkenness and lawlessness confirmed it.

It is hardly necessary to justify the canal port's character as a company town. The canal company, if not directly controlling the majority of the population through employment and tied housing, had a great influence both directly and indirectly on most urban utility and amenity projects, including the establishment of schools, hospitals, markets and fairs, gas and water supplies, and places of worship. Public structures were erected only with the goodwill of the company, which through its canal also had some influence on the affairs of most industrial establishments. Despite the rise of manufacturing, the townsfolk followed the traditional economic and physical orientation of the town in looking to the canal company for guidance in many matters. The canal port image, for example, was still firmly impressed on industrializing Runcorn, for in 1844, over forty years after the duke's death, it was noted: 'The Duke's horses still draw the Duke's boats. The Duke's coals still issue from the Duke's levels; and when a question of price is under discussion—What will the Duke say or do? is as constant an element of the proposition as if he were forthcoming in a body to answer the question'.[2]

Vigorous, economically highly specialized, and exhibiting signs of growth and prosperity, the canal port at mid-century already contained the seeds of functional change or decay. Not only had the canal lost its original raison d'etre through the completion of railroads, but the company was seriously considering the desirability of some form of railway connexion. Add to this a desire on the part of certain railway companies to reach the port and the scene is set for the struggles which were to consume much canal company energy in the Railway Age. 'We

shall do well enough', remarked the Duke of Bridgewater, if we can keep
clear of those damned tramroads'.[3]

The Canal Port at the Eve of the Great War

In 1913 the canal port was still partially under the control of a highly
individualistic canal company. Functionally, however, the town had
grown in importance at the relative expense of the port; throughout the
period 1850–1913 there was a general swing towards manufacturing,
with a consequent reduction in the specialized nature of the town as a
diversity of job opportunities became available. Although still tending to
have more tertiary workers than the national mean of 44·8 per cent of all
employees, and with transport occupations dominant in the tertiary
sector to the extent of at least 40 per cent, the internal structure of
transport employment had radically altered. While canal employment
had remained static, employment on the railways had increased
manyfold. Although manufacturing employed less workers than service
occupations, the canal port was increasingly dominated by a few
specialized heavy industries. In occupational terms, only Goole remained
true to the canal port model of 1850, with a relatively undeveloped
industrial sector and with 'shipping and its adjuncts the chief sources of
employment'.[4] At the other end of the spectrum Stourport alone failed to
construct new dock space after mid-century, and though dying as a canal
port, was the harbinger of industrial diversification in being the sole town
to possess, in textiles, an industrial specialism unrelated to port activities.

Migrant inflow continued during the period, and in 1911 the canal
port remained much more youthful in population structure than the
national urban mean. Males still comprised well over 50 per cent of the
population, compared with the national urban mean of 48 per cent. In
conjunction with this continued growth, Mumford's characteristic
nineteenth century urban triad of railway, factory, and slum appeared in
strength after mid-century.[5] Indeed, the canal town expanded almost out
of recognition. Industrial plant took up a marked linear distribution
related to waterways. Dock and industrial railway branches emphasized
a gradual shift in relative importance from the canal to the river frontage,
to which industry was attracted for better wharfage facilities. Canalside
industries reflected a new evaluation of the canal less as a means of inland
communication than as an adjunct to the dock system.

Railways played an important part in promoting and shaping residential growth. Outside the built-up area of the 1860s a second focus of urban

activity grew up with the establishment of the railway station with its concomitant sidings, cottages, and public house. Though the pull of the still viable industrialized dockland prevented the wholesale obsolescence of the old town centre, there was an unmistakable shift of the canal port's centre of gravity towards the railway (Fig. 23). The street running between docks and station became the main street, and its overall similarity of red brick fabric and pretentious Victorian ornamentation contrasted sharply with the chaste uniformity of building style in the Georgian area around the canal terminus. Beyond the railway line, which soon took on the role of a social divide within the town, a 'new town' area with embryo urban facilities was in the making by 1913. Its regular gridded layout contrasted strongly with the congested area around the canal company nucleus, already regarded by contemporaries as 'old town'.

With these developments the canal port town began to take on attributes common to most small English towns of the period. Its image as frontier town and company town faded, despite its continued dependence on long range contacts. In terms of the frontier analogy, while Goole continued to ride the boom, and the Mersey ports were spurred by the arrival of a new medium into the throes of hurried expansion likened by contemporaries to a gold rush, Stourport, for all its citizens could surmise, was a town that was going downhill. Decline of canal company influence was everywhere apparent after the 1860s. Growing railway influence, continued expansion of population and industry, and the tendency of the town centre to shift away from the docks all contributed to this decline, which was confirmed by the institution of urban local government at the turn of the century.

By 1913 the canal port had fallen under the paternal influence of a few major industrial undertakings. Only Goole retained a lasting special relationship with its canal company. But whereas the four canal ports had been extremely similar in economic function, physical form, and the degree of company influence in 1850, by the eve of the Great War major differences between them had appeared. The canal port model must now be seen as a developmental spectrum, with industrial Stourport occupying, largely by default, the highest point on the scale of economic diversification, with the Mersey ports in an intermediary position as both ports and manufacturing centres, and with Goole remaining most faithful to the original canal port model of 1850. Significantly, while town hall and dock offices in the Severn port lay some distance apart, in Goole the two occupied the same imposing building. Moreover, the continued importance of the port function at this time was indicated by Stourport's

stagnation and the boundless optimism of Goole. Despite the doubts of a
few concerning the future prospects of one-industry towns the spirit of
Goole was buoyant, a consensus of local notables opining: 'with
intelligent management, and a continuous display of that enterprise
which has forced Goole to the front as a port, there should be no fear that
the next period . . . will [not] see a corresponding advance'.[6]

The Canal Port in the Early 1970s

After World War I the contrast between the canal ports increased, as
those with a modernizing industrial structure (Stourport, Ellesmere Port)
increased rapidly in population compared with those with relatively
palaeotechnic economies (Goole, Runcorn). By the 1960s, however, the
canal port, on the whole, was increasingly conforming to national urban
norms in terms of age structure, sex balance and social structure.
Occupationally, service employment suffered a relative decline in favour
of the manufacturing sector, although the greatest decline was found in
the older ports, Stourport and Runcorn. Such a shift in emphasis was due
not only to increased manufacturing employment, but also to the
continued decline of the transport job market, in line with the absolute
decline of the transport sector in the nation as a whole to about 7 per cent
of all employment. Of the canal ports, only Goole differed significantly
from this figure in the 1960s, and with a quarter of its working population
in transport occupations retained an unsophisticated aura of traditional
specialization in the transhipping function. This traditionalism was
reflected in Goole's inability to provide sufficient work for its slowly
declining population; while the older ports had achieved balance
between the daily inflow and outflow of workers, and Ellesmere Port had
caught some of the atmosphere of the booming South East, by the early
1970s Goole had become the canal town Ireland. The relative success of
the canal ports in changing the emphasis of their economic base from
declining transportation to expanding manufacturing is illustrated in
Table XIII.

The traditional linear arrangement of heavy industry along waterways
was accentuated after 1918, although the canal banks were increasingly
vacated in favour of the major river frontage. Lighter plant, established
mainly after 1945, clustered on light industrial estates with compact
roadside sites. Most residential expansion in the period took place in the
unconstricted area on the far side of the railway line from the canal port
nucleus, where urban renewal projects were in operation by the 1960s.

Table XIII
Canal Port Economic Base Shifts, 1851–1951

Year	Runcorn	Stourport	Ellesmere Port	Goole
1851	T_2M	T_1M_1	T_3	T_2
1911	T_2M_2	tM_2	T_3M_3	T_3m
1951	tM_3	M_3	tM_3	T_2m

Explanation of classification:

Manufacturing workers comprise:		Transport workers comprise:	
per cent of workers in manufacturing, retailing, and wholesaling	per cent of all workers	per cent of workers in manufacturing	per cent of all workers
m	under 60	under 25	t	under 5	under 5
M	60–84	25–39	T	5–24	5–9
M_1	75–84	40–44	T_1	25–49	10–20
M_2	85 plus	45–54	T_2	50–149	20–39
M_3	85 plus	55 plus	T_3	150 plus	40 plus

Sources: Enumerators' ms returns, 1851; Census of England 1911, 1951. Classification adapted from C. D. Harris, 'A Functional Classification of Cities in the United States', *Annals, Association of American Geographers* 33 (1943), 86–99.

Here again, the canal town came to resemble the national urban norm; similarity of physical form between the canal ports is now due less to economic forces than to the growth of standardized methods, materials, and layouts in the field of cheap construction.

Canal company influence completely disappeared during the period. Today it is found only in the shape of derelict buildings and central street patterns subject to urban renewal, now wholly subordinate to the modern town centre which by the 1970s was moving over the railway in the direction of recent building. Although the AC retained control of the Goole dock estate until 1948, elsewhere the canal company had no great influence on urban form or function in the twentieth century. In fact, by the late 1950s, it was clear that in the Mersey towns at least, the paternalist mantle had shifted to the shoulders of major manufacturing concerns. Modern paternalism, however, quite unlike that of the original canal company, has been restricted in physical expression to the organization of recreation, tied social clubs replacing company housing as a means of binding the worker to his place of employment.

During the twentieth century, then, the original canal ports diverged widely from the nineteenth century canal port type. On all available criteria, the four towns today exhibit similarities only where they conform to national trends. This assertion is perhaps best supported by the townsfolk themselves, many of whom learn of the existence of the canal which created their community only through local history classes. In urban planning, imageability questionnaires are used by planners to gain insight into how the urban dweller perceives his environment. Such a questionnaire was administered in the canal ports in 1966; one section asked each individual interviewed for a ranked list of all the physical features of the town which he considered to be distinctive. It is immediately apparent that the originating canal is of only minor importance in the perceived townscape of today's canal port inhabitants (Table XIV).

Table XIV

Canal Port Images: Dominant Features Recognized, 1966 (Per cent of sample)

Town	Image 1	Image 2	Image 3	Total	Per cent of sample mentioning canal
Runcorn	40 Mersey road bridge	25 Canals	20 Chemical firms	85	60
Stourport	80 River Severn	—	—	80	25
Ellesmere Port	40 Oil firms	35 Civic Centre	—	75	15
Goole	65 Dockland	25 Boothferry Road	—	90	35

The high imageability of the Bridgewater Canal in Runcorn is due less to its intrinsic importance than to its position, in a highly canalized area referred to as 'Little Venice', as a much-bridged barrier between town centre and the main residential areas. Elsewhere the canal today lies in an area little frequented by the public. In Ellesmere Port, as in Stourport, 'the town . . . now ignores the canal in its decay [and] an air of disjointedness pervades the area'.[7] Goole's rather higher ranking accords with the regular commercial use of its canal and the crossing of it by a major street. Dissimilar in almost all aspects by the early 1970s, the canal towns' differences are emphasized by the subjective verdict of their townsfolk. This confirms the erosion beyond recognition, during the twentieth century, of the characteristics of the formerly valid canal port model.

Testing the Model: Grangemouth

Grangemouth immediately qualifies for study by passing the population, social provision, and administrative standards outlined in Chapter 3.

Genesis

Grangemouth was founded in an area of easily-flooded agricultural land where only hamlets had previously existed. It was sited at the confluence of the Grange Burn with the Carron and Forth rivers. The Carron in the eighteenth century carried some shipping which, passing the site of Grangemouth, penetrated as far upriver as Carronshore, where the famous Carron ironworks had developed on the basis of local iron and coal supplies. Though the meandering lower Carron had been straightened, major improvement came with the implementation of a scheme, envisaged since the time of Charles II, to join the firths of Forth and Clyde by canal. Under the direction of Sir Lawrence Dundas, who began the cut in 1768, the Forth and Clyde Canal was designed not only to connect the two Scottish coasts, but also to link interior mining and manufacturing areas with major seaports.[8]

Although the canal, engineered by Smeaton and Whitworth, was not completed until 1790, Dundas, hoping to initiate trade, promoted the construction of an eastern terminal where seagoing vessels might tranship to and from canal boats. Begun in 1777, the terminal was soon provided with cottages, dock furniture, and the inevitable inn. By 1783 a comprehensive town plan had been drawn up by the architect Henry Holland.[9] This resulted in a company estate nucleus of uniform eighteenth-century stone buildings, some with classical door cases in timber, the whole forming a pentagonal canal town situated north of the single tidal basin.[10] Originally destined to be named Charlotenburg, the town was soon given the more prosaic and accurate name of Grangemouth.

Development

As the volume of trade increased the tidal basin and dock (Old Harbour) were supplemented by the creation of the Old Dock in 1836 (Fig. 24). Upper Dock, Junction Dock, timber basins for the Scandinavian trade,

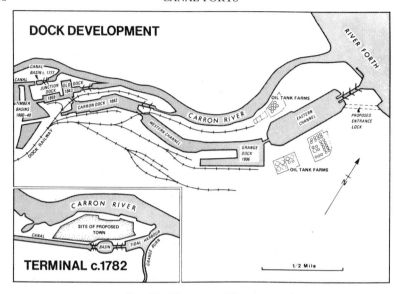

FIG. 24. The port of Grangemouth.

and shipyards followed. From the latter emerged the pioneer steamship *Charlotte Dundas*, a paddle steamer designed for use on the canal but soon laid up because of damage to the canal banks. With the growth of chemical manufacture, grain milling, and general port industries the port had, by the 1840s, taken on the character of a mature canal port, and 'appeared as a miniature Venice with its canals, docks, and . . . timber basins'.[11]

With serious congestion and the periodic freezing of the canal, the appearance of a railway branch in 1860 was a stimulus to port development. Owning much of the Lanarkshire coalfield and desirous of an east coast outlet, the Caledonian Railway Company purchased the canal, and with it the docks and town of Grangemouth. Though both frontier and company town characteristics began to wane after the creation of a burgh in 1862, a second wave of prosperity was initiated, as in Goole, by railway enterprise. Further docks were opened in 1882 (Carron Dock) and 1906 (Grange Dock), by which time the annual volume of coastwise and short-sea trading with northern Europe had reached 2·5 million tons annually. Grange Dock was equipped in 1906 with a lock giving direct access to the Forth for the first time, as the previous entrance via the Carron had proved increasingly difficult. To accommodate a sixfold rise in population from 1,488 in 1841 to 8,386 in 1901 a temporary shack area was replaced by New Town, developed by speculative builders on the opposite side of the docks from the original core. The urban economic base also changed as sawmills, shipyards, and soap, iron, and engineering works were established in dockland locations.

Economic base changes were even more revolutionary after the close of the Railway Age. Excellent transport facilities and good water supplies were among the reasons behind the arrival of a dye works and an oil refinery in the period 1919–24. These required specialized dock facilities and the continuation of estuarial improvements begun before World War I. Company control of a strategic wedge of land fronting both Forth and Carron facilitated these developments, although after 1945 petrochemical works spilled over the mud flats south of the Grange Burn. As with Ellesmere Port, difficulties of approach and the inability to accommodate vessels of over 12,000 tons led to the construction of a crude oil pipeline from Finnart on the west coast of Scotland. Port installations have been modernized in the 1960s, and vessels of up to 14,000 tons now berth at oil jetties and may pass through a 626ft × 80ft entrance lock into the docks. Though the original dock area has been infilled following the closure of the canal in 1961, some early functions still flourish. Shipbuilding, employing about 1,000 workers, still plays a part in the economy. But the town today is wholly dominated by ICI and British Petroleum, over half of whose workers commute daily from outlying areas. Employment has clearly outpaced the provision of amenities, though an ambitious plan for a new city of 300,000 population in the Falkirk–Grangemouth area could redress this imbalance.[12]

Clearly, only detailed investigation of company decisions, migration, railway projection, demographic and economic structure, and the like, could establish whether the detailed genesis and development of Grangemouth follows the same pattern as the typical English canal port. The general resemblance, however, is arresting, and is confirmed by a study of Grangemouth in relation to both the situation and site models previously discussed (Fig. 23). Neither of these would have to be radically altered to accommodate Grangemouth's characteristics. As with the English ports, external influences have always been dominant, and technological innovations in the successive transport eras of inland water, rail, and road movement have had overwhelming influence on both form and function. Grangemouth has experienced a typical migration of the urban focus from its original canalside position to successive rail- and road-oriented locations. Furthermore, the importance of the railway in urban morphology is brought out as strongly in Grangemouth as in Ellesmere Port, the line symbolically and effectively dividing the old canal town and docks from modern residential and industrial developments.

Any (Canal) Port

A single element of major importance to the canal town, at least until the later nineteenth century, the dock system may be compared with the model Any (British) Port.[13] Developed by Bird in 1963, this generalized model of dock system development is intended 'not to display a pattern into which all ports must be forced, but to provide a base with which to compare the development of actual ports. Actual lay-outs that differ markedly from the generalized scheme will provide the greatest interest for the student of port development'.[14]

Initially, a survey of relative defects indicates that Goole, the town most closely retaining canal port characteristics, has one of the most defective port locations, only Stourport, no longer a port, being in a less advantageous position (Table XV).

Table XV

Relative Defects in Canal Port Location, 1973

Element	Runcorn	Stourport	Ellesmere Port	Goole	Grangemouth
Water situation		X		X	
Water site	X	X		X	X
Land situation		X		X	
Land site		X			X

X represents a defect

More advantageous port locations in the three other towns have attracted large scale port-based industry which in turn has swamped port occupations in terms of employment provision. On the whole the canal ports tend towards defectiveness of the water site, largely through their upstream locations, though the Mersey ports are without substantial defect. Shackled to a palaeotechnic economy Goole remains, largely by default, the only settlement still fully dependent upon its port.

As a body the canal ports exhibit a significant common deviation in historical development from the Any (British) Port model (Table XVI).

Table XVI
Any (British) Port and its Relation to the Canal Ports

Any (British) Port Era		Year of termination of era					Era terminated by (canal ports)
		Anyport	Runcorn	Stourport	Ellesmere Port	Goole	Grangemouth	
I	Primitive	1597	1771–6	1771	1795	1826	1777–90	Canal terminal with dock
II	Marginal Quay Extension	1809	X	X	X	X	X	—
III	Marginal Quay Elaboration	1842–4	X	X	X	X	X	—
IV	Dock Elaboration	1921	1894	c. 1929	1894	*	1924	ship canal; oil wharfs
V	Simple Lineal Quayage	*	*	*	*	X	*	—
VI	Specialized Quayage	*	*	*	*	X	*	—

X denotes unrepresented eras

* denotes situation obtaining in 1973

Arriving late on the scene, the canal ports ended a possible primitive era of unmodified creek usage by a process of sublimation. Created during the Anyport periods of marginal quay development and elaboration, which denote the situation prevailing before dock excavation, the canal ports dispensed entirely with these stages, springing Minerva-like into existence as fully-fledged entities of the dock elaboration type.

Unlike that of most major British ports, the development of the canal port has no significant gap between the excavation of an initial tidal basin and the construction of a wet dock. Indeed, in the cases of Stourport and Goole, the initial tidal basin was entirely absent. After a dock elaboration stage of greater than average length, in which dock systems such as those of Goole and Runcorn became elaborate in the extreme, almost all the ports entered the modern phase of simple lineal quayage along the major river front, with specialized wharfs for certain commodities. Here the MSC gave the Mersey ports nearly thirty years advantage over Grangemouth and Stourport, which conformed to the national mean.

Only one town witnessed no such development and, symbol of its economic underdevelopment, remains firmly fixed in the dock elaboration era. The verdict of its citizens has a ring of truth: 'Goole was born, prospered, and died with Queen Victoria'.

The Anyport concept was developed for larger British ports with long histories of occupance. It is clear from the above analysis that the model is hardly applicable to the canal-created port. Indeed, the fundamental similarity in the development of the canal ports, especially in their sudden creation complete with enclosed wet docks, suggests an Any (Canal) Port model. The precise formulation of such a type, however, must be postponed pending the investigation of other ports created in the modern period, notably railway ports, many of which came into existence fully-equipped in like manner.

Conclusion

Ex hypothesi, it seems justifiable to include, in the typology of urban history, an overall canal port model consisting of genesis, development, situation, physical structure, and dock development elements. The canal port, existing in pure form until the mid-nineteenth century, gradually lost its importance in a port town which changed character in the later part of the century, and which wholly reorganized its economic structure after World War I. What remains of the original canal port today is, even in Goole, largely fossil in character. Two hundred years of change have left some derelict relics of the early dockland, historic street names, a few original buildings, the products of early schools of painting and other items of local colour, perhaps an image in the minds of the inhabitants, and a historic orientation of the town around an obsolete canal nucleus, now in the throes of demolition. Towns which have suffered radical economic reorganization while retaining a physical structure geared to earlier functions are not uncommon; the canal port provides a particularly vivid example.

Yet, especially with regard to the general rise to overwhelming dominance of the large scale industries characteristic of industrial ports, even recent trends have been based on a structure of successively earlier functions reaching back to the *primum mobile*, the transhipping function of the original canal port. The relative success of individual canal ports in shedding obsolete functions has indicated a vague but basic economic cycle. In these terms the ports are today located at varying points along a characteristic developmental continuum, stage of advance depending upon the degree to which features of urban development have built up and overlaid those of urban genesis. As with all company towns built to support a specific function, the canal port, in the face of technological change resulting in its potential economic redundancy, has had to adapt or die. The adaptation process has been almost everywhere successful. Today only the stagnant town of Goole, a monument to the high noon of the Canal Age, rewards the curious and patient visitor with a working example of a port created in an era when the canal was thought to be the ultimate in transport innovation.

10. Notes

1. S. Lewis, *A Topographical Dictionary of England*, London Vol. 2 (1842), p. 295; Vol. 2 (1849), pp. 159, 315; Vol. 3, p. 714; Vol. 4, p. 213.
   See also J. Bagshaw, *History, Gazetteer, and Directory of Cheshire*, (1850), pp. 571, 699; Bentley's *History, Gazetteer, Directory and Statistics of Worcestershire*, Birmingham Vol. 4 (1841), p. 109; I. Slater, *Directory of Worcestershire*, Manchester (1850), p. 53.
2. *Quarterly Review*, 72 (1844), p. 314.
3. Ibid., p. 316.
4. MOH report, West Riding of Yorkshire (1901).
5. L. Mumford, *The City in History*, Harcourt, Brace and World, New York (1961).
6. *Goole Times* (31 July 1896).
7. J. Liley, 'Seven Hours on the Severn', *Motorboat and Yachting*, 106 (1967), p. 34.
8. R. Porteous, *Grangemouth's Modern History 1768–1968*, Burgh of Grangemouth, Grangemouth (1970).
9. D. Stroud, *Henry Holland: His Life and Architecture*, Barnes, New York (1966), pp. 59–60.
10. Royal Commission on Historical Monuments (Scotland), *Stirlingshire* Vol. 2 (1963), p. 318.
11. D. Semple, 'The Growth of Grangemouth—a note', *Scottish Geographical Magazine*, 74 (1958), pp. 78–85.
12. *Daily Telegraph* (9 July 1968).
13. J. Bird, *The Major Seaports of the United Kingdom*, Hutchinson, London (1963).
14. J. Bird, *Seaports and Seaport Terminals*, Hutchinson, London (1971).

Appendix I

Abbreviations (of Company Titles) Used Frequently in Chapters 4–9

AC	Aire and Calder Navigation
BWB	British Waterways Board
BCR	Birkenhead and Chester Railway
BLJ	Birmingham and Liverpool Junction Canal
CH	Calder and Hebble Navigation
ECC	Ellesmere and Chester Canal
GJR	Grand Junction Railway
GSS	Goole Steam Shipping Company
GWR	Great Western Railway
GB	Gloucester and Berkeley Ship Canal
ICI	Imperial Chemical Industries
LNWR	London and North Western Railway
LBR	Liverpool and Birmingham Railway
LMR	Liverpool and Manchester Railway
LYR	Lancashire and Yorkshire Railway
MSC	Manchester Ship Canal
MIN	Mersey and Irwell Navigation
NER	North Eastern Railway
OWWR	Oxford, Worcester and Wolverhampton Railway
SURC	Shropshire Union Railway and Canal Company
SCCC	Severn and Canal Carrying Company
SK	Stainforth and Keadby Canal
SVR	Severn Valley Railway
STW	Staffordshire and Worcestershire Canal
TM	Trent and Mersey Canal
TS	Thames and Severn Canal
WCI	Wolverhampton Corrugated Iron Company

WPGR   Wakefield, Pontefract and Goole Railway
WB   Worcester and Birmingham Canal

Abbreviations in References

The following abbreviations refer to manuscript company minutes located in the British Transport Historical Records (BTHR) archives.

ACN   Aire and Calder Navigation;
ECC   Ellesmere and Chester Canal Company;
ELC   Ellesmere Canal Company;
STW   Staffordshire and Worcestershire Canal Company;
SURC   Shropshire Union Railway and Canal Company.

Other abbreviations used are:
BM   British Museum.
BWB   British Waterways Board.
CRO   County Record Office.
JHC   *Journal of the House of Commons.*
MIN   Mersey and Irwell Navigation Company (manuscript records, Bridgewater Department, Manchester Ship Canal Company).
MOH   Medical Officer of Health (local authority annual reports).
PP   *Parliamentary Papers.*

Appendix II

Data Sources for Figures

Figure 5.　　Runcorn Tithe Award (1844); Bridgewater Papers, Northampton County Record Office (CRO) EB (1459–64); Ordnance Survey (OS) field sketch 1822 (British Museum); OS maps (various dates); MSC Bridgewater Department; field work.

Figure 7.　　Canal line plans, BWB Wolverhampton; Fig. 8; OS maps (various dates); field work.

Figure 9.　　Canal line (1802), BWB Leeds; OS maps (various dates); field work.

Figure 12.　　British Transport Historical Records (BTHR) ACN 3/7, 8; OS maps (various dates); field work.

Figure 13.　　BTHR: ACN 3/7, 8 (George Leather's 'Plan of the Harbour and Docks at Goole' (1825) and 'Plan of the Port of Goole with Intended Improvements' (1828)).

Figure 17.　　Deposited plans, Chester CRO; BTHR: ELC and SURC (throughout).

Figure 19.　　Deposited plans, West Riding of Yorkshire CRO; BTHR: ACN (throughout).

Appendix III

Population History of Major Canal Ports (uncorrected from Census)

Census Date	(No. of inhabitants)			
	Runcorn	Stourport	Ellesmere Port	Goole
1801	1,379	1,603	170	294
1811	2,060	2,352	75	348
1821	3,103	2,544	250	450
1831	5,035	2,952	234	1,671
1841	6,951	3,012	839	2,850
1851	8,688	2,993	909*	2,960
1861	10,063	2,958	729	3,479
1871	12,066	3,081	1,084	4,186
1881	14,812	3,358	1,488	4,823
1891	20,050	3,504	5,107	4,853
1901	16,491	3,111	4,082	16,576
1911	17,353	4,434	10,366	20,332
1921	18,476	4,777	13,063	19,111
1931	18,127	5,949	18,911	20,239
1951	23,931	10,146	32,653	19,234
1961	26,035	11,748	44,681	18,891
1966	27,150	n.a.	50,990	18,470

*The Port, excluding Whitby village, 617.

Appendix IV

Population History of 1970 Local Government Areas

Census Date	(No. of inhabitants) Runcorn	Stourport	Ellesmere Port	Goole
1801	1,541	2,127	1,259	294
1811	2,249	2,923	1,219	348
1821	3,397	3,063	1,642	450
1831	5,567	3,526	1,826	2,203
1841	7,577	3,704	2,635	3,571
1851	9,621	3,689	2,564	4,619
1861	11,028	3,788	2,629	5,937
1871	13,526	4,005	3,448	7,700
1881	16,496	4,834	4,011	10,687
1891	22,389	5,596	9,908	15,416
1901	18,498	5,280	6,956	17,120
1911	19,498	5,567	13,292	20,916
1921	20,722	6,462	16,502	19,679
1931	21,910	8,280	23,126	20,885
1951	23,931	10,203	32,653	20,293
1961	26,035	11,748	44,681	20,010

Besides small corrections for parts of neighbouring parishes absorbed from time to time, Runcorn includes Weston until absorption; Stourport includes Upper Mitton and Areley Kings, until absorption; Ellesmere Port includes Overpool, Netherpool, Great and Little Sutton, Childer Thornton, Ince, Stanlow, Great Stanney, and Hooton, until absorption; Goole includes Hook from 1831.

Index